Praise for Mark Gungor's
Laugh Your Way
to a Better Marriage

"Mark Gungor uses a brilliant combination of humor and no-nonsense straight talk to address the frailties of modern marriage and offers practical solutions to make it better."

> —Ken Davis, author, comedian, and radio host of
> *Lighten Up and Live!*

"What could be better than to be able to *Laugh Your Way to a Better Marriage*? Mark Gungor has a gift. His passionate message about marriage breaks through the current myths and misinformation in our culture and renews hope that anyone can achieve a happy, sexy, satisfying marriage. Gungor is a national treasure. It's wonderful to see that he's as good on paper—as immediate and as life-changing—as he is in person at his Laugh Your Way seminars."

> —Diane Sollee, founder and director of Smart Marriages

"I love it when I can read a book about a serious subject written by an author who doesn't take himself so seriously. Mark Gungor has all the credentials and experience to weigh in on the issue of marriage, but his street-level perspective and his tongue-in-cheek way of conveying his wisdom make it easy to absorb the truth that he shares on a subject that—for many couples—is no laughing matter. This book will help you ramp up your understanding of each other, step up your ability to fight fair, and juice up your sex life."

> —Dr. Tim Kimmel, president of Family Matters and author of
> *Raising Kids for True Greatness*

"This was more than a book to us, it was an experience. We felt understood, empowered and completely covered. This book will help you!"

> —Matt and Laurie Crouch, Trinity Broadcasting Network

"Marriage books? I've read them all. This one's the best—absolutely rock-solid advice, delivered in hilarious prose. This is the first marriage book that's totally fair to men, and totally liberating to women."

> —David Murrow, author of *Why Men Hate Going to Church*

LAUGH

Your Way to a
Better Marriage®

Unlocking the Secrets

to Life, Love, and Marriage

Mark Gungor

ATRIA PAPERBACK

New York   London   Toronto   Sydney

ATRIA PAPERBACK
A Division of Simon & Schuster, Inc.
1230 Avenue of the Americas
New York, NY 10020

The information contained in this book is intended to be educational and not for diagnosis, prescription, or treatment of any health disorder whatsoever. This information should not replace consultation with a competent health care professional. The author and publisher are in no way liable for any misuse of the material.

First Atria Paperback edition March 2009

ATRIA PAPERBACK and colophon are trademarks of Simon & Schuster, Inc.

For information about special discounts for bulk purchases, please contact Simon & Schuster Special Sales at 1-800-456-6798 or business@simonandschuster.com.

Designed by Karolina Harris

Manufactured in the United States of America

10   9   8   7   6   5   4   3

The Library of Congress has cataloged the hardcover edition as follows:
Gungor, Mark.
    Laugh your way to a better marriage : unlocking the secrets to life, love, and marriage / by Mark Gungor.
        p. cm.
    Includes bibliographical references.
1. Marriage. 2. Man-woman relationships.   I. Title.
HQ734.G88473 2008
248.8'44—dc22   2007023091

ISBN-13: 978-1-4165-3605-5
ISBN-10:   1-4165-3605-1
ISBN-13: 978-1-4165-5879-8 (pbk)
ISBN-10:   1-4165-5879-9 (pbk)

TO MY DARLING DEBBIE

When we married we were very young (eighteen and nineteen), extremely poor (we were essentially hippies—our first home was an eight-by-ten tent), and unbelievably dumb (see points one and two), but our journey together has been one that millions of people envy. Our life together is proof that all people need to succeed is a stubborn commitment to do what is right. Thank you for being my girl.

Acknowledgments

To my brother Ed, whose valuable insights and skills have made this book possible.

To Terry Kohler, whose vision and compassion have helped to positively touch millions of marriages.

To the Uhlmann Family for their love and support.

To Diane Brierley and Joy Groblebe, who have read, re-read and then read this book again more times than anyone should legally be allowed.

To my mother, who planted in my mind the grand delusion that I could accomplish anything I set my mind to.

And finally, to my kids, Leslie & Ross, Phil & Kirsty and my grandsons, Parker, Keyan and Monty. Ultimately, marriage is about building a strong and successful family. It's all about family.

Contents

CONTENTS

LAUGH

Your Way to a
Better Marriage®

Introduction

DESPITE its title, this book is not about the benefits of laughter in marriage, nor is it a collection of funny stories about marriage. This work is based on a seminar I offer, called "Laugh Your Way to a Better Marriage®," which is a very serious effort to improve the married lives of those who attend it. The name refers to laughing simply because many of the points I share are, well, funny. In fact, the live seminar is more a standup comedy show than an episode of *Dr. Phil,* and yet tens of thousands of couples testify that the seminar has enriched, and even saved, their marriages. So while many of the points and stories herein may cause you to smile or laugh, what you will ultimately find is a serious attempt at providing helpful information that will empower you to succeed in married life.

I agree with David Viscott, who writes, "Relationships seldom die because they suddenly have no life left in them. They wither slowly, either because people do not understand how much or what kind of upkeep, time, work, love, and caring they require or because people are too lazy or afraid to try."[1]

People have a lot of strange ideas about love and marriage. Some think that if a marriage is meant to be, *it will just be.*

Some think they should be able to follow their instincts and arrive at happiness. And true, relationships *do* have a kind of "instinct" to them; however, experience shows that people cannot rely on instinct alone.

Others think *romance* is the key to marital bliss. My bride, Debbie, and I are childhood sweethearts. That may *sound* romantic, but truth be told, romance has had little to do with it. Sure, it's played a part, but only a small part. Like the salt I threw on my eggs this morning—the main factor in *that* story was the eggs, not the salt. If I had tried to make it a story about the salt, it would have made for a lousy breakfast. Romance is a great "salt" to sprinkle on the hard work of sharing a life with another human being, but the main ingredient of a happy marriage can never be romance. (You'll see why later.)

The thing that makes marriage wonderful is *work*. But we need more than work; we need *skill*. Just because we are willing to work for a great marriage does not mean we have the skills to actually pull one off. Those skills take time and knowledge. The longer we wait to learn those skills, the more apt we are to tumble from one painful relationship to another—each one building a case on the past one, convincing us we will *never* be able to be happy with the spouse we are with. We then become the *walking wounded*: ever more cautious, less vulnerable, and fearful about trusting the one we are supposed to be with for life. Marriages like these start to generate more pain than they appear to be worth, and people start to bail.

The good news is that marriage problems are fairly easy to resolve. Whenever a husband and wife are willing to study the dynamics of marriage and willing to take the time to understand each other, they will come together in love. That is the *why* behind this writing.

Now, ladies, if your husband doesn't want to read this

book, don't take offense. *Most* men won't want to read whole books about *relationships*. You can, however, find success in asking him to read short sections that you wish he would read. As you will learn in chapter 5, men like to compartmentalize things. Asking him to just read a small section will make him much more likely to respond than trying to get him to read the whole book. Then try to discuss *just that one subject* with him. Men don't mind talking about specific issues. What they hate is when one issue leads to another and then another and then another. . . .

Girls, also keep in mind that men *don't like* working on their relationships. A guy will assume, that if it ain't broke, don't fix it. Men think that the best possible thing one can do for a relationship is to leave it alone. To a guy, the idea of reading a book on relationships rates right up there with root canals and rectal exams.

Women, on the other hand, *like* to work on their relationships. A woman enjoys tilling the relational gardens of her life—planting, fertilizing, weeding, pruning—all the while cherishing each and every improvement she sees, as her relational "garden" grows and thrives. The idea of reading a book about marriage is a welcome one, and she will sit down at the first opportunity to begin exploring these pages. So my assumption is that most of *you*, my readers, are women. But not to worry, the information you will find here is *so* good and will be *so* transforming for your marriage that it will take only *one* of you to tango your marriage into happiness. Believe me, if you do this stuff, *he'll start dancing.*

Now, before we move forward, I need to ask you to be patient with the generalizations I make throughout this book. Generalizations are just that. They are what is *generally* true, but not *always* true. For example, generally speaking, men are more interested in sex than women. There are many marriages, however, in which the wife is more interested in sex than her husband. (Now, if you are a man reading this and your wife is more interested in sex than you are, I think I speak for all men when I say, "We hate you.") When you read these kinds of generalizations, take time to calibrate them to your unique situation, personality, and experience. But, though there may be exceptions to these generalizations, the stereotypical gender differences are too strong to ignore; hence, I discuss them.

One of my favorite verses in the Bible reads, "Where no oxen are, the manger is clean, but much revenue comes by the strength of the ox."[2] The meaning is clear: If you have an ox, you're going to have ox *poo*. If you don't want any ox poo, then you have to get rid of the ox. But an ox is a good thing—we get "much revenue" from having an ox. So there's the quandary: If you want the benefit of having an ox, you're going to have to endure the *poo* that comes with it.

Marriage is a good thing. We get "much revenue" from being joined to another person. However, there are problems. There is no such thing as a poo-free marriage. That's why the apostle Paul gave us this advice: "It is good for a man not to marry."[3] Why does he say that? Because, he continues, "those who marry will face many troubles in this life, and I want to spare you this."[4]

You don't hear these verses read at many weddings. You don't see very many greeting cards that reference this. Why not? Because we don't like to admit that when you get a marriage ox, you will also be getting a pile of marital ox poo. But that is precisely what happens. Nevertheless, marriage is wonderful. I love being married! And what's the alternative? Being alone for the rest of your life? That's no picnic, either. The point is, challenges come with every choice we make.

Now, if all you are getting out of your marriage is a pile of poo, you have yourself one sick ox. I can help you with that.

The problem is, many don't expect to find any poo at all in their marriage, and when they encounter stuff that stinks, they see it as a sign that they married the *wrong person*.

One last thing before we begin our journey. Albert Einstein said, "The significant problems we face cannot be solved at the same level of thinking we were at when we created them." The point is, if you want to tackle significant relational issues, you have to be willing to think at a *new level*. I'm going to help you do that. You will run into some new ideas that will thrill you and some that will make you mad. But don't reject what I say out of hand. Listen. Think. Ponder. Dare to go to the next level and watch your marriage follow you there.

MARK GUNGOR
Green Bay, Wisconsin

Part

Setting the Stage

1

The Perfect Mate

DEB and I had flown into Raleigh, North Carolina, to do one of our *Laugh Your Way to a Better Marriage* seminars. Usually during my weekend events I speak for up to six hours or more, so if I am not careful I can overwork my voice. In preparation for an event, I try to limit my jabbering and generally turn down any requests to meet with people, do interviews, and so on. However, the Friday morning before the start of the Raleigh event, my good friend and host pastor, Steve Coronna, asked if I would join him and his wife Connie on the set of their TV program, *Making Your Marriage Work*. My reluctance to do three television programs on the day of a seminar was mitigated only by my friendship with Steve.

The plan was to leave the hotel at 9:15 a.m. and drive to the studio to meet them. I am not exactly a morning kind of guy, and being true to form, I slept in as late as possible and began to shower and get dressed only at the last possible minute. After I shaved and combed what hair I have left, I went to get a fresh pair of underwear out of my suitcase. However, I could not find any. Since I am a typical man and unable to find something even if it's right under my nose, I did not panic, but simply called out to my wife, who was now in the bathroom.

"Hey, Debbie, where are my underwear?"

"They're right there in the front of your suitcase," she answered.

"No," I retorted. "I looked. There's nothing there."

Exasperated, Debbie shot out from the bathroom to the suitcase to try and find what I had obviously missed. After a few moments, however, she started to giggle and said, "Well, I guess we didn't pack any."

Didn't pack any?! I started to panic. *No underwear?!* My mind began to race: *I have people to meet; television shows to tape! I don't have time to deal with, 'I guess we didn't pack any.'*

Perhaps yesterday's undies, I thought, switching from panic to resolution mode. A little gross, but it seemed like a plausible plan at the time. Then I realized my drawers were lying wet on the bathroom floor and there was no time to dry them out. I had to go *now* if I was going to be on time.

Only two options lay before me: a) go au naturel with no restraints—*freely,* as it were; or b) do the *unthinkable*—wear my wife's underwear. As I pondered the options, a pair of my wife's undies caught my eye. They were made of simple cotton, and, were it not for "Victoria's Secret" stamped all over the elastic band, they almost looked like a pair of men's skivvies.

Dare I? I mused.

Now, every man I have ever shared this story with has told me they would have chosen option "a," and never option "b," even under threat of death or bodily harm. For most men, wearing women's underwear is *not* an option—there are *way* too many conflicting implications. But I just could not see spending my day underwear*less.* I can't handle that much *freedom* in my life. I would have found it extremely distracting.

So, option "b" it was. I quickly slipped on my wife's undies, finished getting dressed, and headed out the door, giving what I had just done very little thought.

About five miles down the road, it started to dawn on me that I was sitting in a pair of underwear that had *"Victoria's Secret"* imprinted over and over again on the waistband. I thought to myself, *Good grief! What if I'm in an accident?* I imagined myself lying on the side of the road while the medics tried to remove my pants to save my life. I saw myself fighting them off, screaming at the top of my lungs, "Let me die! Let me die!"

Soon I was at my destination, and I tried to focus on taping the programs to be aired over the next three weeks. You can imagine the irony I felt as I looked into the camera and threw out a challenge for the men in the audience to be *real* men, not the all-too-familiar men who live in a virtual world of TV, video games, and computer porn—yet all the while I was sitting in a pair of women's underwear! It was a struggle to concentrate on what I was saying.

After the taping, while we were waiting to be seated for lunch, I could hold my secret no longer. I leaned over to Steve and Connie and told them I had a confession to make. Few things get people's attention like an open confession, so they gathered close to me as I whispered the events of that morning. When I finally got to the part where I revealed I was standing there with them in a pair of my wife's underwear, which I had been wearing all morning, Steve screamed and tried to get as far away from me as possible. (Did I mention guys have issues with this kind of thing?) He continued with lunch only as long as I agreed not to touch him. He also asked me to never mention his name when telling this story. (But, *hey,* what are friends for?)

The Moral of the Story

I reveal this self-deprecating story to illustrate a point. If you are going to survive unexpected circumstances and disappointments, you are going to have to be willing to change, to adjust, to work with what you have, and to commit to doing things you normally wouldn't have chosen to do. Despite our best efforts and intentions, life doesn't always turn out the way we have hoped and planned. This is especially true when it comes to relationships between men and women.

Love can be deceitful. It starts out so easily. In fact, it is the ease of the relationship that convinces us that the other person is "the one." We are so comfortable with them. They are incredibly easy to talk to. We can just be ourselves around them. With seemingly no effort at all, we experience a sense of joy just by being around them.

"It is so easy," we reason, "this person must be *the one*!"

"Yes," your romance-starved heart answers, "this is it—true love is *always* easy!"

So we take the plunge, we make the big commitment, we promise, "Till death do us part." And we know it's right because it's easy. *Easy* is always a sign from God that things are right. *Right?*

But after the "I do's" have been exchanged, life kicks in. And guess what? *It ain't easy.*

Men and women begin their journey believing that fate has caused them to meet each other, and then they date and end up at the altar. They think that since they have spent so much quality time with each other, they truly know each other. They know what to expect and, therefore, feel the relationship is safe—they have discovered the *perfect one*. However, due to the intoxicating nature of the dating process, people don't know each other nearly as well as they think.

So when life hits, *shock and awe* set in. *Shock* because the differences that attracted them to each other now repel them. *Awe* because they are now frustrated and angry and feel that their whole marriage is simply *aw*ful.

We read in the Old Testament, "Hope deferred makes the heart sick."[1] Simply stated, when things don't go the way you hoped they would, it is easy to get "heart sick"—to lose your *oomph*, to want to quit and get away from what disappointed you. But that is a mistake.

The truth is that such lofty ideals of romantic perfection actually work to make people's marriages worse, not better. Since these ideals are rarely if ever realized, dissatisfaction rules the day. You were smoking marital ganja if you expected marriage to be a life filled with constant waves of joy, where every morning birds sing you awake and little bunnies help you sweep the floors as the chipmunks wash the dishes.

It may be a hard pill to swallow, but it doesn't take the ladies long to discover that—though they were worshiped and coddled like beautiful princesses during the dating experience, *and* though they married the guy expecting to step into a long life of being the object of worship and coddling—it doesn't last. Generally, women end up feeling as if they are the property of the Pumpkin Eater (who, according to Mother Goose, has his little woman neatly tucked away in his pumpkin shell, there to keep her very well). Women discover that their Prince Charming is more pauper than prince, and the man of her dreams morphs into looking more like the monster from her nightmares.

Similarly, men get disappointed and offended, but only by the idea that we could ever disappoint a woman. "How can this be?" men reason. "Our moms always said we were perfect."

And we guys hate to lose the "Prince Charming" label. The problem is that we can't begin to comprehend why being married would take anywhere near the energy dating did. We have won the girl. The girl said "yes." The boy said "I do." Everything seems set, so we assume we can now begin to redirect our attentions, formerly used to chase our bride-*to-be,* to new pursuits. There are new hills to climb, new wars to win, new seas to cross, and of course, video games to play. Sadly, many men think "I do" means "I'm done." This is because we generally approach relationships with a conquer-and-possess mind-set. And once men *possess,* we are ready to move on to new ground.

In a way, what we possess "disappears," kind of the way a new car disappears after we own it for six months, and we often cease to give those we love significant attention. We don't do it to be cruel, we just don't get *why* we would keep fighting and striving to secure something we *already have.* Sadly, the romantic chase of courtship gives way to the thoughtlessness, inconsiderate behavior, and even rude assumption of ownership. (I'm not saying this is right or that it has to stay this way, it just *is* for the average guy.) Our shock and awe in marriage have to do with the discovery that our wives no longer think we are the cat's *meow.* After all, we are men, the bearers of the magic that accompanies our gender—endowed to us by the male penis.

Ah, wretched disappointment—it makes us sick. And when marriages are filled with disappointed wives and offended men, it doesn't take long for them to become convinced they have made a terrible mistake. Why? Because it is no longer *easy;* now it's very, very hard.

This can't possibly be love! our disappointed heart cries. *I must have made a mistake! I shouldn't have married this guy (gal). There is no way he (she) is my true soul mate.*

It is here where the battles begin to rage, and *how* a couple fights those battles is critical (we'll talk more about that later). Some couples fight openly, some quietly. But a couple must be willing to wrestle till there is a win for *both* parties involved. A win/win often requires flexibility: some push and pull, some lovingly compromise, and—dare I suggest it—even wearing each other's underwear (should the circumstances warrant).

But many are unwilling to fight *or* compromise. When their expectations are *not* met, their hearts feel "sick" and they want *out* of the marriage. Unmet expectations in marriage tend to erode the relationship. And when the marriage deal begins to feel like a bad deal, many head out looking for a new deal. They view conflict, which is inevitable in any healthy relationship (intimacy is forged in conflict), as evidence that they have married the *wrong* person. After all, the promise of true love can be realized only if one finds and marries their predestined *soul mate,* right? Wrong.

I know this won't make me very popular with a lot of people, particularly many of the ladies, but the idea of the perfect "soul mate"—that God made one special person just for you—is the stuff of sweetsy, twenty-five-cent romance novels, and has no footing in Christian thought.

THE MYTH

"When you grow up," the wind whispered in the young girl's ear, "you'll meet your soul mate—the one with whom you can share your life and experience ecstatic, joyful love. You will find yourselves entwined as one in conjugal bliss."

"How will I know who it is?" the little girl questioned. "How will I find the right one?"

"Oh, don't worry," said the wind reassuringly. "Destiny dictates the meeting of our soul mates. You will meet the one who is right and you will live happily ever after."

The idea that there is just *one special person for me—my soul mate—* comes from an alleged altercation between the human race and the Greek god Zeus. According to Greek mythology, we humans originally had four arms, four legs, and a single head made of two faces. Because Zeus feared that the authority of the gods might be compromised by this race of beings, he decided to split each person in half, condemning us to spend the rest of our lives wandering unrequited until we find the half we were separated from—our lost *soul mate.* It was thought that our undying pursuit of perfect love is the result of Zeus's scheme to keep us busy—far away from meddling in the domain of the gods.

According to this account, a person's soul mate is the *one-and-only* other half of one's soul—we would always be *less* happy with any other person. Today millions base their hope of marital bliss entirely on the Zeus account.

If this is true, then when a relationship fails, it isn't that *we* have done wrong or failed to do what is right, it is that we have not found Mr. or Ms. Right. Hence, when relational failure comes, the best we mere mortals can do is cut our losses and return to our quest for the *one* who, once found, will cause us to live *happily ever after.*

But come on. Doesn't the idea that we were once two-faced, four-armed, and four-legged beings who got split by a paranoid Greek god come across as just a *little* crazy? And aren't thoughts founded in a mythical story really just . . . *myth?* Yet this idea has been successfully universalized; most people today hold to this view, even the non-Zeus followers.

Mixing Myth and Faith

The view that there is a predestined *one-and-only* out there for each of us has permeated even the Christian view of courtship and marriage. We have spiritualized it. We teach, "God has made one special person *just for you.*"

Really?

If that is not the epitome of self-centered, narcissistic thinking, I do not know what is. God did *not* create another human being *just* to satisfy your needs or to make you feel complete.

Yet many believers pray for God to lead them to the "right one," instead of negotiating through the decision-making process of selecting a mate in a down-to-earth, biblical approach.

Those of us in Evangelical circles have even taken this to a whole new level by encouraging parents to start praying for that "one special person" that God has chosen for our child while he or she is still young. Rather than praying for our children to embrace righteousness, justice, wisdom, sacrifice, goodness, et cetera—all things that would make them wonderful mates to *whomever* they chose to commit their lives to—we are praying for that "special one" God has already chosen for our child. *Zeus be praised,* I guess.

Surprising to many, there is absolutely *no* biblical evidence to substantiate such behavior. The Bible *never* tells us to find the one *God* has chosen. It teaches us how to live well with the person *we* have chosen. And there is a distance of infinitude between those two thoughts. The first assumes that life, love, romance, and marriage are part of God's divine plan and, therefore, depend more on God than on us. The second, and more biblical, line of thought tells us that successful life, love, romance, and marriage are the result of a couple living by God's principles—principles that never fail. But this version, which places true love and marriage on the footing of human choice and responsibility, just isn't nearly as romantic or seductive.

Many people of faith bristle when I take this position and ask me, "But what about when Isaac prayed that God would bring the right woman to him at the well?"

First of all, Isaac never prayed such a prayer; it was Abraham's servant who did. Abraham had sent his servant back to his homeland to find a relative for his son, Isaac, to marry. True, the servant *did* pray at the well that God would help him find the right girl, but he wasn't looking for some divine soul mate, he was looking for a relative of Abraham. In fact, when you read the story in Genesis, the servant does not begin to praise God until he learns that the girl is, in fact, one of Abraham's relatives.[2]

Now, if you are comfortable with one of your dad's employees searching for a cousin for you to marry, I guess it would be appropriate for you to pray that God will lead him to the "right one." But beyond that, the Bible is clear that marriage is *your* decision—not the result of a divine edict. In point of fact, I can find only *two* places in the Bible where God ever told someone to marry a particular person.

One is when God spoke to Joseph to take Mary as his wife. Joseph wanted to abandon her when he learned she was pregnant, knowing *he* wasn't the father. But God revealed to him that her pregnancy was by the Holy Spirit—obviously, an unusual situation. But even in this case, Joseph had *previously* chosen Mary.

The only other time God told someone to marry a particular person is when God told the prophet Hosea to marry a prostitute. (And I will concede that if you are considering marriage to a prostitute, you probably should have a divine revelation before doing so.) But even then, God did not tell him *which* prostitute to marry. It was still up to Hosea!

Though it is not supported in Scripture, there is something about the soul mate blather that is a siren song to the human soul. We want to believe it—it is so . . . *romantic.* And with this longing deeply embedded in our psyche, we inadvertently impress these thoughts onto the Bible as we read it. Sad to say, but the sacred Scriptures, which have brought unspeakable comfort and blessing to countless mortals, have also been used over and over to justify numerous untenable positions.

I'm suggesting that the problem is that we don't understand the dynamics of true love. We *think* we do. Our songs, movies, romantic novels, and TV shows all echo the belief that true love will always *appear* when we meet the right person, our destined soul mate. And this love will hit us hard out of the blue—an idea charged with mystery and romance. So the search for romantic love continues to occupy the minds of people, even those who are married! The result? High divorce rates and a plummeting marital happiness index.

The truth is, a successful marriage is *not* the result of marrying the "right" person, feeling the "right" emotions, thinking the "right" thoughts, or even praying the "right" prayers. It's about doing the "right" things—*period.*

Why doesn't God have a special person just for you? Because He knows that His principles of love, acceptance, patience, and forgiveness work, and they work all the time, every time—no matter to whom you are married. That is why the apostle Paul never told us to find that "special someone," but rather to make sure we find someone who truly believes and lives by the principles of love, acceptance, patience, and forgiveness. He referred to such a person as a "believer."

Now, here's an honest question: If being a believer is the key, then why do so many marriages fail, even with people of faith? Simply because many people of faith fail to live out these principles. The apostle James touched this problem when he said, "Faith without works is dead."[3] In other words, if you don't actually *do* the right thing, *believing* the right thing won't do you any good. In fact, he teaches that our lack of action can nullify the very faith we claim to have. It doesn't matter how spiritual or holy you *think* you are, if you are an impatient, demanding, whining, unforgiving person, your marriage will suffer.

Marriage Physics

We are all subject to the laws of physics no matter how we look, what we say, whom we are with, or even what we believe. For example, if you drive a car seventy miles-per-hour around a fifteen-mile-per-hour curve, you are going to get hurt—even if you feel lucky that day; even if you are listening to a Christian radio station at the time; even if you have a bobble-head statue of Jesus on your dashboard (though he may have his hands over his eyes with a look of "Ahhhhhhhh!!!" on his face). Why? Because the laws of physics still apply to you— they apply to everyone.

Just as there are laws of physics that affect everyone regardless of who they are or what they believe, there are also laws of *marriage physics*. Sadly, people keep breaking all the laws and then are stunned by the fact that their marriage stinks. "Why is my marriage so bad?" they ponder. Then the unwise voices of modern convention scream in their minds, *Wake up and be honest with your feelings. If things are bad, you married the wrong person. It's not supposed to be this hard. You've made a mistake. God doesn't want you to feel unloved. Be courageous and bail.*

And bail they do—by the millions.

But the problem isn't that people marry the *wrong* person; it's that people act in ways that are *wrong*—ways that destroy. If your marriage stinks, someone is breaking the rules of *marriage physics.* Unfortunately, most are unaware that rules even exist, much less know what they are.

Even though I don't think there is such a thing as a soul mate, I'm not saying the dating process shouldn't involve a hunt to find a special someone—someone compatible with you, someone with whom you have made a connection. If you are single, I think you should expect that, even strive to find a person with whom you can share feelings of deep affinity, friendship, sexual attraction, and compatibility. That being said, I think *finding* someone to journey with in marriage is the slenderest part of a life-long relational journey. A great marriage is mostly about two people committing to each other and then employing principles such as love, acceptance, patience, forgiveness, sacrifice, and unselfishness, to enrich that committed relationship. Marriage is more about *work* than about divine *luck,* more about finding someone to *love* than about finding someone to meet your own laundry list of personal needs.

2

Putting Things into Perspective

MAYBE you have looked around you and seen a number of happy couples and you've wondered, *What's the secret? How'd they do it? Can anyone show me some new techniques that will give me the intimacy and the love I long for?*

People grab books or attend seminars in hope of learning some new methods that will help them experience true satisfaction in their marriage. But what if better relational techniques and practices don't get to the root of marriage problems? Certainly, learning techniques that improve communication and intimacy can help a marriage grow (that's why I have written this book), but what if they are *secondary*?

I believe people often have the wrong *perspective* about marriage, about their spouse, and about love in general. They carry a perspective that is hurtful to their marriage. Problems are not the result of a delinquent marriage or the fault of the person we married; problems are rooted in how we *view* marriage. How we view our marriage will always trump what we do in one—what we *do* is secondary.

We should ask ourselves, *Could there be something I need to see in a deeper, more fundamental way—some kind of a shift in how I look at marriage, period?* I'm suggesting that marriage is more of an *inside-out* process than an *outside-in* one. The danger of making it an *outside-in* enterprise is that you actually set yourself up for feeling victimized and emotionally paralyzed when your techniques and marriage-enrichment practices don't work.

The bottom line is that there are no quick-fix techniques for a happy marriage. All the marriage-enrichment techniques and new behaviors only work like aspirin or Band-Aids when it comes to producing a strong marriage. There are a host of marriage-enrichment steps we'll talk about later, but the really hard work has to do with what's going on in between your own *two ears*—your expectations about marriage. Wrong thinking always produces bad results; and whenever your expectations are one place and your experience is somewhere else, you start to experience an emotional meltdown.

So what is the *right* view of marriage?

Buck-Naked

In a way, marriage is the great revealer, because you're living in very close quarters. If you ever want to get to know people, go camping with them for a week. Not only will you get to know them, they will get to know you. Somehow *who we really are* starts to poke out whenever we get close to others over an extended period of time. How we act under pressure in unguarded moments is always telling. Most of us are pretty good at covering up our negative parts under *normal* conditions; we even fool ourselves into thinking we are better than we are. But close relationships rat us out. This is especially true in marriage.

In the beginning, the Scriptures teach us, Adam and Eve "were both naked, and they felt no shame."[1] In an open, naked

17

relationship, if there are things to discuss, they are discussed. If there are issues to resolve, they are resolved. (Anyone up for naked arguing?) An open relationship means you can discuss misunderstandings and miscommunications, as well as how one spouse feels about what the other is doing. In a relationship free of shame, a husband and wife can even risk sharing their different ways of approaching love, friendship, and life in general, and do it *openly*—no smoke and mirrors.

In marriage, God intended that we be "naked" (so to speak)—that all the ways we are unique and different from each other come to the forefront. But sin changed our willingness to do that. Because of sin's effect on the human race, most are not comfortable with marriage being a revealer; we want marriage to be a *cover*. We don't go into marriage to face ourselves; we get married to get away from ourselves, to camouflage who we are.

Ever walk past a mirror and are shocked or mortified by what you see? Your hair standing up in a weird way, your slip showing, your fly open, egg stuck in your teeth? Mirrors can be real lifesavers. Had it not been for that mirror, you may have gone the entire day looking ridiculous.

Marriage is a mirror. By living so closely with another human being, you start to get a picture of what you *really* look like. You start to see where you need to adjust and change. This is why marriage is so effective at making people's lives more rich and productive—*if* they adjust to the needed changes. Unfortunately, many expect marriage to be something that makes them look better, not something that reveals where they don't look so good. Additionally, rather than see where *we* need to change, we opt to project our own negative images on our spouses and point out where *they* need to change: *She is so irritating. . . . He is such a lazy slob. . . . I don't want to act this way, but she brings out the worst in me.* Adam played the blame game like this: "That woman *you* put here with me—*she* gave me some fruit from the tree, and I ate it."[2]

If we believe our spouse is present in the marriage to make *us* look better, instead of being a mirror to help us see who we *really* are, we will think our marriage is inadequate whenever one of *our* faults is revealed. Like the witch in "Snow White" who became angry at the mirror for not telling her what she wanted to hear, we criticize the mirror—our spouse—in the marriage. We end up communicating to him or her: *This marriage isn't good. You're doing something wrong. We need to get this fixed.*

Once you are *internally* convinced that your marriage is *wrong,* you will never be able to change it *externally,* no matter how much you work on your attitude or behavior. People in troubled marriages seldom grasp the fact that bad marriages cannot become good ones by external pressure. External marriage-enrichment techniques do not work unless you begin by changing your *perception* of the marriage.

How do you see your marriage *now?* Is it precious to you? Do you honor, appreciate, and place worth on your marriage—as it *is?* If your view of marriage is fundamentally flawed, all the energies and strategies you are using (thinking your marriage will be better *if we just* do this or we just change that) will end in failure.

Unless you honor your marriage union *first*—without conditions—your tactics will come across as manipulative strategies to get your spouse to do what you want. This smacks of duplicity and insincerity. You must work on your marriage *because* you believe it *is* valuable, not because you are trying to *make it* valuable. Quick-fix manipulations do not a good marriage make.

Wrong Places

Have you ever planned to meet someone at a restaurant and you show up at the *wrong place* without realizing it? You search all over the restaurant before you sit down just to make sure your friend didn't beat you there. And you wait . . . and wait. Then you get up to scope the joint again, this time harder and faster. It hasn't dawned on you that diligence isn't going to help you at all, not when you are in the *wrong place*. You try to think positively: *They just got caught in traffic . . . they'll be here any minute.* You have no idea that your positive mental attitude is powerless to change the situation. Eventually you get frustrated and angry with the person you were supposed to meet.

Then you get the call. *"Where are you?"* the voice on the line asks.

In a moment you realize you have been at the *wrong place* all along. All your waiting, diligent searching, and positive attitude meant nothing.

Many are in the wrong place *mentally* when it comes to their marriages.

We think marriage is the place where we are *promised* happiness and love, not the place where we *learn* to love each other and face the ugliest parts about ourselves. We think marriage is the place where we should experience unending romantic love, where husbands are a girl's best friend, and where wives give their husbands all the sex they want when they want it. Ahhh, sweet dreams.

But this is *not* where marriage is—if you are there, you are in the *wrong place*. You can wait and search and wait some more. You can work harder and faster, but your work is in vain. If you don't change your view of marriage, you will eventually conclude that your marriage is flawed; that *it* is wrong. You will begin to think thoughts like: *I must have married too young; I probably married the wrong person; Maybe this marriage was never meant to be; My spouse must be the second-cousin of the antichrist.*

The Power of Understanding

When you are willing to understand each other, new vision and hope will emerge. You will immediately become energized to work on your marriage, even if it is rife with trouble. Here is a story that illustrates the power *understanding* has on our willingness to stick to a difficult relationship.

Once there was a boy who lived with his mother and grandfather. His grandfather was not really an elderly man, but he was confined to a wheelchair and had very little use of his arms. His face was badly scarred, and he had a difficult time swallowing his food.

Every day the little boy was assigned the task of going into his grandfather's room and feeding him lunch. This the little boy did faithfully, but not joyously. It was quite a mess to feed Grandfather.

As the boy grew into adolescence, he became weary of his responsibility. One day he stormed into the kitchen and announced that he had had enough. He told his mother, "From now on, you can feed Grandfather."

Very patiently his mother turned from her chores, motioned for her son to sit down, and said, "You are a young man now. It is time you knew the whole truth about your grandfather." She continued, "Grandfather has not always been confined to a wheelchair. In fact, he used to be quite an athlete. When you were a baby, however, there was an accident."

The boy leaned forward in his chair as his mother began to cry.

She said, "There was a fire. Your father was working in the basement, and he thought you were upstairs with me. I thought he was downstairs with you. We both rushed out of the house, leaving you alone upstairs. Your grandfather was visiting at the time. He was the first to realize what happened. Without a word he went back into the house, found you, wrapped you in a wet blanket, and made a mad dash through the flames. He brought you safely to your father and me.

"He was rushed to the emergency room suffering from second- and third-degree burns as well as smoke inhalation. The reason he is the way he is today is because of what he suffered the day he saved your life."

By this time the boy had tears in his eyes as well. He never knew; his grandfather never told him. And with no conscious effort on his part, his attitude changed. With no further complaints, he picked up his grandfather's lunch tray and took it to his room.[3]

Once you understand *why* your husband acts that way, or *why* your wife thinks that way, it will change how you feel about him or her, though nothing has really changed. Compassion will come with an accompanying perseverance—all because you now *understand*. I cannot overstate the importance of understanding.

Fighting to Understand

In the pages that follow, I am going to work hard at helping you *understand* what's going on in the enterprise of marriage: what men think, what women think, what men expect, what women expect, how men are wired, how women are wired, et cetera. In a way, marriage is a cosmic joke; we are so different from each other. But if marriage is about revealing weakness and sin, and is about being challenged to get beyond ourselves to truly love another person, as I contend, then *understanding* will bring the fruit of newfound energy and strength for the task of getting along—not unlike the shift that happened to the grandson on that fateful day.

Dare to believe marriage is good, that the one *you* are in is good. Dare to ask God to help you treasure it, appreciate it, and stay committed to it, even though there are times you feel a little shaken-up and buck-naked with your needs going unmet. Until we have the right perspective about marriage, our efforts to make it better are futile. When we see things correctly, our efforts are met with real, lasting, authentic change that fosters a healthier, stronger marriage.

Part

2

The Laws
of Marriage Physics

3

Marriage Physics

ONE hundred percent of divorces start with a marriage. Marriage can be dangerous. But marriages don't have to fail. There *really* are things you can do to ensure that the sparks of love reignite in your marriage. The good news is, the laws that govern relationships don't discriminate regardless of whether you are small, fat, tall, short, cute or a tad less cute, young, or old.

As I said earlier, we are *all* subject to the laws of physics. And just as the laws of physics affect everyone regardless of who they are or what they believe, so do the laws of *marriage physics.*

Don't misunderstand me. I do think *grace,* which is God's unmerited favor, gives us an advantage in life, but it does not afford us sloth or negligence, God doesn't bring grace to bear so we can become slobs. I think grace gives us an advantage *after* we have done all we can do, while trusting Him to take our efforts beyond what one would normally expect—like the fellow who gave Jesus the five loaves and two fishes.[1] The guy gave his best, his all, but it wasn't much. Yet Jesus took this small quantity of food and fed a multitude with it. That's what faith does. It trusts God to do more than we could have ever thought or imagined as we do our absolute *best* in obedience to

Him.[2] The great apostle Paul wrote, "But by the grace of God I am what I am." But then he immediately said, "I worked harder than all of them."[3] No matter how you slice it, faith isn't for dillydalliers.

We must commit to discovering and practicing the laws that govern relationships if we want to enrich and empower our marriages to be great. And we must learn to avoid the things that rob and destroy relationships. As we talk about these laws, I will be describing the fundamental differences between men and women. As I noted before, these are generalizations. Not everything will apply to you; however, a generalization is *generally* true. If the shoe fits, wear it. If it doesn't, move on.

4

Law Number One: Men and Women Are *Not* Created Equal

JACK SPRAT could eat no fat, his wife could eat no lean, and so, between the two of them . . . *they argued and fought and lived miserably.* One would think they could have celebrated their differences and enjoyed the savings of a clean plate instead of starting the war of the worlds. But that would have been way too . . . compromising. Attacking and judging each other for being *different* came much more naturally.

The differences between men and women are colorful and pretty self-evident. In fact, the only thing we seem to have in common is that we come from the same species. Other than that, we have different views of the world, different values, and we operate by a different set of rules.

Take the bathroom. Men visit the bathroom with a single goal in mind; he goes in, does his business, and walks out avoiding eye contact and conversation. Women, on the other hand, think of the bathroom as a social area or therapy office. A woman can meet a *stranger* in the bathroom and begin a conversation as if she were her new best friend. Men don't make friends in the bathroom; it just doesn't happen.

Men have sex; women make love. Men like things;

women like people. When women get lost, they ask for directions. Men don't get lost—getting lost would make a man look stupid. A man may take a scenic route, which adds travel time, but men don't get lost. Men are hunters; women are gatherers. Men protect; women nurture. As we will see shortly, men and women even have different brain structures. We think differently, believe differently, handle stress differently, and behave differently.

Yet it is amazing how many men and women resist recognizing or discussing their differences. But these differences are the fingerprints of our gender. They are neither good nor bad; they are simply who we are. Birds fly, frogs croak, horses sleep standing up, and men and women do what they do. A loving, intimate marriage relationship will leave room for gender differences without making the assumption that the other is *wrong*.

To value the *uniqueness* of another person—how they *differ* from us—is a very mature position to take. Most don't because we tend to see differences in others in terms of flaw and affliction. For example, consider how differently men and women approach problems and how we "dis" each other because of it. Men are ordinarily logical and women generally are more in touch with their feelings. (Again, this is clearly a generalization that doesn't *always* hold true and may sometimes be exactly the opposite.) So because of our inward bias against differences in others, a feeling wife doesn't understand her logical husband's position. She doesn't describe her husband as "levelheaded" and "clear-thinking," she thinks, *Why is he so mean and hard-hearted? He is without the milk of human kindness!* The husband makes the same mistake. He doesn't see his wife as someone who understands and cares deeply for others; he wonders, *Why is she so fuzzy-thinking and emotional? She wears her heart on her sleeve. She is too illogical and seems incapable of standing up in the face of opposition!*

Actually, both the logical and feeling types are perfectly capable of understanding each other. The feeler *does* have logic and the logical *does* feel. It's just that they prefer to make decisions *in their own way.* It is simply a matter of preference. Once a feeler understands that a logical does have feelings and is not ice-veined, and a logical understands a feeler isn't just muddle-headed but understands logic, they are well on the road to deciding which approach is best for a particular situation.

The point is, we are different, but if we learn to understand and accept each other, there can be some pretty nice harmony. But understanding and accepting differences do not come easily when one sees those differences as bad or stupid. Hence, as husbands and wives we work hard to correct the "flaws" we see in our spouses—to make the one married to us just like us. We assume our gender distinctions are "right" for both genders. But the truth is, men make lousy women and women make lousy men.

Sadly, there is great resistance in our culture to identify or discuss gender differences, much less applaud them. For most of the twentieth century, people said the differences between men and women were socially engineered. Social pressures made girls play with dolls and dress in pink, and made boys play with trucks and wrestle in the mud. But an explosion of biological research since the 1980s has shown that the stereotypical differences between men and women are *not* learned or socially engineered—they just are. If you put little girls and little boys on a desert island, the girls would make dolls out of sticks and grass and play house, and the boys would grunt, hunt, and establish a leader. The boys compete; the girls cooperate. This research demonstrates that men and women are wired to behave in certain ways, just as animals behave instinctively in various environments. One way is not *better* than another way; it is just *different.*

Refusing to understand and appreciate our male/female differences, or trying to cover them up, results in tragedy. Chaos, conflict, and unhappiness rule. When individuals in a marriage cannot *be* who they are or feel marginalized for being who they are, they retreat into fake behavior, fight, or flee. There is certainly no intimacy, where one can be known and loved.

But every marriage has hope for intimacy. Working to gain understanding of how the one you are married to thinks about life will inject your marriage with energy. I have the joy of watching thousands of couples have their marriages transformed during my weekend seminars, not because anything really changes, but because *understanding* comes. They begin to *get* the *why* behind the things that make them want to strangle each other, and it is like a shot of adrenaline into their relationship. Understanding is an amazing thing. It's weird. Nothing has actually changed—no new patterns have emerged and no new practices have been established—yet these couples begin to look at each other with a new set of eyes. They literally *fall in love* all over again!

Here is a story told by Stephen Covey that captures the power that understanding has on our emotions:

I remember a mini-paradigm shift I experienced one Sunday morning on a subway in New York. People were sitting quietly—some reading newspapers, some lost in thought, some resting with their eyes closed. It was a calm, peaceful scene.

Then suddenly, a man and his children entered the subway car. The children were so loud and rambunctious that instantly the whole climate changed.

The man sat down next to me and closed his eyes, apparently oblivious to the situation. The children were yelling back and forth, throwing things, even grabbing people's papers. It was very disturbing. And yet, the man sitting next to me did nothing.

It was difficult not to feel irritated. I could not believe that he could be so insensitive as to let his children run wild like that and do nothing about it, taking no responsibility at all. It was easy to see that everyone else on the subway felt irritated, too. So finally, with what I felt was unusual patience and restraint, I turned to him and said, "Sir, your children are really disturbing a lot of people. I wonder if you couldn't control them a little more?"

The man lifted his gaze as if to come to a consciousness of the situation for the first time and said softly, "Oh, you're right. I guess I should do something about it. We just came from the hospital where their mother died about an hour ago. I don't know what to think, and I guess they don't know how to handle it either."

Can you imagine what I felt at that moment? My paradigm shifted. Suddenly, I *saw* things differently, and because I *saw* differently, I *thought* differently, I *felt* differently, I *behaved* differently. My irritation vanished. I didn't have to worry about controlling my attitude or my behavior; my heart was filled with the man's pain. Feelings of sympathy and compassion flowed freely. "Your wife just died? Oh, I'm so sorry! Can you tell me about it? What can I do to help?" Everything changed in an instant.[1]

We're Not Equal

Let me go ahead and say it: Men and women are *not* created equal. We are pretty defensive about equality in modern culture today, and rightly so. But when I say this about men and women, I am *not* suggesting that men are better than women, or that women are better than men, or that one sex should be afforded more opportunity than the other. I am saying there are *differences* between the sexes that must be acknowledged and understood for marriages to be successful.

People who claim the sexes are *equal* (or the *same*) are well-meaning, but do both sexes an injustice by ignoring the fundamental differences in men and women. Everything from language (using "humankind" instead of "mankind") to fashion (unisex everything) has been redesigned in an attempt to mask the ways men and women are different. There is nothing inherently wrong with those things; in fact, they may be beneficial in confronting gender bias. But when they are the result of a quest to eliminate gender distinctions, I think that is a mistake.

Certainly, both men and women should be *treated* as equals in terms of respect, opportunity, pay, influence, and so on, but that is *political* or *moral* equality. The essential differences in the sexes are the result of the created order and are easily demonstrated scientifically. We should not ignore or try to cover up those differences. Doing so sabotages male/female relationships. We refer to each other as the "opposite" sex for good reason.

Equality was never the goal of creation. Not everything is the same. Differences are everywhere in God's created order. He loves diversity. There is not just one type of flower. Every snowflake is different. He didn't create just one kind of fern, but fourteen *thousand* different kinds. Astronomers estimate there are at least a million different galaxies in the section of sky framed by the cup of the Big Dipper. God loves that men and women are different, and I think He wants us to showcase our differences, not fight over them. He wants us to be "naked" about them.

The Way We Were

When the first man met the first woman, there was good chemistry. The Bible says Adam took one look at Eve and said in essence, "Now, a guy would leave both his mom and dad for one of these!"[2] They were open, honest, and naked with each other and not ashamed. There was no infighting or blame shifting. It was a sweet deal.

But then *sin* entered.

The moment sin appeared, the first couple responded by retreating from each other and sewing "fig leaves" together to "make coverings for themselves."[3] *Naked* became too risky. What is interesting is *what* was covered. They didn't cover their mouths, though their mouths were involved in their sin. They didn't cover up their hands, though they, too, were involved. They covered the parts that were *different* from each other. Why? Because *different* is most often the fodder for judgment and rejection. We tend to push against those who are different than us.

Once sin came, the first couple pushed against each other by inaugurating the *blame game.* Adam claimed coldly that the "woman" God had given him was to blame for the mess. Eve said the devil made her do it. One-upping each other became the norm, but that was never God's dream.

Celebrating the Differences

People waste tons of energy trying to camouflage male and female distinctions (they are fig-fashion experts). Something about sin makes us want to ensure that our differences go unnoticed. But what if God wants us to acknowledge and celebrate the differences? I think we resist acknowledging our differences because when we talk about differences, people immediately attach judgments about those differences. There is something in the human condition that wants to believe there is *one* thing that is "best," which means it is better than everything else. We think something or someone must be at the top of the heap—"Best of Show." So we are forever making comparisons and assigning judgments. When one thing is judged wonderful, the other is not nearly so.

You are going to lose in the marriage enterprise if you don't stop, drop, and roll over the fact that men and women are *not* equal. We may be equally valuable, but we differ in a litany of ways. If we don't recognize and adjust to those differences, our marriages will not be what God intended them to be.

When we are able to talk openly about our differences, we will learn how to actually enjoy and celebrate them. If we can't be "naked" about how different we are from each other, we will never be able to experience intimacy in our marriages. We'll just be playing roles. Conflict may come when we first start discovering and discussing our differences, but conflict eventually gives way to appreciation and celebration. When we *don't* give our spouse room to be himself or herself, conflict comes, too, but it comes to stay.

Remember this law the next time you hit a rough patch when your expectations are not met: *Men and women are not cre-*

ated equal (the same). Manage your expectations and endeavor to better understand each other. Learning about each other, and accepting, celebrating, and negotiating differences are not natural practices for us. But we must learn these skills if we want to have great marriages.

5

Law Number Two: Men and Women Think Differently

MEN and women are different. We just are. Our bodies are obviously different; our behavior is different; and as it turns out, our brains are different, *too*. Why would God create us to be so different? For two reasons: 1) He wanted each of the sexes to face ourselves, so we could discover our strengths *and* our weaknesses; and 2) He wanted us to learn to depend on each other's strengths, which would end up covering for each other's weaknesses. Facing ourselves—being open, honest, and naked about our differences—is an unnerving undertaking. Yet denying our differences ultimately accounts for our undoing.

Understanding the different ways men and women think and feel about life helps us more accurately interpret what is *really* going on in our marriages. How a person views the world affects how they interpret things. Imagine a Martian watching an election on Earth. The Martian would think the human beings were simply putting pieces of paper in little tin boxes. A politician of the time might view it as a very tense election in progress, one that affects his livelihood. A historian in the future might see it as the turning point at which a country moved from one era to another. The point is, your perspective colors your understanding of what is happening. And it will ultimately govern your responses.

It's All a Misunderstanding

In the words of John Gray, *men are from Mars and women are from Venus.* In other words, we come from two completely different worldviews. Our differences are "head" differences, not "heart" ones. If we would dare to learn how the opposite sex thinks, we would spend less time judging each other for having a wrong "heart" and could spend more time discussing which "head" view is most appropriate for any given situation. We could actually experience a kind of *synergy.* Learning about the thought patterns peculiar to the individual sexes, and learning to discuss them, or even celebrate them, is like mastering a foreign language.

Wars usually start over misunderstanding. If you work on *understanding,* you can avoid a *hundred-year war* and actually experience marital bliss. Those who fail to learn each other's "language" will end up seeing their relational energy *lost in translation.* Misinterpreting your spouse's actions will cause you to believe there are hidden dragons lurking in your spouse's soul—something "deeper" is going on that is not good. This explains the tendency we have to create "heart" problems out of things that are inherently "head" problems.

Consider how men and women view feelings. Men typically don't share feelings very well with their wives—or with *anyone,* for that matter. Many women view this male reticence as a "heart" problem. *There is something wrong and he won't admit it,* she thinks. *There are dragons afoot.* Worse still, this problem gets translated into, *He does not love me.* Why? Because when a *woman* doesn't share her feelings, it is because her heart is sick or she no longer cares. It's easy to project why *you* would act a certain way onto another person, but that does *not* mean doing so is valid. *Judgment* is all about arbitrarily assigning a specific motive to an action when you have no idea why the person *really* did what he or she did. Jesus said, "Do not judge, or you too will be judged."[1]

Men do this to women as well. If a wife tries to "improve" her husband or their relationship, it comes across to him as criticism. Unsolicited advice always comes across as criticism to a man. He interprets his wife's attempts as, *Why is she criticizing me? I haven't done anything to deserve this.* He assumes his wife has a "heart" problem she's not facing. Again, *dragons.* He concludes, however unfairly, that there is only one explanation: She is a card-carrying "witch" (or something rhyming with "witch").

Judgments always preclude us from really understanding each other, and they foster alienation and conflict. What we have to realize is that those misinterpreted actions are really the result of how our spouse processes information.

Tale of Two Brains

News Flash: Both sexes *do* house brains. However, they operate very differently. Though the search for brain differences is nothing new, the modern (and more sophisticated) hunt for differences began in the 1960s, when researchers first discovered that a part of the hypothalamus called the *preoptic* area was substantially larger in males than in females. Since then, image technology has made mapping male and female brain differences easier.

The 1990s became the *decade of the brain,* as research skyrocketed all over the world. What have scientists found? The deeper they dig, the more they discover there *are* big differences between the male and female brains. Men tend to be better at analyzing systems (better systemizers), while women tend to be better at reading their environments and reading the emotions of other people (better empathizers). The evidence is indisputable that these distinctions arise from biology, *not* culture.

Though men have four percent more brain cells than women and about 100 grams more brain tissue, women have more *dendritic* connections between brain cells, which means they use their brain cells more efficiently and effectively than men do. A woman's brain also has a larger corpus callosum, which allows a faster transfer of data between the right and left hemispheres than in a man's brain.

Somewhere between eighteen and twenty-six weeks into a pregnancy, a male baby's hormones (testosterone) start to kick in gear and the results are significant. The bundle of nerve fibers (corpus callosum) connecting the right and left hemispheres of the brain starts to disintegrate. This causes a breakdown of communication between the two hemispheres. This is important because of the activity that takes place in these two hemispheres.

The left side of the brain houses the logic and reasoning centers of the brain. The right side houses emotions, feelings, judgments about beauty, and social relationships. It turns out that about 85 percent of men end up being *left-brained* thinkers; they are extremely logical in their approach to life, impacting the way they problem-solve and act in relationships. Consequently, men are very *task-oriented*. It's not that the *right-brained* functions, such as feelings and aesthetic judgments, which foster strong relationships, are impossible for men, but we function from the right side *less* well, and when we try to, it come across a tad contrived. Why? Because the male's left-brained disposition has to be overcome with a tremendous amount of concentration and energy. We men do not "get in touch" with our feelings easily, and it is precisely this struggle that women end up misinterpreting as *lying*. But men aren't necessarily lying when we come across as phonies, it is that men can't move from being left-brained to being right-brained with *ease*.

Men were therefore born to think unilaterally. We think in either the right or left hemispheres, but seldom in both at the same time. It is sort of like having two computers—one on the right shoulder and one on the left—but there is no inter-facing cable between the two of them. They both work, but they don't communicate with each other in any meaningful way.

Women, on the other hand, have no such breakdown be-tween the two hemispheres. *Plus,* the female hormone estrogen prompts nerve cells to grow *more* connections within the brain and between the hemispheres while the female is still in the womb. The female connecting tissue doesn't deteriorate; hence, the two hemispheres of their brains interact and process infor-mation *together.* Because of this, women process their environ-ment from more than one point of view. They have logic and reasoning juxtaposed with feelings and relationships—much more complex than a man's thinking. Hence, women are more in touch with their feelings and can more easily express them than men can. They have an increased ability to bond and be connected to others. This is why women are the primary care-takers for children. There is no society on earth where men take on this role. Because of *brain differences,* women have a more acute sense of smell, better hearing, and keener eyesight than men do. Now, many women assume this stronger connection system makes their brains more efficient and productive than a man's brain. Men, on the other hand, see this connection process as proof of faulty wiring—the two sides keep getting in the way of each other.

All Boxed In

Men's brains are specialized. Compartmentalized. Because of the separation of the two hemispheres, men must focus on *one thing at a time.* If you take a brain scan of a man while he is reading, you'll find he is virtually deaf. Before a man answers the phone, he has to ask everyone to quiet down, the TV needs to go off, and the environment needs to settle *before* he picks up the receiver. A woman does no such thing. The TV can be blaring, she can have a baby on her hip and be in the middle of making dinner, and she simply picks up the phone without pause. Why? Her brain can differentiate among all the sounds and activities in a way a man's brain does not.

Generally speaking, men don't multitask well. It is as if men's brains were a collection of little boxes. We have a box for everything. There's a box for the job, a box for the wife, a box for the kids, a box for the money, a box for the mother-in-law (taped up and stuffed somewhere in the basement), et cetera.

Basically, men have a box for all the important facets of their lives. And here's the basic rule: *The boxes never touch!* When an issue arises, we men reach for the appropriate box. We take hold of that box and slide it out, being ever so careful not to touch or disturb the other surrounding, unrelated boxes. We open the selected box, discuss the contents of *only that* box, then carefully pack it up and put it back among the other boxes until needed again. This is why men tend to be single-taskers. We do one thing at a time; we open one box at a time.

The Nothing Box

There's a special box in a man's head that most women don't know about. This particular box has nothing in it. We refer to it as the "nothing box." It's called that because it contains, well . . . *nothing*. It's just an empty box. And amazingly, of all the boxes stacked in a man's brain, his "nothing box" is his favorite box. If given the opportunity, a man will always go straight to his "nothing box."

Ever wonder what a man is doing when he looks comatose and dead to the surrounding world for hours on end? Picture him fishing, channel surfing, or playing a video game—as long as the activity requires little or no mental energy, men love it! We revel and wallow in it like joyful pigs in the mud.

Researchers have discovered that men do, in fact, have the ability to think about absolutely nothing and—*get this*—still breathe. Neurophysiologist Professor Ruben Gur of the University of Pennsylvania showed that 70 percent of the electrical activity of men's brains shut down when they were in a resting state. Think of that: *70 percent*! Women's brains, on the other hand, maintained a full 90 percent of their electrical activity. This demonstrates that women are constantly receiving and analyzing input from their surroundings. Women with children are completely aware of how those children are feeling, what their emotional state are, who their friends are, what their hopes, dreams, and fears are, and if they are plotting any mischief. Contrariwise, men maintain only a vague knowledge deep in the back of their minds that they have a wife and some shorter, nondescript people wandering around.

Not to underestimate men—we actually *can* think very intensely. Women may be great multitaskers, but men can go head-to-head with women in the arena of single-minded focus. Men are the gladiators of focused thought, champions who think with laser-like precision. This is what makes men so good at what they do. Men will usually rise to the top of any profession, even those dominated by women. The best chefs in the world are usually men. The best hair designers in the world are usually men. The best clothing designers in the world are usually men. (Remember, we are generalizing.) This is because men have the ability to block out every distraction and focus on one task and excel at it.

Here's the glitch: When a man is not driven by a specific task, something he can fight for or dominate, *he will drift.* A man will drift to the comfort and solitude of his "nothing box" every chance he gets.

Women can't think about nothing. Why? Because their minds are constantly abuzz, always reviewing, always processing numerous bits and bytes of information about what may or *may not* need doing. Consequently, a woman who doesn't understand the *nothing box* will surmise that her husband must be in a place of meaningful contemplation whenever he is quiet. Then, thinking he is surely primed for intimate, meaningful conversation, she engages him by asking a simple question.

"What are you thinking about?" she inquires.

"Nothing," he replies glumly.

"Nothing? You have to be thinking about something!"

He pauses. "No . . . *really* . . . I was thinking about nothing."

"You're lying," she says with a hint of hurt in her voice. "No one thinks about nothing. You just don't want to tell me."

"I'm not lying!" he says defensively. "I really was thinking about nothing."

So off she goes, annoyed that he's holding out on her
again. All she wants to know is *why he won't share with her*. She
doesn't even consider that he really might be thinking about
nothing, because it is an experience with which she is entirely
unfamiliar.

According to columnist John Scalzi, men are well ac-
quainted with this line of questioning:

> Every male in the world has had to deal with this ques-
> tion, which is more often than not uncorked at entirely in-
> appropriate times, such as when you are watching sports,
> locked in a passionate embrace, or reeling in a feisty marlin
> from the Gulf of Mexico. Regardless of what you're doing,
> you must come up with a complete and satisfactory answer,
> or stand accused of *hiding your true feelings*. Which means, of
> course, you'll spend the next week pretending to be sorry. So
> you've got to come up with something. And it had better be
> good.[2]

The truth is, men *love* to think about nothing. It's a kind of
cherished quality among our gender. *Nothingness* is every man's
quiet reward in this life. In our search for great joy and peace,
we men will look for the stone clearly marked "nothing." *Nothing* is the froth on the top of a man's life. *Nothing* is the reward
for engaging in a day chock full of "somethings." We love *nothing*; we relish it.

The problem is, this drives women *crazy*. Few male behaviors are more frustrating to a woman than when a man sits
joyfully content doing—you guessed it—*nothing!*

How can he just sit there? she frustrates.

Incapable of thinking about *nothing,* she fails to comprehend such a thing. Her mind is constantly flittering as one thought after another shoots across her mind with the precision of a skilled tightrope walker. She multitasks her way from one activity to another, which just adds to her angst as she observes her silent, *I-refuse-to-disclose-my-true-feelings* husband. She concludes he must just have a cold, resistant *heart.* And all this time she thought *he was "the one."*

Back to John Scalzi:

Go up to a woman and ask her what she is thinking. I have just done so with my wife, and this is what she is thinking about: "Off the top of my head, I'm thinking about the party we're having Saturday, and how I'm going to fix that chandelier in the front room so that people can walk around without hitting their heads. Underneath that I'm thinking about my work schedule this week and whether or not I'm going to have time to do some of the things I need to do at home as well. And under that I'm wondering if it's too late to get tickets on a plane to Ohio for Christmas. *And* I'm thinking about getting a snack."

Not only is she thinking about something, she's thinking about four separate things. If I check back in five minutes, she'll still be thinking. Women are always thinking, and often about practical things.

Men, on the other hand, are actively thinking about five minutes out of every hour (usually not in sequence). So, at best, you have a one in twelve chance of catching a man actually having a thought.[3]

The problem for a man is obvious: If he lets a woman into the "nothing box," *something* would be in the box and it would no longer be the "nothing box." And he doesn't want *something;* he wants *nothing.* And truth be told, if he *did* let a woman in, she would be both shocked and disappointed. For when she entered the nebulous realm of the "nothing box," she would witness a vast wasteland, an empty space, an immeasurable black hole.

In the battle of the sexes, women often have asserted that their brains are somehow superior to a man's because they are always thinking. But I have *never, ever* had a man say he wishes he could do the same. I have, on the other hand, met countless women who have expressed great envy and exclaimed, "I wish *I* had a nothing box!"

Where Is the Salt?

As I noted before, the female brain has an amazing ability to receive and differentiate auditory and visual stimulus. Because of this, women are often said to be able to read people's minds, or of having eyes in back of their heads. The truth is, women are not mind readers, but they are experts at processing verbal, vocal, and body language. When men don't demonstrate the same capacity, women tend to think they are insensitive and uncaring, when, in fact, they are just being *men.* On the other hand, when men see this tendency in women, they think, "Who cares about the underlying messages? Just focus on the facts!"

Women have a greater variety of cones (color receptors) in their retinas. The X chromosome, of which women have two, is responsible for the development of the cones. That means women don't just see in color, they see in *full* color. A man may be able to tell the difference between red, blue, green, and purple with relative ease, but a woman's perception of color is far more detailed. She notices such colors as salmon, magenta, taupe, aqua, and even sea-colored aqua, as easily as a man sees red from blue. A man may say a particular car is green and his wife will stare at him as if he is playing the village idiot and say, "It's not green, it's teal." The man may respond, "Who cares *what* shade of green it is? It's still green!"

Women have a much wider peripheral visual perception than do men. So in a way, they *do* have eyes in the back of their heads—or at least they see more than a man does. A man's eyes are longer than a woman's, but his brain configures his eyes to act like a pair of binoculars. He pretty much sees only what he focuses on, which means he misses much of what goes on *right in front of his eyes.*

It is a woman's amazing visual skill that makes the following scene familiar to all married couples. It goes something like this:

Husband: "Honey, where is the salt?"

Wife: "It's right there in the cupboard. I just put it there."

Husband: "I can't find it. It isn't here! You must have put it somewhere else."

With an exasperated exhale, she marches over to the cupboard, reaches in, and *presto,* she produces the salt.

Inexperienced husbands think she has just performed a magic trick. We old guys just shake our heads in puzzlement. Because many women don't understand how a man sees, they tend to think they have witnessed just one more example of how men are muddleheaded and lazy. But the truth is, men are geared to look up and down, right and left, and from one spot to the next when searching, as if scanning a field with a pair of binoculars. Not so with a woman. Her peripheral eyesight can see *and process* the entire cupboard at one time. She claims superior awareness of detail. He claims she has a faulty filtering system and gets distracted with too much detail.

The Better to Hear You With, My Dear

The female brain has the amazing capacity to identify and categorize sounds, as well as make judgments about what those sounds mean. A woman can have a conversation with one person while monitoring another conversation nearby. Women hear the voices of babies and crying kittens much more easily than men do, and from farther away.

It is this capacity for receiving and processing such information that makes a woman more aware of what's going on in her environment. This is why women are masterful multitaskers; they can juggle several projects at one time. One of the reasons women are more successful with small children is that they can be aware of where each one is, what he or she is doing, what each one *should* be doing, and working on some unrelated task like doing the laundry, *all at the same time.*

This can become a problem. For example, if a woman walks into the kitchen and sees her husband reading the newspaper, she assumes, *I multitask, therefore he must multi-task,* and she starts talking to him. Being a single-tasker, however, he has all of his attention on the newspaper and is not hearing a single word she is saying. When it becomes apparent that he has not been listening, she assumes he does not care about her and incorrectly perceives his "head" problem as a "heart" problem.

Ladies, if you see a man busy doing something, you will have very little success, if any having him recall *what* you are saying, even if he is responding, "Uh huh . . ." Unlike a woman, when a man is doing something, all of his energies are focused on that one thing, and for all practical purposes he is as deaf as a doorknob. If you want him to actually *hear* what you are saying, you will need to disrupt his activity and get him to *look at you.*

This, of course, is not without peril, since he will not want you to stop him from what he is doing. You may want to wait until he is finished before engaging him *in* important conversation. The challenge in this is that men seem to always be doing *something*. Even when they are in their "nothing box," they are doing something—which in that case is *nothing*.

Eye, Ear . . . and What?!

After discovering this for myself, I found I was much more successful in *hearing* what my wife had to say. Inevitably, however, I still found myself in situations where she insisted that she had told me something and I had no recollection of any such conversation. In my attempt to be a better listener, I was careful to watch out for my single-tasking proclivities and to stop whatever I was doing so I could focus on what she was saying. But oddly, I still found myself missing things she claimed to have told me. After a while I became concerned that I might be losing my hearing. I actually called our family doctor and made an appointment.

When I saw my doctor, I explained why I believed I might be losing my hearing. He said that since I was getting older, I was probably correct—the ears are usually one of the first things to go as we age. He said he would have his nurse give me a screening.

I followed the nurse into a room where she had an electronic box. She explained that a series of tones and beeps would be played. Each time I heard one, I was supposed to raise my hand. We began the test.

As expected, she played a variety of tones and beeps, one after the other. As instructed, I raised my hand each time I heard one. Finally the nurse stopped the test.

"You can hear all that?" she asked, suprised.

"Yeah," I responded. "Why, is something wrong?"

"Well, according to this machine you can hear what cats and dogs hear," she said, sounding confused. "Something must be wrong with this thing," she concluded. "I'd better send you to an ear specialist. They have much better equipment."

She called and got an appointment for me to see the specialist that same afternoon, and grabbed a pad of paper to write down the name of the place she was referring me to. She wrote down "Eye, Ear" and abbreviated "Associates." Then she handed me the paper. You can imagine my confusion as I read that I was to visit an "Eye, Ear and *Ass* doctor."

I looked for a moment and asked, "What kind of doctor is *this?*"

"Why do you ask?" she responded.

"Well . . . I've heard of an 'Eye, Ear and Throat' doctor, but I've never heard of this—"

"*What?* Let me see that. . . ."

Realizing her error, she quickly apologized and proceeded to write out "Associates." Feeling reassured I was not being sent to a place of profound discomfort, I left to go to the office of *Eye and Ear Associates.*

At the specialist's office, I was escorted to a room where there was state-of-the-art ear-testing equipment.

The lady behind the glass gave me the same instructions as before, reminding me to raise my hand only when I heard a tone or beep. As before, I found myself responding to a large variety of sounds and was raising my hand constantly. Finally the test operator asked the same question I had been asked at my doctor's office? "Really, you can hear all that?"

The specialist said I had better hearing than he and was curious why I had bothered to take the test. Though I explained I came in because my wife claimed she had been telling me things I had no recollection of ever hearing, I still felt like an idiot.

When I got home, Debbie asked, "Well, what did the doctor say?"

"According to them I can hear what cats and dogs can hear," I replied.

"I knew it," she said. "You can hear fine. You just don't pay attention!"

But I *had* been paying attention. I knew I was a single-tasker, but I was being careful not to perform any tasks when being spoken to. Yet I was still missing stuff. So, I decided to do a test of my own: *I would watch how far Debbie would get from me before I could no longer hear her.*

She was unaware of my impromptu test as she started talking to me in the kitchen. I kept my eye on her as she moved to the far side of the room, noticing I could still hear her fine. She then proceeded into the living room (I had not moved from my position) and then took a left and went into the dining room—the whole while still talking to me. She was now *on the other side of the house,* in a completely different room, still disseminating vital information on which I was certain I would have to pass a pop quiz later.

"*Hey!*" I yelled.

"*What!?*" she yelled back.

"I'm on the other side of the house! How am I supposed to hear what you are telling me?"

She paused for a moment, then responded, "Awww, you don't listen anyway. . . ."

Ah ha! Now it was all beginning to make sense. It wasn't that I was too much of a single-tasker and not paying attention. It was that she was too much of a multitasker and would keep talking to me as she flitted about doing all her tasks. Never mind that I was in a different part of the house. In her mind she was still talking to me!

The next day I caught her doing the same thing, only now she was on the second floor while I was still on the first! Women are often quick to blame their husbands for not listening and will complain, "I told you!" She told him all right—while she was in a different area code!

I remember sharing this story at a men's retreat, thinking it was just something funny that had happened to me, but heads everywhere started to nod. At the break, one guy came up to me and said, "Pastor, I'll be in the bathroom. The door is closed; the fan is on; sounds are bouncing against all the tiles in the room; all I can hear is the sound of rushing water—and *she's still talking to me!*"

Multitasking women. Once they start a conversation, they can't seem to stop. They just keep wandering around the house, dealing with the many tasks on their plate while they continue their important conversation with you. Of course, whether or not you are in the same building seems to be completely irrelevant to them. You will still be responsible for the information.

Intuition vs. Interpretation

What people refer to as women's intuition is simply their acute ability to interpret small changes that men usually miss (facial expressions, a slight change in mood or attitude, body language, tone of voice, and so on). This is why some men have a hard time lying to women—their eyes and slight facial expressions give them away. Women are like walking lie detectors.

If a man and a woman walk into a party, the man's tunnel vision and focused hearing pick up bits and pieces of what's going on. He notices Joe across the room but completely misses Pete, who is standing two feet off to his right. He catches some laughter at one side of the room, but misses the "hello" from a friend who just flanked him from the side. He does instinctively scope out an alternative exit, as well as where the kitchen and bathroom are, but that's about it. On the other hand, in just a few minutes (usually within ten) his wife has picked up on who is there, what the women are wearing, what moods they are in, if any flirting, arguing, or scheming is going on, and which couples are mad at each other.

Women have an amazing ability to multitask unrelated activities because their "bandwidth" is much larger and can transfer information faster between the two hemispheres of their brain. However, this creates some spatial problems for women. They may be able to pick up on the smallest change in voice or body language, but can't seem to tell north from south. Around 50 percent of women have difficulty telling their left hand from their right and have to use their wedding bands or some other trick to remember which is which. Men, who are used to unilateral thinking, can more easily make these distinctions. Women's inherent spatial challenge is the result of how their brain processes. This is why women can easily *find the salt* but can often have difficulty reading a map or not hitting the garage door with the car.

The way a woman interprets her world is nothing short of amazing, but that is also why men can't really follow women. It isn't that men aren't smart. It's that we don't follow *how* women arrive at conclusions. Let me explain.

Men are a lot like those old, clunky adding machines that used to take up half of an office desk. They had huge arms that worked like the *one-armed bandit* slot machines. Each time you added a number and pulled the lever, it registered the action sequentially. When you pressed the "total" button, not only did you see the answer, but a tape logged the logical process that was taken to *arrive* at that answer. A man usually comes to his conclusions very much like this. He is logical and sequential; you can predict his "total" from the steps he took before he hit the "total" button and pulled the lever.

Women are not nearly so easy to follow. They are much more like a computer with a sophisticated program. It does amazing calculations, but you can't really see *how* the program arrived at the answer. This uncanny ability in women is the primary reason seventeen-year-old girls function like adults while boys of the same age are still clowning around and lighting farts.

With vastly differing brains, we must learn to communicate with each other.

6

Law Number Three: Men and Women Communicate Differently

THE captain of Road Prison 36 in the movie *Cool Hand Luke* claimed, in his thick Southern drawl, "What we have here is a failure to communicate." He could have easily been talking about the communication between men and women in general. This is not good news for married couples, because *how* we communicate affects *everything:* the issues we deal with, whether or not conflict gets resolved, and ultimately how we behave toward each other.

Communicating Can Be Difficult, Even on a Good Day

Communicating can be a challenge even outside of marriage. I remember some years ago, back in the early 1970s, when I was first getting involved in ministry, I was in a mall in Peoria, Illinois. Malls were pretty new back then. Before malls, everyone went shopping downtown, which involved struggling to find a place to park and braving whatever weather elements presented themselves. Plus, there was always the tricky task of negotiating past people you did not want to talk to. Downtown shopping districts were magnets for people who wanted to push their ideas on everyone else. From bizarre chanting cults and pan handling bums to political campaigners and people preaching on soapboxes, downtowns were a virtual potpourri of opinions, requests, and verbal assaults. Not only did the new malls provide great parking and shelter from the elements, they were a haven from all the people soliciting their opinions. Much to the dismay of the new mall owners, however, these "solicitors" followed the crowds into the malls and bothered their customers. Despite their best efforts, the mall managers had a difficult time discouraging these merchants of opinion. On the particular day that I was visiting, the mall had decided they had had enough and would arrest any and all who were proselytizing or soliciting in any way, shape, or form on their property.

Keep in mind that I was not standing at the door of the mall, handing out religious leaflets. Neither was I in the middle of the mall fountain shouting, "The end is near!" I was sitting in a coffee shop discussing spiritual matters with a friend, and I had my Bible resting on the tabletop. But in other parts of the mall, zealous young people were walking up and down the halls, handing out flyers and doing their best to promote their faith. The mall called the police and soon arrests were being made everywhere. An officer walked into the coffee shop where we were sitting and noticed my Bible on the tabletop. "Excuse me, is that your Bible?" he asked. I acknowledged that it was, and the officer quickly took me into custody and threw me into a paddy wagon. Needless to say, I wasn't expecting to be thrown into jail just for having a Bible in public.

As I was sitting in the paddy wagon, I started to get angry. I knew that the situation was ridiculous and that my rights had been violated. I considered getting into the faces of the officers and demanding my rights. (Something I would not have had a problem doing. I'm Puerto Rican. We get into people's faces just for the sport of it.) But I decided to quiet my Latin blood and was instead determined to be sweet and nice, to reflect the love of God in a less-than-ideal situation. Yes, that would be the plan: Be nice and show the love of God to all.

Upon arrival at the police station I was kind and respectful, and offered smiles to all the officers who were processing me. I stayed relaxed and calm, maintaining the demeanor of one who was among friends. The entire time I was fingerprinted and photographed, I smiled and let the officers know that I was appreciative of everything they were doing. I smiled from ear to ear and just knew they could sense the peace and love of God that I felt in my heart for them.

Soon after I was photographed, however, an officer approached me and requested that I follow him into another room. I thought it odd that I was the only one singled out, but politely agreed to follow, smiling at everyone I passed. Once in the room, the officer looked sternly at me and told me that I needed to remove my clothes. He then walked out of the room.

Remove my clothes? Why would I need to remove my clothes?! While I was not particularly comfortable with his request, I felt it wise to just do what the man requested. I proceeded to disrobe and was soon standing in the room in my underwear.

As I was standing there, I looked over at the far end of the room and saw another guy sitting in a small holding cell. He looked at me and said, "Hey." I quickly responded with a "hey" of my own.

"So . . . what'cha in for?" he asked.

I thought that was kind of cool (just like in the movies). I'd never been asked such a question.

"Well," I replied, "I was talking to somebody about God."

"Oh . . ."

I really expected more of a response than "Oh." After all, how many people had he met who had been thrown into jail for talking to somebody about God! Oh well, I decided I should return the question—kind of a "jail etiquette" thing.

"What are *you* in for?" I asked very politely.

"I killed somebody," he whispered.

Killed somebody? They have me in a room in my underwear with a man who *killed somebody!?!* I was stunned. How do you respond to such a statement? I mean, what is the proper response to "I killed somebody"? *Gee, that's nice? Way to go? Bet they had it comin'? Ah, don't worry about it—everybody has a bad day?*

Why did he tell me that? After all, if you *do* kill somebody, aren't you supposed to keep that a secret?! Why was he spilling his guts to some stranger standing in his underwear!?! Felt he needed to be honest? For cryin' out loud, he just *killed* somebody! I think a little white lie to my question would not have been that big of a deal at that point.

Suddenly the officer reentered the room. Considering my recent conversation, I was really glad to see the guy. He looked at me standing there in my underwear and said, "No son, you need to take your underwear off."

This was getting weirder by the minute. I still had no idea what was going on or why, but when a man with a gun tells you to take off your underwear, you take off your underwear. Then, as if things could not *possibly* get any weirder, the officer said, "I need you to bend over and spread your cheeks."

Spread my cheeks!? For crying out loud! What was going on?

Then it finally hit me. Here I thought I was communicating the love of God, but all they were hearing was, *This boy is high on drugs.* And now they were looking for my drugs!

Thank God all that was required of my "interrogation" was a simple visual inspection of my—well, you get it. Gotta tell ya, though, it was pretty humiliating. All I could think was, "Thank God I don't have *this* guy's job."

So there I was, flashing the vertical grin to some cop who thought I was on drugs. Once convinced I was not smuggling anything, he finally put me in a cell. Later, when the judge heard the details of the case, he immediately dismissed all the charges, and I was soon a free man again.

Trust me when I tell you, communicating is not as easy as you would think.

Learning to Communicate

A man called his neighbor to help him move a couch that had become stuck in the doorway. They pushed and pulled until they were exhausted, but the couch wouldn't budge.

"Forget it," the man finally said. "We'll never get this in."

The neighbor looked at him quizzically and said, *"In?"*[1]

Marriage communication is often exactly like that. We think we are saying one thing but the other person is hearing another. In fact, because of the presuppositions and points of view we bring into a relationship, we often hear things that were never said and don't hear the things that were. It's one thing to talk *at* each other; it's an entirely different matter to be *understood,* which is the *goal* of communication. Clear, effective communication is one of the most complex things to learn. This is not for the faint of heart. The truth is that verbal and nonverbal, *push-and-pull* communications ultimately forge the "rules" that govern our marriages. It's the training ground where the long-haul legacy of interaction is created. We need to get good at it.

There's an inherently human notion, however, that prompts the thought, *Hey, we're married, we'll communicate! After all, communication is like sex, you just kind of . . . well . . . do it. Right?* No, that's wrong. Whether you've been married for one month, one year, or fifty years, you have to work on communicating with each other; it does not come naturally. Communication is the fresh, breathable air of every relationship. Without communication skills, couples suffocate under the stress of unrealized expectations.

Differences Foster Conflict

Because marriage is the place where two very different people, emerging from two completely different families of origin, come together to live for a lifetime, there will be conflict. The ways each partner makes decisions, resolves differences, spends money, et cetera are often Grand Canyons apart. This means there are going to be misunderstandings, incorrect assumptions, and flat-out fights through which we must navigate. But do not fear. Conflict is not a sign that you should not be together and it is not necessarily a bad thing. In fact, intimacy (where we know and can be known) can only be forged *through* conflict.

As a couple matures, conflict appears less and less often because the spouses' understanding of each other becomes greater (if the marriage is healthy). But initially, conflict pops up fairly frequently and can be intense. There is no way a husband and wife will be able to resolve all their differences in a few weeks; it will take time and truckloads of love and hard work. The strongest couples with the greatest marriages have wrestled through bagfuls of conflict. Looking back, they all realize conflict helped them move toward understanding by highlighting both their differences and their preferences.

Make friends with conflict. Through conflict we discover that not everyone thinks like us, not everyone has the same perspective we have, and not everyone feels the same emotional and spiritual needs we feel. The real danger of conflict is ignoring it, or just hoping it will go away on its own. The Scriptures warn about this. Paul writes, "Do not let the sun go down while you are still angry."[2] That means we must *address* conflict when it happens; we cannot let it linger.

But even talking things out sounds simpler than it really is.

Talk Ain't Cheap

Women love to talk. Just get a few women together to watch television and they will carry on conversations with each other about a variety of things *during the show.* Like juggling experts, they can juggle several subjects with each other and no one ever seems to drop a ball. If there are men present, they will usually be begging the women to be quiet. Men can't watch the screen and carry on a conversation, so they assume women who talk must *not* be watching the show. But they are. The reason they are motivated to talk while watching the TV is that women bond and build relationships through casual chatter. To just sit around like couch potatoes, watching a show in silence, is considered by women as insulting to the others in the room.

This is one of the main reasons women become upset when men don't talk. They assume that since the man doesn't talk, he must not care about their relationship. But men talk to communicate information or facts, not to build relationships. The reason many men avoid their wife's "let's talk" request is that they don't get why they should. If the facts have already been stated and the pertinent information disseminated, why engage in meaningless banter? Why waste the time? The problem is, women *need* to talk.

However, women need to understand that talk is a very costly emotional enterprise for a man. Men struggle with talking much more than women do. Why? For men, language is generated in the dominant hemisphere of their brains (usually the left side), while women seem to be able to use both sides for language (talk comes more easily). Though men's brains are great for processing information in highly compartmentalized ways and have the capacity to separate and file information, they have no efficient way *to talk about it.* Go ahead and ask a five-year-old boy, "How are you?" and chances are his mother (or younger sister) will answer, "He's fine, thank you," while the boy is still searching to find words with which to respond. This is why men tend to use many more "uh" and "um" fillers than women do. And this is also why most speech pathologists work with boys.

Silence Is Deadly

Men tend to talk inside their own heads. We can sit for long periods of time without uttering a word. We are not mad or trying to be distant; we are just being quiet. If a man and woman share the same physical space, the woman will perceive the quiet man as distant, sulking, or not interested in jumping into conversation, when it fact, he's just not talking. There's nothing going on emotionally; he is not trying to make any kind of relational statement.

Whether a man intends to or not, his silence speaks volumes to his wife. Guys, if we are not careful, silence will speak *for us*; and it will say things we do not want to say. It will say, "You're not worth my time," or "I don't really care what you think," or "Go away, you're bothering me." How many times have you husbands had your wives accuse you of saying something negative when you *know* you never said anything negative? You may not have said it *verbally,* but you said it with your *silence.* When a man goes silent, a woman starts to feel unloved. Silence is deadly to a relationship with a woman.

One of the most intimacy-enhancing activities you can do in a marriage is *talk.* For most men, the kind of intimacy they are looking for is sexual intimacy. What they fail to realize is that one of the keys to sexual intimacy with a woman is something most guys would *never* think of: *talking.* Guys, we need to talk more and learn to listen *better.* New levels of marital intimacy are reached when a man learns to converse with his bride. Sometimes this is the only adjustment a couple needs to make for romance to be rekindled in a marriage. Real intimacy begins above the waist. Listen to her; talk to her.

Processing Life

Remember that men's brains are made up of little boxes (see chapter 5). We have a box for everything. When we discuss an issue, we go to the appropriate box, pull the box out, open the box, discuss only what is in that particular box, and then put the box away until it's needed again.

To deal with the challenges of life, men think things over without talking out loud. We stick our problems in the appropriate box and then mentally go back and forth from the problem to our "nothing box" until a solution begins to emerge. The whole time we can appear blank-faced, statue-like, and nearly comatose. Women tend to interpret this activity as, *he must be bored, or lonely, or depressed,* and then they will try to engage in some lovely, relational-building chatter to make us feel better. Of course, a man sees this as an invasion of privacy and resents the effort. Ladies, guys love sitting silently. This is why buddies can spend a whole day on a boat fishing, saying little to each other, and feeling refreshed and complete at the end of the day.

Women, on the other hand, can't understand this, because if they don't talk openly about things, they feel like they are suffocating. Women's brains are more like a big ball of wire, where everything is connected to *everything else.* It's like the information *superhighway,* where any computer in the world can talk to any other. When a woman discusses an issue, she reserves the right to refer to any other issue at any given time, since she is connected to *all* issues at once. This is why a woman cannot resolve the issues she faces in silence. The problems she faces keep going around and around in her head until she *talks them out.*

But just as it drives women crazy when their husbands go silent in order for their problems to resolve, men tend to go crazy with the gabbiness of a woman processing her issues out loud. Understanding "why" men and women solve problems the way they do will eliminate much conflict here.

Code-Talking

A movie was released some time ago called *Windtalkers.* It was about a soldier who was significant to U.S. military reconnaissance because he was a Native American who used his native language as code to prevent the enemy from deciphering sensitive data. He was referred to as a "code-talker."

Similarly, men and women communicate in their own unique codes. It is very easy for us to misunderstand each other unless we take time to learn each other's codes. Men are literal; women are more emotive—they want to communicate emotions rather than facts. Men are direct; women are indirect.

A man will ask his wife, "What are you upset about?"

"Nothing," she responds.

Good, he thinks to himself. *All is well, then. We've communicated.*

But does he get off the hook that easily? No way! At this juncture the man commits a major communication faux pas. He assumes her "nothing" means just that: nothing. But men need to learn that in a woman's code language, "nothing" really means "something." When a woman says, "Nothing is wrong," she is really saying, "I'm angry at you because you are an insensitive jerk!"

On the other hand, women must learn the code-talk of a man. If a woman *really* wants to communicate effectively with a man, she must grasp the inescapable truth that she needs to say what she means. While this sounds completely inappropriate to most women, it's a must. Men do not get subtle hints, or even obvious ones, for that matter. To a man, hints are like fancy hors d'oeuvres at an all-you-can-eat buffet. We reason, why waste your appetite on one-bite appetizers, with fancy names, skewered on toothpicks, when there's limitless chicken fried steak and mashed potatoes to be had?

Getting Beneath the Surface

When men communicate, we generally say what we mean and mean what we say. If we didn't say it, we didn't mean it, and if we did say it, we meant *only* what we said—not what you *think* we meant by what we said. Women don't buy that.

They are constantly looking for the "deeper meaning." But when you dig and keep on digging to search for a man's deeper meaning, you won't find anything.

It's not that men are shallow. Men have depth, but we don't give hints as to what's going on inside our hearts. A man's emotional depth requires some direct excavation—flat-out interrogation, really. Like Shrek tried to explain to Donkey in the movie *Shrek*, men have layers. He explained that males were like onions. You can't tell what's inside from what's on the outside—you need to peel back the layers. Sadly, some men guard their layers like Fort Knox, while others are less layer-sensitive. But either way, when communicating with a man, a woman must understand she has some layer-removal to do. She can't assume he is sending out signals through the tone of his voice or with his body language. Men don't do that.

Women, on the other hand, are masters of nuance. For women, *words* are just a piece of the conversation. Women send out and analyze facial expressions, hand gestures, and voice inflections in the communication process. And they use these things to "message" to others on purpose. A woman's brain has the capacity to distinguish tone changes in voice volume and pitch in a way men often miss. She can literally hear emotional changes in others. For every *one* man who can sing in tune, there are *eight* women who can. When a woman says, "Don't use that tone of voice with me," this is one of the few places where she is being literal. She can *actually* hear disrespect in the tone of a person's voice.

Because a woman is so in tune with communication nuances—which help her read between the lines—what is said to a woman is not nearly as important as *how* it's said, or what is potentially *implied* by what is said. A husband has to be vigilant to make sure that his implications are accurate, not just his *words*. The implications come with consequences. If he misses this all-important detail, he risks placing another barrier between himself and the real issues about which he and his wife are seeking to communicate.

There is an old episode of *Star Trek* where the characters encountered a species that was hypersensitive to nonverbal communication. The *Enterprise* crew diligently prepared for the meeting, studying every possible protocol and nuance. One wrong eye blink, sudden movement or incorrect voice inflection could result in a perceived insult, thereby unleashing an intergalactic war. Sounds much like the species known as *Woman*.

Much to the chagrin of men, women often communicate on levels men do not understand. Here is a sample of a casual encounter between two women:

"Hi, Susan!" Marie says.

"Oh, hello Marie," Susan responds.

"Oh, I love that outfit you have on today. It makes you look very nice," Marie remarks.

"Thanks, Marie. I appreciate that," Susan says as warmly as she can.

As Susan walks away, she turns to her husband and says, "She is such a witch!"

"What?! She was very nice to you!" he retorts.

"No she wasn't! She said I was fat!"

"What are you talking about? She said you looked nice."

"Oh, she was just rubbing in that I need to wear loose-fitting outfits like this because she thinks I'm a cow!"

The husband is stunned.

"Are you doing illegal drugs?" he says.

"Oh, you could tell by the way she smiled that she hates me," Susan asserts.

"You are just being crazy!" her husband complains.

"Oh, so you think I'm fat, too!" Susan exclaims.

Don't Play God

Though women have an amazing capacity to "read between the lines" during communication, they are not always right. Jesus warned about judgment. Judging occurs when someone does something and you don't know *why* but you decide to assign a motive to it anyway. Rather than jumping to unnecessary and unproductive conclusions, women need to work on *understanding* their men. Don't assume your husband thinks you're stupid when he gets quiet. Don't assume you know what he is thinking. The Scriptures teach that only God "looks at the heart."[3] (Perhaps this is subtly implying, *Wives can't.*)

I'm not suggesting that all mind reading is bad. Sometimes we have had enough experience with each other that we can sort of "guess" what our spouse will do without asking him or her directly. Women are notorious for being able to guess how their husbands will respond to different things, though men do so as well. Truth is, this is not always bad. Mature couples "mind read" each other all the time so they can meet their spouse's needs without having to conduct a formal interview. However, if there has been a lot of hurt or judgment between the couple and they are in relational distress, mind reading can make things worse.

Assumptions jam the communication gears and this factor alone leads to much marital discord. Wives, with their *below-the-surface* intuition, always probing for the deeper meaning, will reach one conclusion, while their husbands, who assess situations *on-the-surface,* come up with another. While women see communication as digging for treasure, men see it more like raking leaves from the lawn. A man will rake (scrape up the exterior stuff), efficiently bag it up, and consider the matter settled—leaving his wife, who longs for what's below the surface, unsettled.

But whose approach is right? The man's surface approach or the woman's below-the-surface approach? The answer is, *both* are right. Effective communication is about *understanding,* and because we are different from each other, we must work harder at understanding. Understanding requires asking questions. Dr. Stephen Covey, in his classic book, *The Seven Habits of Highly Effective People,* encourages people to *seek to understand, before seeking to be understood.* This principle can narrow the communication gap, and once mastered can alleviate much of the difficulty we experience in trying to understand each other.

Seeking to understand creates fresh communication. It helps us to arrive at: "I can see *how* you would feel that way." If couples would practice a "seek to understand" approach when communicating, instead of judging each other, there would be more dancing in the streets and less divorce in the courts.

7

Law Number Four: Men and Women Want Different Things

MEN and women want *different* things. No surprises here. Those who take the time to find out what their spouse wants or needs, and do something to see those needs are met, have the stuff of a happy marriage. This is a little tricky, because it's easy to assume that the wants and needs you feel are the same as those of your spouse. It is the assumption that our needs are the same that drives us to treat our spouses the way *we* want to be treated, to love them the way *we* want to be loved. However, when someone is trying to love you in a way you don't really want to be loved, or they try to meet needs that are *not* felt by you, it will mean little to you, and may even seem annoying. Scratching feels good only if you *scratch* where it *itches*.

Find the *itchy* places—the places where there are wants and felt needs—and decide to "scratch" (meet) those wants and needs. No one pushes to go to divorce court because their spouse is meeting too many of their needs. Met needs always produce the feeling of being loved, valued, and appreciated. Contrariwise, unmet needs make relationships unbearable and precipitate all kinds of inappropriate activities.

What Men Want

Before we discuss what it is men want, let's point out a few things they *do not* want. For instance, *men don't want to become women.* If you ask women to describe their ideal man, many will describe a man who loves to converse and open up. They want someone who enjoys the little details of life, someone who remembers all the things that are important to them, and someone who would rather *share* with them about the day than *stare* at the TV all night. In short, women describe their favorite *girlfriend.*

Sorry, ladies, but we men make terrible girlfriends. We don't like to talk and open up. We generally forget the little things. And sadly, staring at the flashing boob tube is often more appealing than sharing minor details of the day with you. But don't take it personally—we don't really want to share with *anyone.* Men do not share. We conquer, we protect, we compete, we work, we insult, we make disgusting noises, we leave the toilet seat up, but we generally do not share. You *can* train us to share (more on *that* later), but sharing doesn't come naturally. And at the end of the day, we will never be women.

Work-Free Zone

Here's another thing men don't want: *Men don't want to "work" on their marriages.* Why? Because most often, men like their marriages the way they are. A survey taken by the *Chicago Sun-Times* showed that of 2,301 men, 1,788 said they would remarry their wives. In another survey by *Women's Day* magazine, women were asked how they felt about their husbands. Only half of the women who wrote in to the magazine said they would marry their current husbands if given the chance to do it over again. David Roadhouse, a Chicago psychotherapist, suggested the reason for the disparity might be that "on the whole, men experience fulfillment more easily than women do. Women are filled with all these romantic yearnings and romance is finite, limited, difficult to sustain."

For years, I believed men were primarily responsible for the rise in the divorce rate and for marital problems. When it comes to relationships, men in our culture are generally referred to as clueless, insensitive, heartless, cruel, et cetera. Every man is the hapless nitwit portrayed by Ray Romano in *Everybody Loves Raymond*.

Not long ago I attended a play called *The Male Intellect— An Oxymoron,* in which men were mocked for their relational incompetence. (It was a one-man play performed by—*yep*—a guy.) In my early presentations I confidently asserted, "The biggest problem in marriage is that there is a man involved."

Now, after countless hours of working with troubled marriages and after speaking to tens of thousands of couples, I no longer believe that is the case. When it comes to relationships, men are not stupid, clueless, twisted, broken, perverts, or sickos. We're men. And the truth is, we are not much different today than men have been for thousands of years. It is not the men who have dramatically changed; it is the women.

In most cases, it is women who are upset with the whole marriage enterprise. Eighty percent of all divorces are filed by women. It is usually the woman who seeks out marriage counseling. Women of our day are the ones frustrated to the hilt. It is the woman who always seems to have her heart broken. It is the woman who is the most *disappointed.* I now believe women of the twenty-first century have completely unrealistic expectations when it comes to living with and dealing with men. And I am convinced divorce rates will continue to rise if women do not bring their expectations about marriage back to reality. *Unrealistic expectations* are often the culprits responsible for the misery women feel—not their husbands. The unsustainable, unreasonable romantic longings of women are ripping marriages apart.

At one of my *Laugh Your Way to a Better Marriage* seminars, a woman came up to me and admitted that she had spent the first eight years of her marriage in a constant state of disappointment. Her husband (poor fellow) could *never* live up to all the expectations she had. Finally she decided to sit down and write down all the expectations she had brought with her into the marriage. She said she filled out one page after another after another with all the ways she wanted to be treated by a man. After writing out every expectation she could think of, she put all of the pages in a shoebox, grabbed her husband's hand, and went into the backyard. She dug a hole with her husband and, together, they had a funeral for all those *unfulfilled* expectations. That night she changed her perspective on marriage. Her eyes lit up as she told me the funeral took place over twenty-five years ago and that she had been happy ever since.

Sadly, millions of women seem completely clueless about this. And trying to reason with many of them is like trying to explain advanced algebra to a person who just smoked several joints of marijuana. So pervasive is their "drug-like" romantic thinking that many women enter marriage with the expectation that a man will meet *all* the emotional needs of her heart. But God never designed a man to meet *all* the emotional needs of a woman. He is supposed to meet some of them, but there is not a man on planet Earth who is wired to meet all the emotional needs of a woman.

"But isn't he supposed to complete me?" you may ask.

No, he's not. And while we are on *that* subject, let me say this: A successful marriage is *not* the result of two empty souls finding each other in an attempt to "complete" each other. Two empty, unfulfilled souls who get married will just be a marriage of two empty, unfulfilled souls. A successful marriage is possible only when two complete and happy people get together for the purpose of building a life together. They do not need the other to be truly happy, complete, or emotionally whole. They are *already* whole people who are joining together to enjoy the benefits of marriage. The Bible says that "two are better than one." But that is only true if they are two healthy, emotionally stable, and complete human beings. If you are a single, miserable, lonely, incomplete, and hollow soul, for the love of God, do everyone a favor and get yourself whole before you get yourself married.

Who's to Blame?

For most of human history, multiple generations of a family lived within close proximity to each other. Chores such as cooking, planting fields, washing clothes, caring for children, and harvesting crops were often shared by the family clan. Women grew up their entire lives with the same women around them. They had a network they could trust and garner support from. Sadly, today those kinds of networks no longer exist for most married women.

A shift in Western culture has resulted in young brides being separated from their mothers, sisters, and friends as their new husbands drag them away to distant lands while seeking their own fame and fortune. The result is that these emotionally isolated women then try to get all of their needs met by their husbands, when no man was ever designed to meet all the emotional needs of a woman.

I believe this rarely acknowledged issue is one of the main contributors to so many women being unhappy in their marriages today. My best advice to young would-be grooms is this: Don't take the girl away from her support structure of friends and family. If you want to live in L.A., then marry a girl from L.A. Any man who marries a woman and then moves her a thousand miles away from her friends and family may feel like she is sucking the emotional life out of him while she tries to get all of her emotional needs met by him alone. The Scriptures say, "For this reason a man will leave his father and mother and be united to his wife."[1] I find it interesting that it doesn't say a woman should leave *her* father and mother. Is it possible that keeping a woman near her emotional support structure has always been an essential key to a happy marriage?

Practically speaking, however, staying close to family and friends is just not an option for many couples. This makes it absolutely critical for couples to develop safe relationships outside of marriage. If they don't, their marriages will go bankrupt, and they will end up lonely, frustrated, and angry. Men need to find a band of brothers they can connect with, and women need to find good girlfriends who can fill the void that was once filled by their mothers, sisters, and childhood friends. Unfortunately, many women do not make friends as easily as men do, which is why I strongly suggest making sure the wife remains near her original support structure if at all possible.

I Can't Get No Respect

So what is it that men *want*? In a word, men want *respect*. That means a man wants to be held in esteem and to be shown consideration and appreciation—even when he makes mistakes. He wants to be seen as a hero, especially in the eyes of his bride. He needs someone to believe in him when the odds are stacked against him. If a man doesn't *feel* respected, he's destined to act in a way reminiscent of the obnoxious, *"I-can't-get-no-respect,"* Rodney Dangerfield. He becomes insulting, bug-eyed, and generally gross.

What women don't understand is that men don't believe they need to *earn* respect; they feel it is owed to them because they are *men.* That may sound sexist, but it really isn't. What I'm saying is, men need to be respected for *who they are,* not for what they do. If they don't feel respected, they can't survive. It gets harder and harder for them to breathe (emotionally). That is why it is *so* important for a woman to learn to give her man *unconditional* respect.

Most women are willing to show respect, but they want their men to be worthy of it. If he is not, a woman feels that showing respect is disingenuous and she moves into *"I-had-better-correct-the-situation"* mode. She believes she can respect her man only if she can get him to *act* respectable. But that is not how it works. Respect is too great a need for a man to have it *come and go* based on performance. If a woman will learn to risk respecting her man when he is not perfect, he will open his heart to her and will become pliable to change. A man needs respect to feel safe enough to open up. When he feels he is being looked up to as the "head" in a relationship, he will auto-matically allow his wife to become the *"neck"*—she will be able to point her man in the right direction. Women generally have no idea how much sway they have over a man. The book of Proverbs says, "The wise woman builds her house,"[2] but "a dis-graceful wife is like decay in his bones."[3] A wife is either build-ing up or tearing down her husband.

Most women are not aware of this, but the majority of men feel very unsure of themselves. In a recent survey, 75 percent of men admitted that they feel like an imposter. Many spend their entire lives fighting the voices in their head that constantly shout, *You don't really know what you are doing! It's just a matter of time before everyone discovers you're a fake! You are a fraud!*

A man's home should be the one place in his life where those voices of criticism are silenced; where he is assured he is wonderful and competent. The ultimate ego boost of a man's life is when his wife willingly and enthusiastically makes love to him (as opposed to lying there counting ceiling tiles and asking, "Are you done yet?").

Sadly, for millions of men, their home is a place where the voices of criticism are amplified, not silenced. I heard one woman say to her husband who had just received a special plaque at an award banquet, "Everyone thinks you're so great, but I *know* what an idiot you are!"

Women frequently make the mistake of insulting their husbands in an attempt to motivate them to change. *"What's the matter with you?"* they'll quip. *"Can't you do anything around here? Can't you pick up your dirty clothes? What kind of loser are you anyway!"* Women who do this assume that if their "criticisms" and "rejections" are properly received, they will correct the faults and character flaws of their husbands and make them better men. But nothing could be further from the truth. Those criticisms and rejections create only anger and frustration inside the man. The result will be a man who is disconnected, bitter, and unemotional.

The reason so many women use insult as a tool to try to motivate men is that insults generally work on women. If you insult or embarrass a woman, she tries to do something about it; she tries to change. But this thinking does not work on a man. The insult of insults for a man occurs when he tries to make love to his bride and she rejects him and pushes him aside as she would set aside a pile of dirty laundry. Insulting a man will only end up robbing you of his heart, and you will not see the changes you want in the relationship.

Ladies, don't ignore your man's need for *respect*. When you disrespect your man by being unappreciative, corrective, demeaning, ridiculing, ignoring, or discounting, it will hurt him. But don't misunderstand me: *Respecting* a man doesn't mean you can't work on him. You just need to be smart about it. If you are not careful, your attempts to change him will communicate to him disrespect. If you want a man to act differently in your relationship, you are going to have to put insults aside and learn to be *unconditionally respectful*.

Even God Deals with Men Through Respect

If there ever was a person who had the right to disrespect men based on their performance, it would be God. God is intimately aware of every flaw and defect in a man's character. Yet look at how God dealt with men throughout the Bible.

Abram was so cowardly that he denied Sarah was his wife so that a king would not kill him in order to get her. Yet God did not respond to the obvious coward, He looked deep within and saw a man of great faith. Even though Abram was not able to have a child at the time, God called Abram "Abraham," meaning "father of a multitude." God gave Abraham the *respect* due a father and a patriarch long before he became one.

The Lord called Gideon a "Mighty Man of Valor" despite the fact that, at the time, Gideon was a chicken and was hiding so no one could hurt him. But God looked deep inside Gideon, saw what he was capable of, and treated him with the respect due a great warrior long before he was worthy of such honor.

Gideon went on to achieve one of the most lopsided military victories in history.

Look at Simon. The guy was a flip-flopping, not-sure-of-himself, run-when-the-heat-is-on kind of a guy. This is the one who told Jesus he would willingly die with him, yet fled when Jesus was arrested and three times denied that he even knew Jesus. But when Jesus first met him He said, "Simon, from now on you will be called Peter—the rock!" And sure enough, Peter went on to be a bold and compelling witness of the Gospel of Jesus Christ. God knows that the key to unlocking the potential in a man is to treat that man with unconditional respect, long before he deserves it.

If It Ain't Broke . . .

When a man falls in love with a woman, his thoughts go something like this: *I love her, she's great—in fact, she is perfect. I love her just the way she is and I hope she never changes.* It was this thinking that inspired Billy Joel to write the song "I Love You Just the Way You Are." On the other hand, when a woman falls in love with a man, her thoughts are generally something like this: *I love him, he's great, but he really needs some work.* This is a disaster in the making. Divergent expectations always lead to conflict.

When a woman thinks a man needs work, she is not trying to be negative or demeaning. In fact, she rather enjoys the thought. Do you know why? Because women *like* to work on relationships, and because marriage represents her *greatest* relationship, she enjoys working on it. But the thought of working on *any* relationship makes most men feel ill. You see, to a man, work is something you do to earn money. *Relationships* don't fit into a man's definition of work. We think relationships are the one class of things we should *never* have to work on.

So when a woman wants to work on the marriage relationship, the husband usually gets nervous and uncomfortable. The reason is simple: She says she wants to work on "the relationship," but men view that as code for *she wants me to change.* And men don't want to change. To a man, "change" is a four-letter word. This is primarily because we men have fragile egos. We don't handle *there is something wrong with you* very well.

That being said, it doesn't mean men don't think very highly of themselves; we do. Most men love themselves dearly and don't *really* think there is much need for self-improvement. So if a wife is pushing for improvement, he feels insulted that she even made the suggestion. It's not that he is completely against change, it's that he thinks his wife is wonderful the way she is and she should feel the same way about him. Women don't catch this because they don't think of working on the relationship as insulting a man's ego—it's more a matter of *improving* him. And the truth is, women *do* improve men.

In their book *The Case for Marriage,* Maggie Gallagher and Linda Waite make the case that married men are happier, healthier, and make more money than single men. In other words, *marriage improves men.* Statistics also show that married men live longer than single men. In fact, statistically, being single is one of the worst things a man can do. It is equivalent to smoking two and a half packs of cigarettes a day! (I suppose the worst would be a single guy who actually smokes two and a half packs of cigarettes a day.)

Girls, don't take offense that your husband is having a hard time with your efforts to *work* on your relationship. Don't interpret his resistance as a sign that he doesn't care—he does. Men look at things *differently* than women. Though men need improvement, women must learn to be patient and not destructive to the male ego in the process. Women need to see the men in their lives as long-term projects and learn how to encourage change without fracturing their egos. (The good news is, you ladies really *can* eventually get us to where you want us to be. The bad news is, after you get us there, *we die.*)

Strong Women

Just because men are resistant to "improvement" and women need to be careful *not* to fracture a man's ego, this doesn't mean women can't be strong. Ladies, the truth is, you *need* to be strong. Women play a critical role in helping men leave boyhood to become men. But you must learn to be strong in ways that don't cross the line of disrespect.

History shows us that one of the strongest factors in determining whether or not men will be barbarians or become civilized creatures is the absence or presence of strong, confident women. In the late 1800s, men rushed to the new opportunities found in the American West. Without the presence of significant women in these men's lives—women who demanded a certain standard of behavior—it did not take long for the West to become known as the "Wild West."

By the early 1900s, however, the men of the West had been tamed, becoming responsible husbands, fathers, and members of their communities. What made the difference? The presence of women—strong, confident women. When these women came to the West, they demanded that men behave in a civilized manner if they wanted them as their wives. The result? Men acted civilized.

Can you imagine if the women of that era thought like so many women today? Many modern-day women are more desperate than strong, more devoid of self-esteem than confident.

If this ilk had been the ones who headed west (freely having sex and willingly caring for deadbeat men without requiring proper behavior), these men would have never changed their dispositions. When men are not held to the fire of relational discipline, they take advantage of all the freedoms women afford them, and in the end, they will abandon their women and children (either emotionally or physically) in the pursuit of their own personal pleasure.

Today our entire Western *civilization* is "wild." We have multiple generations of boys who have failed to become men— they are extremely self-centered individuals who think of little more than what they want next. These boys have been nurtured by guilty mothers and needy women who often have little to no self-esteem and who take care of their man's every need, while requiring little to nothing back from him. Mothers believe they are to "protect" their boys from others who try to demand things from them (teachers, coaches, spiritual leaders, or any strong male figure). These boys have girlfriends who freely give them sex, live with them, cook for them, wash their clothes— all while demanding *nothing* from them. These foolish girls cross their fingers, vainly wishing and hoping that these broken boys will become men who love and truly commit to them. They drift in a romantic fantasy of *if I just keep loving him he will change.* Sadly, these women don't realize that they are creating a hopeless situation. Boys do not get inspired to become men by being smothered with kindness.

What will get boys to *stop* being boys is a generation of healthy, confident women who rise up and demand that the males in their lives become men. Sadly, our culture is chock-full of insecure women who fear losing their boys so much, they will do *anything* to keep them, but, in doing so, they produce males who aren't worth keeping anyway.

Though the role of a man in the home is fundamental to its success, women have allowed men to become an option with which to "accessorize" a family. This needs to stop. Women need to challenge the men in their lives to mature so they can shoulder their role in society. Men are supposed to guarantee the welfare and safety of their wives and children. If a man believes he is an optional "accessory," he will have no stimulus to deny himself frivolous pleasures in order to pursue the interests of his family. The "optional" dad will worry more about how to buy a new boat for himself than about buying a life insurance policy or investing in a college fund.

Let me be clear here, ladies. I am not saying we need women who degrade, criticize, and otherwise emasculate the men in their lives. There is already plenty of that. Mine is not a call for more whining, nagging, complaining, and disrespect. Only those who have no power resort to such behavior; people who understand influence don't need to emotionally threaten anyone. Whining and criticizing do not produce real men; challenge and respect do. Notice I said challenge *and* respect. If you want to challenge him, you need to treat him with the respect due the man you believe he is capable of becoming.

The women of the frontier West did not need to resort to tactics like whining and criticizing. They knew they held power. These women took the position of, *you want me—you behave in a way worthy of me.* It was that simple. They didn't disrespect men; they treated them in a way that communicated *you are better than that.* The results were transforming: men competed for such women, with only the most worthy candidates winning out. The only "easy" women to be had were at the brothels. With enough money, *any* man could score with one of those. There were also women who could be paid to cook or clean for a man. But no one competed for those women. The ones who were greatly valued and respected by men were the ones who greatly valued and respected themselves. What kind of woman are you?

Open Your Eyes

Even a casual perusal of the healthy marriages in our culture will reveal that they contain strong women. These women will not tolerate irresponsibility from the men in their lives. I often hear reports from women who tell me of how their "man" stays out till two a.m. without calling them. Or how he entertains old girlfriends or goes out with his buddies instead of spending time with the family. Then they ask in a soft, insecure voice, *"What can I do?"*

I often sit there for a moment asking myself, *Why don't I treat my wife that way?* The answer is straightforward and always the same: *I don't because my wife would kill me.* I think of all the men I know who have good marriages and I ask myself, *Why don't they stay out all night and chase other women?* The answer is always the same: because *their* wives would kill them.

One woman came to me and told me that she had discovered her husband had taken pictures of his genitals and e-mailed them to another woman. Aghast, I quickly asked, "What did he do when you confronted him?!"

"Oh, I didn't say anything to him," she replied in her soft, insecure voice. "I was wondering what *you* thought I should do."

Good grief! My wife would *never* ask "What should I do?" She would more likely say, "You better hang on to that picture, because that is the last time you will ever see your genitals. . . ."

Obviously, I don't think my wife would *literally* kill or dismember me (at least, that is what I keep telling myself), but what she would *not* do is continue taking care of me, making love to me, and otherwise making life comfortable for me while I continued to treat her irresponsibly and neglectfully. Most likely I would come home and find myself shut out of the house with a set of keys that no longer work.

I recently had a woman tell me, "My husband only bothers to come home about one week a month. When he does, he ignores me and doesn't even want to have sex with me." This thin, attractive woman told me that her husband, who is a hundred pounds overweight, no longer finds *her* attractive!

I didn't have the heart to tell her that he was probably having an affair, or satisfying himself with porn and strip clubs. However, I did urge her to take a stand: to change the locks on the house, to shut him out, to dial "9-1" and wait to dial the final "1" till he came back and tried to get in. But she was afraid—afraid to live on her own, afraid of financial stress, afraid he might leave her forever, afraid she would spend the rest of her life alone. It was clear there was no way she was going to do anything close to what it would have taken to motivate that male dog to change. The irony is, most women like her *do* eventually leave their absent, abusive husbands, but they do it too late for the relationship to survive. Let me explain.

A woman had been coming to me for a year or so, complaining that her husband would stay out until all hours of the night and come home whenever he was "good and ready" to come home. I told her to kick his sorry butt out of the house until he decided he could treat her with dignity, but she was too afraid to act. Eventually (as is usually the case) she got to a place where the pain of being around him overpowered the fear she had of being without him, and she threw him out. What was his response? As I had predicted, he begged her to let him back in and promised to go to a counselor or do anything she wanted, but she was too hurt to want to have anything to do with him. She filed for divorce and ended it.

What went wrong? She waited until she no longer cared. If she would have taken a tough stand while she was still invested in the relationship, she probably could have saved her marriage, but she waited till she snapped emotionally and then it was too late.

I'm not talking about kicking your husband out if he doesn't pick up his socks or watches too much TV. I'm talking about extreme cases: Your husband is seeing other women, he calls you a "bitch" and a "whore" and treats you with contempt, he comes and goes as he pleases with no consideration toward you, he hits you, he mistreats the children, he neglects you sexually, et cetera. I know each case is different and demands careful consideration (this is where guidance from pastors, counselors, or strong, mentoring women will help).

Years ago, a high school friend of mine called me and said she was concerned that she and her husband were at a stalemate in their marriage. "He's a good man," she said tearfully. "It's just that he is absent when he is present. I can't even get him to talk with me or engage with the children. It's destroying our marriage and our kids. They are still small, but they are at the place where they don't even *try* to communicate with their dad anymore."

"Do you still love him?" I asked her.

"Yes, I love him," she assured me.

"Then here's what you need to do," I continued. "Pack up the kids and go to your mom and dad's house. When he calls to ask what's going on, tell him that you are not willing to go any further with him if he is not willing to deal with the issues that are hurting your marriage and the family."

"Are you serious," she asked, surprised. "Is that even Christian?"

"Absolutely," I told her. "Christians are to be the salt and light of the world. Salt preserves and prevents *rot*; light dispels darkness. You are trying to salt and light your home. Most women wait too long to do the thing that will get their husband's attention and then, when the attention comes, they are too hurt to care. Do this while you still care!"

She did exactly what I suggested. She packed up the kids and headed to mom and dad's. Within hours her husband was on the front porch crying. She held out for the weekend and went home to a man begging to change. The whole time she still loved and respected her husband—she didn't *mouth off* to him or do things to demean or criticize him. But neither did she continue tolerating his destructive behavior. That happened over twenty years ago and they continue to enjoy a happy and healthy marriage today.

The Role of the Church

The Church needs to support these women and discipline the men who act irresponsibly in the home. Too often in the Church, the biblical command for women to "submit" has been overstated. Submission was never supposed to be an escape clause for men to remain unchallenged and immature. If a man does not love, support, and connect with his family, he has no business being in any position of authority in the Church— even if he is just directing traffic in the church parking lot. Women will never feel safe about demanding higher standards from their men as long as the Church continues to protect their irresponsibility.

Second, the Church must create an atmosphere that is conducive to cultivating strong women. The Bible teaches us that the healthy, mature women should be teaching the younger women *how* to live. Churches need to put mentoring programs in place so that strong women can begin to teach the confused and insecure younger ones how to be strong as well. And I mean *practical* teaching: *This is how you deal with a man, this is how you raise your children, this is how to approach a particular problem, this is when you kick the bum out of the house.*

There are scads of lofty, high-minded female Bible studies where women address the following questions: *What does true love mean?* or *How can we be more spiritual?* or *What does it mean to submit?* But I'm suggesting there needs to be less chatter about theory and more teaching about the everyday, practical stuff of family and marriage.

Finally, the Church has to stop giving women false information. When it comes to the area of love and relationships, rather than giving them sound biblical teaching, many churches simply repackage the faulty ideas found in secular culture. Our secular culture teaches women that *true love never expects anything in return,* and the Church passes this along under the guise of Christian love. We teach them that unconditional love demands an unconditional *relationship.* In other words, we tell them that they should love the men in their lives, take care of them, have sex with them, do *everything* for them while expecting nothing in return. We use twisted, false spiritual concepts to delude them into thinking such logic is biblical, but it is not.

God loves us unconditionally, but He *demands* a conditional relationship. For example, God forgives us *when we repent.* He will meet our needs *when we ask Him.* He will come close to us *when we draw close to Him.* The Bible is *full* of the conditions we must meet if we are to have a successful relationship with God—even though God loves us unconditionally. The truth is unconditional love *demands* a conditional relationship. You must

love your child unconditionally, but if you have an unconditional *relationship* with him, you will raise a hellion. Love your
teen unconditionally, but have an unconditional *relationship* with
him, and he will destroy himself. Love your husband unconditionally, but if you have an unconditional relationship with him,
you will have a terrible marriage and a weak, selfish man.

While it is important for the Church to challenge these
immature boys to grow up and start acting like the men God
intended them to become, there is little hope that anything
will ever change as long as weak and needy women continue to
empower these "men" to remain boys. We need a new generation of women with the same kind of confident, strong, frontier
spirit that the women of one hundred and fifty years ago had—
the kind of spirit that demanded they be treated with the kindness and respect they were due. Only then are we likely to
reclaim and retame the wild, wild West.

What a Woman Wants

Gentlemen, let me have your attention. I am about to
give you the single most sought-after pearl of wisdom that men
have craved since God made a woman out of Adam's rib. I'm
going to tell you *what a woman really wants.*

This is particularly significant because most women don't
even know what they want. They sense an inner longing, an
inner need—a need as basic as the need for food, water, or oxygen. They may not know how to articulate it, but they are desperate for it.

This unidentified, desperation-producing need often drives
women to become aggressive complainers in marriage—not unlike a man who has had a hard day and comes home yelling at the
dog and kicking the cat. The animals are innocent, but he is pent

up with unprocessed anxiety and emotion, so Fido and Felix have to bear it. Women do this to their husbands. Often, wives complain about things that have nothing to do with the unmet need motivating them to complain to begin with.

For example, a wife may attack a single behavior in her husband, such as *"You watch too much TV!"* It's not that she cares so much about TV, it's that on some level she feels the TV is *competing* with her. Of course the man, who is a fact-based, logical being who loves to look at life in terms of measurements, quickly goes to his brain to see if, in fact, he *is* watching "too much TV." Since his brain is not exactly sure how much "too much" is, it quickly assures him that that he does *not* watch too much, but rather watches just the right amount of TV. So he dismisses his wife's complaint, which, of course, adds to her angst.

Or a wife may complain, *"You don't do enough around the house!"* Again, she is debating about a *measured* item with a man. He goes to his *measure-loving* brain, measures whether or not he is doing "enough," and quickly comes to the conclusion that he *is* indeed doing enough. Again, he dismisses her criticism, and again her desperation grows.

Then she tries another approach: "I want you to love me."

"I do love you," he responds, adding, "Can you hand me the remote?"

To which she retorts with heightened emotion, "Why don't you care about me?"

"I *do* care about you," he says, wondering for a millisecond why she's being so weird and irrational. "Could you just grab me another beer?"

Despair and frustration do not a nice evening make. She's mad; he believes her illogical emotions and behavior are reason enough to disconnect from her—further isolating her from the very thing she longs for. Truth be told, he really *does* love her and wants to care for her. In his mind he wouldn't be there if he did not love and care about her. His continued presence, the check he brings home, the fact that he is there to protect her and the children from dangers seen and unseen, are evidence in his mind that he *does* love and care for her. And the very suggestion that he *does not* is insulting.

Husbands usually melt down in situations when their wives get unreasonably critical. For the life of him, he cannot begin to understand what the problem is. His wife makes no sense to him. The odd thing is, women admit that while in critical moods, they don't make sense to *themselves*—they just hurt. This inner ache is too deep to articulate, so they cannot make it clear to their husbands what's really going on.

She *says* she wants to be loved, but that cannot be the truth, for she is *already* deeply loved by her family, her children, and her closest friends—and she knows that. She *says* she wants to be cared for, but that cannot be it, because her husband is already working as hard as he can to provide for her and the family—and she knows that. She *says* she wants him to pay more attention to her, but what exactly does that mean? How much is *more*? How much is *enough*?

What a woman wants—what she is longing for in her deepest heart of hearts—what all women want—is simply this: *She wants to be chosen.*

Pick Me

For a woman, the whole of life is like a junior high school dance where she stands alone thinking to herself, *I want to dance.* But what she really means is, *I want somebody to choose me.*

Men may not feel it as intensely, but they all know what it was like as a child, to be picked for teams on the playing field.

Every guy was thinking, *Pick me! Pick me!* No guy wanted to be the last one picked. The higher up the picking ladder he was, the more status he held with all the other guys. Everyone likes to be picked. But for a woman this feeling is overwhelming.

Rabbi Shmuley Boteach, the affable host of the television show *Shalom in the Home,* says it perfectly:

> Why do women want to get married? Looked at logically, marriage is a terrible proposition for a woman. She has to risk her life to have a man's children (up until the 20th century one in three women died in childbirth). She literally loses her name, as she takes her husband's name, as do the kids. She makes a man a home and assumes, even in our egalitarian age, most of the domestic workload. And today she has to hold a job to provide that all-important second income.
>
> Why would a woman leave the parents who love her unconditionally for a man whose love is so inconsistent? Why would any sane person agree to so rotten a deal? Because a man can give a woman the one thing her parents cannot. Her parents can love her. But only he can choose her. He can make her feel special and unique.[4]

When a man proposes marriage to a woman, he is saying to her, *Of all the women in the world, I choose you.* On her wedding day, at the greatest party of her life, in front of her family, her friends, and God, she is celebrating, *I have been chosen!* This fact is what causes her single girlfriends to rejoice with her and envy her at the same time. They think to themselves, *She has been chosen, great! But when will someone choose me?*

Before Adam met Eve, he had been hanging out with all the animals, and the Scripture says there was nothing found in creation that was "suitable" for him. Nothing on this planet was worthy of being *chosen* by him to love, adore, and orient his life toward. Adam lights up *only* after God forms the woman and brings her to him. He does a basic *stop, drop,* and *roll* when he sees her. She gives him *fever.* He knows he wants to be with *her!* He knows she is worth choosing no matter what that means. And as he gazes at her, he starts to predict the future of other men. He claims men of the future will end up leaving their moms and dads (the foundational relationships of their lives) to be with one of these new *"womb*-men." Intrinsically, Adam knows nothing in the world will catch a man's attention like meeting and making a life with a *woman.* And it is when a woman knows this—when she knows she is the *one* a man wants to be with *over everything else in creation*—her longing heart is satisfied.

The man who understands this holds the key to what a woman truly desires. Love is *not* enough. She must be *chosen. Choose* her. The complaining wife doesn't really care that her husband watches too much TV, or plays too many video games, or works too long; it is that he does those things *instead of choosing* her. The man who will regularly demonstrate to his wife that she is his top choice will be the man with an extremely happy wife. As comedian Jeff Allen says, "Happy wife—happy life."

Guys, despite what you may have come to believe, your wife doesn't need your attention twenty-four/seven, nor does she really care that you have other interests. She just needs you to exhibit, with regularity, that you intentionally choose *her.*

Here are some suggestions: Instead of watching your favorite show, say to her, "How about I turn this off and let's go for a walk?" Instead of sticking your nose in a laptop for hours on end as you bring work home, tell her, "How about I shut this off for a while and you can tell me about your day?" Dare to skip a golf date or a day fishing and tell her, "You know, the guys wanted me to go with them today, but I decided to stick around and give you a hand around the house." That act of *choosing her* reaffirms to her your love and commitment. *Watch out,* her response will be pretty dramatic!

Truth is, guys, if you will make the effort to demonstrate to your wife that you are choosing her, she will push you out to enjoy more time with other activities you find enjoyable or productive. But you must demonstrate, *Instead of this, I choose you. Instead of that, I choose you. Instead of my buddies, I choose you.* Thinking it will do you no good. You must *show her.* But at the end of the day, she will show you just how good of an idea it was to have chosen her. Guys, you can scour the planet in search of happiness and fulfillment, but *there's no place like home.* When you have a happy, loving wife—it's the closest thing to heaven on earth!

8

Law Number Five: Women Are Givers; Men Are Takers

GOD created men to be providers, which means there is a tendency in every male soul to go into the world to *gather* and *get* things. Women, on the other hand, were created to be nurturers, which means they were designed to go into the world to *give* and *care for* things. And though modernity has afforded couples the opportunity for role reversal, our basic makeup and motivations remain much like they were in the ancient world.

Women are "givers" by nature. They love to give; they define themselves by giving. Put a bunch of women together and they'll compliment each other uncontrollably: *"I love your hair!" "Oh, I love your outfit!" "That color looks great on you!"* Contrariwise, men are takers by nature. They love to take; they define themselves by how much they can "get." Put a bunch of guys together and they insult each other: *"Hey ugly!" "Look who's saying I'm ugly."*

Most women believe the key to a good relationship is simple: *give.* If you want an even better relationship: *give more.* If you want the best relationship: *give and give and give till you drop.* While that *might* work when dealing with other women, it most certainly does not work when dealing with men.

Many women live in a false romantic fantasy world that says *the key to getting a loving response from your man is to give and give until he returns the favor.* But that is not true. If you keep giving and giving to a man, he will simply take more—he'll take as much as you will give him. You will burn out giving long before he returns the favor. Men don't give back without being asked to do so. This may make you hate all men forever, but usually the only reason men *give* is to *get* a reward.

Jesus knew this about men. When He taught His disciples about giving, He said, "Give, and it will be given to you. A good measure, pressed down, shaken together and running over, will be poured into your lap."[1] He could have just said "Give," and been done with it. Indeed, for most women, that would have been the only word required. But to get men to respond, He had to show them the reward that would follow. Read the verse again; only one word was dedicated to the command while twenty-three words were dedicated to the reward. In fact, the majority of God's dealing with men recorded in the Bible is replete with promises of reward. There are over 1,800 promises in the Bible. In a relationship as close as marriage, there is no such thing as altruistic *giving* in a man's heart. Even things that *look* like giving are often just bartering chips for something he wants. If you want to get something out of your relationship with a man, you have to *take it* from him. It's the way it works. Women, however, are very uncomfortable with *taking* in the context of their relationships. It goes against their very nature.

When I tell my audiences across the nation that I am going to show them how a woman can get her husband to do stuff for her, the women usually cheer. They expect that I am going to beat up on their husbands for not being more sensitive and responsive and caring. But believe it or not, the problem is not with the men, it is with the women. And the cheers quickly turn to groans as I try to snap women out of their romantic fantasyland.

Giving to men in order to motivate them to give back seems logical, even *Christian,* but it just doesn't work. It is not unusual for a marriage counselor to hear a woman say, "I have given and given to that man. I have nothing left to give!" The counselor then looks at the husband, to hear him say something like, "Well . . . I thought we had a good marriage." And truth be told, it has been great—*for him.*

If you interview the women who *do* feel their husbands are being responsible and doing their fair share of giving in the relationship, you will discover they are well aware that having a marriage with a giving husband does not happen naturally; they have had to make some demands. Sadly, these women are in the minority. Most women sit around with their hearts constantly broken, living with the false assumption that a man who *really* loves them will attend to their every whim and need—like he did when they were dating. These women don't understand that men act the way they do during the dating season for one reason and one reason only: to win the girl. The women never cared and gave for the sake of caring and giving. Men don't do that.

Girls, you can either sit in shock at the revelation that the man in your life is a taker who generally will never naturally *get* that he should do nice things for you without your asking for them, or you can decide to do what you need to do to get some attention. If you want something from a man, you have to learn to ask—to take it. Let me state that again: *If you want something from a man, you have to take it!*

I am about to show you how you can get more out of the man you are married to. Keep in mind, however, that these points are guidelines, not hard science. Nothing works all the time, every time. But if you start approaching your husband while keeping these simple steps in mind, you will find that he will become much more responsive to your requests.

How to Get a Man to Do Stuff for You

Ask for What You Want

It seems odd to my male brain that women are resistant to ask for what they want. Some seem to believe, *If my husband really loved me, I wouldn't have to ask.* In such cases, I can't help but wonder if estrogen causes a kind of crazed, drug-induced state in these women. This may be hard for some ladies to understand, but husbands do not have ESP—they have ESPN. If you need something, want something, desire something, crave something, long for something, pine for something, yearn for something—you are going to have to *ask for it.*

This is completely counterintuitive for a woman, because women tend to *feel* the needs of those they care for and they give whenever they can, without being asked. When a woman loves she instinctively gives; and the more she loves, the more she is motivated to help out the object of her love. From a woman's standpoint, if you really love someone, you will see what they need and respond to that need *before* they ask. To a woman, *love means never having to ask.* The problem is, women assume men think the same way. But they don't.

Ask More Than Once

Asking a man to do something *once* is like never having asked him to do anything at all. This is because a man is not looking for things to *do* to make his relationship better. As the hunter, the competitor, the provider, he is in a constant state of *take.* To him, life is about taking and winning. He is not likely to remember your request *unless* it is somehow attached to something he might *get* for doing what you ask.

This is completely foreign to women, who are in a constant state of wanting to *do* whatever they can to enhance a relationship through giving. Ask a woman to do something once, and she responds. Fulfilling a request from someone she loves is an easy thing for her, and if she can't get to it right away, she simply puts it into her internal queue of to-dos and gets to it as soon as she finishes the dozen other tasks she is currently working on.

Not so for a man. He goes about happily in his mode of take, take, take. When his wife asks, "Honey, will you do such and such for me?" he pauses momentarily as his right brain asks his left brain, "Did you hear something?" Before answering, his left brain assesses if there is anything to *take* or to *get* in the transaction, and if not, the left brain responds, "Nope. I didn't hear anything." And the man is off again in his mode of take, take, take.

His wife will likely become very upset with him because she assumes he remembers what she has requested, but has willfully chosen to ignore her. She falsely assumes this is an indicator that she means less to him than he does to her. However, the truth is, her request went in one ear, spun around his "nothing box," and shot out his other ear. Unless a man knows what he is going to get out of fulfilling a request, the request won't stick in his mind. No gain, no male brain.

One day I was listening to a relationship expert tell how women do not like to ask more than once. I had a difficult time believing what he was saying, since my personal experience was nothing like that. My wife has no problem asking me to do something more than once. Being skeptical about what I had heard, I decided to prove to myself that such thinking was misguided nonsense.

The next church service I attended, I decided to do a little survey of my own. I approached one of the women before the service and asked her, "Do you ever have a hard time getting your husband to do things for you?"

"Oh, pastor," she replied, "you have no idea. I asked that man to paint the ceiling in the living room. That was back in October. Now it's May and he hasn't made a single effort to do anything about it. He walks in the living room every day and just ignores the fact that I had asked him to paint the ceiling."

She was getting agitated just telling me about it.

"Okay," I said, "but how many times did you ask him to do it?"

Much to my surprise, as soon as I asked the question, she stared at me like a dog looking at a new dish.

"Only once!" she stated in a way that communicated she thought I was being silly for asking the question.

I was stunned. I continued to press, "Why wouldn't you ask him more than once?"

"I shouldn't have to!" she retorted.

I suggested she may want to try asking her man more than once, and quickly went on to find another woman I could survey. I found another candidate and asked her, "Do you ever have a hard time getting your husband to do things for you?"

"Pastor, you have no idea. I will put his laundry in a basket in the middle of the living room and say, 'Honey, put away your laundry,' but he doesn't do it. It's like he can't even see it. Pastor, can't men see laundry?"

I laughed.

"Well, yeah," I said, "we see it. It just doesn't mean a

whole lot to us." Then I quickly asked her, "Tell me, how many times do you ask him to put it away?"

I immediately received the same bewildered look I got from the first lady.

"Once!" she snapped.

I was stunned. "Why wouldn't you ask him more than once?" I inquired, truly trying to understand this behavior.

"I shouldn't have to!" she exclaimed.

I had to try one more time. I found another woman and asked her the same question: "Do you ever have a hard time getting your husband to do things for you?"

"Pastor, you have no idea . . ." she said.

She started to relive in excruciatingly painful detail the transgressions of her husband and how he ignored her requests. As soon as she finished, I quickly asked, "So how many times do you ask him to do these sorts of things for you?"

"Once!" she answered.

I could not believe what I was hearing. "For crying out loud," I asked, exasperated by this point. "Why wouldn't you ask him more than once?"

"I shouldn't have to!" she quipped.

Three different women in the space of fifteen minutes, and I got exactly the same response. Since then, I have spoken to thousands of women about this issue and their answer is always the same: "I shouldn't have to!"

But ladies, let me give you some critical advice you *will* need *if* you want to get your husbands to do things for you: Despite what you think, *you have to!* You *have to* ask him to do things more than once. To sit and stew and get angrier and angrier over the fact that you asked your husband to do something *one time,* and he didn't do what you asked, is a testament that you have *not* heard this advice. You need to ask him *again.*

"But," you protest, "isn't that nagging?"

No. Asking more than once is *not* nagging. Nagging kicks in when you add an *attitude* to your requests.

"But I shouldn't have to ask more than once," you cry.

Well, if you were dealing with another woman, you might not have to. But you are dealing with a man. Which brings me to another critical point: Many women *say* they want a man, but then get mad at him because he doesn't think, act, and respond like a *woman*. I don't think you *really* want us to become women, but I can tell you that your frustration with men will continue if you do not learn how to successfully motivate one.

Many women complain to me, "But I told him five times and he *still* didn't do it!" As I stated earlier, this is not hard science. If you have asked your husband half a dozen times to fix the leaky faucet and he still hasn't done it, do yourself a favor and call a plumber! Or do it yourself. It makes little sense to drive yourself insane if you cannot get a man to respond. As I said early on, marriage is full of poo. At times there will be turds that will just stay turds. Don't forget to pick your battles.

Another reason a woman doesn't like asking her husband to do things more than once is she doesn't want to feel like she is *making* her husband do what she wants. She wants her man to *want to* do it on his own. However, this is not logical to a man. If the man had *wanted* to do what you asked him to do, he would have already done it. Men are used to doing what they *want*. And though this may sound cold and heartless, takers don't automatically want to do what you ask just because you ask them. Your man will probably *never* want to do what you ask him to do.

So you have to ask yourself, *Do I want my husband to do things for me, or not?* If you do, stop worrying about whether he *wants* to do it. I promise you, all those women you envy (the ones whose husbands are *always* doing stuff for them) they generally ask their husbands to do what they want as many times as it takes to get them to do it. They really don't care whether or not their husbands *want* to do it.

Ask the Right Way

You need to ask without the hint of a threat or an insult. You need to be nice. As I mentioned before, men do *not* respond to threats and insults, they respond to rewards and praise. Unaware of this, women frequently try to use insults to motivate their husbands to do things for them.

But this strategy does not work on a man. The more you insult a man, the more resistant he will be to you.

Okay, by now a lot of women readers may be feeling that my first three points are ridiculous, but I want you to forget about your husband for a minute and think about your relationship with God. If you want something from God, what do you have to do? One: You need to ask for what you want. Jesus taught that even though God (unlike your husband) *knows* what you want *before* you ask him, if you don't ask, you're not going to get what you want from God. What else did Jesus teach us?

Two: You need to ask more than once. (I laughingly tell my audiences that point alone proves God is a man.) Jesus taught us that we need to bring our requests before God again and again. Finally, three: You don't *insult* God if He doesn't respond as quickly as you want.

Okay, think about your relationship with your husband again. I believe that one of the fundamental reasons so many women are upset with men is that they try to hold men to a higher standard than God Almighty!

Train Him with Positive Reinforcement

I tell my audiences that training a husband is like training a chimpanzee. Now, that may seem a bit demeaning to men, but consider my point. You might not like the idea of "training" your husband, but you will have to, unless you are okay with him staying the way his mother trained him. Training someone to do what you want follows the same rules whether he is a child, an adult, or a chimpanzee. You reward the behavior you like, and ignore the behavior you don't. If your chimp does something you want to encourage, give him a reward for that behavior. If he doesn't do what you want, don't give him any reward. It is never appropriate to just beat up the monkey—that will only result in the monkey running from you when you enter the room. Husbands will respond in the same way. However, if you come bearing rewards, men (and chimps) will line up and do whatever you want them to do.

Ladies, don't underestimate the power of the reward. Animals (including the male *Homo sapiens)* respond to rewards. You may not like it, but this is *exactly* how to get a man to do what you want. Men are not wired to think and value the same things women do.

So how do you go about rewarding a man? By appreciating the things he does for you—even the small, everyday things he should do without appreciation. Men love to be appreciated. The more a man is appreciated for the small things he does, the more things he will want to do for you. It really is that simple.

One day I was home alone. I had a dirty dish in my hand and had gotten trained to the point that I would put it in the dishwasher. I opened the dishwasher and saw that it was already full of clean dishes. This can be a real moral dilemma for a man: *Do I stick the dirty dish in with the clean ones, or put the clean ones away?* I decided to put away the clean dishes. So I emptied the dishwasher and put everything away. Not long afterward, my wife returned from the store and started to empty the dishwasher. When she saw that the dishes had already been put away, she smiled, came over to me, patted my cheeks, and said, "You're such a good husband!"

I lit up. When she appreciates me, it makes me want to do more.

Now, by all rights she could have said, "Well, it's about time! I have to do this every day while you sit on your butt! You finally did something useful!" But such edifications would certainly not have been received very well, and she is smart enough to know that insulting me would not have caused me any desire to repeat the effort.

The reason some women hate the idea of giving out rewards is that women tend to appreciate only unexpected kindnesses. If you do something a woman doesn't expect, she will light up with thanks and compliments. However, if you do something that *is* expected—well, you generally get *nothing.* However, ladies, if you will be careful to let your husband know you appreciate *whatever* he does for you—expected or unexpected, big or small—you will find he will continue to do *even more* for you. It takes a while, but we train pretty well.

Learn to Barter With Him

Men live in a world of barter. As I have already stated, virtually everything we do is because we get something for it. This is what takers do. While the idea of bartering may be offensive to most women, men love it. When a woman offers to barter with a man, she is speaking a man's language. Men like it because they clearly know what is expected of them and what the rules are; and most important, the reward is clearly spelled out in advance. Here's how it works: First, you find out the things your husband likes to do. Then, when you have something you want him to do for you, you ask him, "Honey, would you like to do that thing you would like to do?" He answers, "Uhhh, yeah . . ." Now you say, "Well, do this thing for me and then you can do that!" Then stand back and watch. *More than likely,* the job will get done.

I have had women complain that this is just a form of manipulation. Some have said to me, "I know women who constantly manipulate their husbands by bartering with them. They even use sex as a tool to get what they want!" What I find interesting is that the men involved in such "manipulations" never seem to complain. Why? Because men don't mind bartering. They get it. They like it.

Many women think two mature, loving adults should never have to resort to such barbarian tactics. What these women need to realize is that many of the men are only doing what they're being asked to do because of a bartering wife. The women who a) ask for what they want, b) ask more than once, c) ask the right way, d) reward their husbands, and e) barter with them are the women who get their men to *give* back to them.

The bottom line is: *Do you want your husband to do stuff for you or not?* If the answer is yes, then you need to start *taking* from the man in your life in the way I have just described.

In talking about the process of husband training, John Gray writes:

I first became conscious of this process when my wife asked me to buy some milk at the store when I was on my way to bed. I remember grumbling out loud. Instead of arguing with me, she just listened, assuming that eventually I would do it. Then finally I made a few banging noises on my way out, got in my car, and went to the store.

Then something happened, something that happens to all men, something that women don't know about. As I now moved closer to my new goal, the milk, my grumbles went away. I started feeling my love for my wife and my willingness to support. I started feeling like the good guy. Believe me, I liked that feeling.

By the time I was in the store, I was happy to be getting the milk. When my hand reached the bottle, I had achieved my new goal. Achievement always makes men feel good. I playfully picked up the bottle in my right hand and turned around with a look of pride that said, "Hey, look at me. I'm getting the milk for my wife. I am one of those great generous guys. What a guy."

When I returned with the milk, she was happy to see me. She gave me a big hug and said, "Thank you so much. I'm so glad I didn't have to get dressed."

If she had ignored me, I probably would have resented her. Next time she asked me to buy the milk I would have probably grumbled even more. But she didn't ignore me; she gave me lots of love.

I watched my reaction and heard myself think, What a wonderful wife I have. Even after I was so resistant and grumbly she is still appreciating me.

The next time she asked me to buy the milk, I grumbled less. When I returned she was again appreciative. The third time, automatically I said, "Sure."

Then a week later, I noticed that she was low on milk. I offered to get it. She said she was already going to the store. To my surprise a part of me was disappointed! I wanted to get the milk. Her love had programmed me to say yes. Even to this day whenever she asks me to go to the store and get milk a part of me happily says yes.[1]

A trained man is a wonderful thing for a woman to have. But women have to get out of their comfort zone to train one. Remember, ladies: With men you get what you *take,* not what you *hope for.*

9

Law Number Six:
The Law of Desire

MICHAEL and Janet were at an impasse when they came to my office. I told them they could overcome all the disappointments and hurts they had experienced in the past, and that God had promised to help them. But as I began to talk about the laws that govern relationships, Michael shut me down. At first, I couldn't understand his reluctance. It *seemed* that he was open to a better relationship, but I couldn't figure out why he wasn't willing to *do* anything to develop one.

Then the truth came out. Michael had let his *desire* for Janet die. He had come in for counseling only as a last resort. He had been hurt and frustrated for too long and wanted the relationship to continue only if Janet changed *immediately.*

In order to cultivate a successful, long-term relationship, you have to learn how to cultivate a genuine desire for each other, and *desire* has to be constantly rekindled. I'm not talking about sexual desire, though that is included; I'm talking about the spark that affirms in your gut, *I want to be with that person for the rest of my life.*

When Desire Dies

Most couples who have a conflicted relationship fight hard to make the marriage better, and they will do so over a long period of time. But just because you work *hard* on your marriage doesn't mean you are working *smart*. And when you don't work smart, your efforts can actually make matters worse. Then, over time, when you don't see any discernible change, hopelessness sets in. This is usually when couples seek outside counsel. But by this point they are in such an awkward place emotionally, they don't believe anything will ever change. Their experience has proven that change eludes them *no matter how hard they try*. Couples in this state of mind have already begun to internally disconnect from each other; their *desire* has already begun to wane.

When desire leaves, your heart is no longer present in the relationship, which means you are only *going through the motions*. The loss of desire in a relationship causes the loss of strength necessary to change it. No desire means you no longer *care*. And desire is the *lifeblood* of any relationship.

This happens often in marriages, even Christian ones. A Christian wife, for example, may no longer love her husband, but she will often go for years submitting to him (in obedience to the Scripture), secretly despising him, hoping someday he'll change. But unless he does, she will refuse to desire him in her heart—she'll only put up with him. Often these women wonder, "Why hasn't God moved in my home?"

God promises to help married couples, but He does not do so by magically changing our spouses into what we want them to be. He helps marriages by helping the husband and wife keep their desire for each other stoked while they discover and work through the laws of relational physics. Unbridled, unconditional *desire* is a power that compels us to *"keep on keepin' on"* till our homes become "as the days of heaven upon the earth."[1]

God Desires Us

Even though we behave horribly at times, God still remains committed to us. God has said, "Never will I leave you; never will I forsake you."[2] Because of God's omniscience (all-knowing ability), our thoughts and actions are never a surprise to him. He knows our capacity for evil; yet He chooses to love us in spite of all the hideous things we have done or ever will do. Even when we are in sin and our actions offend His holy nature, He still keeps us as the object of His love and affection: "God demonstrates His own love toward us, in that while we were yet sinners, Christ died for us."[3]

In her book *Healing in His Presence,* Virginia Lively claims she had a vision of Jesus. Her description of the encounter gives us curious insight into God's attitude toward us:

> As I turned back in my chair, first I stared, and then I started to smile. I smiled because he was smiling at me. For I saw that in the center of the light was a face.
>
> How can I put into words the most beautiful countenance I have ever seen? The first thought that came to me was, he is perfect.
>
> His hair, as nearly as I can describe it, was like candle-light—neither brown nor golden, but vibrant with color and life. It hung to his shoulders in deep, loose waves, and his beard was like his hair. His forehead was high, with little wisps of hair moving gently at the hairline.

His eyebrows were thick and masculine but even, and His eyes exceptionally large. I could not fix the color of them, any more than I could the color of the sea. His nose was straight and slender; His mouth the most magnificent I have ever seen, with full lips that revealed, as He smiled, large white teeth, perfectly matched and even. His complexion, while masculine, was absolutely flawless. It reminded me of thick, heavy cream with a blush of rose in His cheeks.

But much more than his individual features was the impression of life—unhampered life, life so brimming over with power and freedom that all living creatures I had ever seen until that moment seemed like lumps of clay by comparison.

Not for a moment did I hesitate to call this Life at my side Jesus. I knew instantly who He was. And two things about Him struck me in particular. The first was His humor. I was astonished, as I gazed at Him, to see Him break into outright laughter. It was the most beautiful sound I had ever heard.

The second thing that struck me was His utter lack of condemnation. I realized at once that He knew me down to my very marrow. He knew all the stupid, cruel, silly things I had ever done. But I also realized that none of these things—nothing I could ever do—would alter the absolute caring, the unconditional love that I saw in His eyes.

I could not grasp it! It was too immense a fact. I felt that if I gazed at him for a thousand years, I still could not realize the enormity of that love.[4]

When God enters into a relationship with us, it carries an eternal and permanent perspective—He never loses interest in us. Jesus expressed this by saying, "Jerusalem, Jerusalem, who kills the prophets and stones those who are sent to her! How often I wanted to gather your children together, the way a hen gathers her chicks under her wings, and *you were unwilling.*"⁵ Here we see Jesus telling of His love for a people who rejected Him, yet He still longs for them and *desires* to be in a relationship with them. Wow! It is precisely this kind of commitment to us that makes us feel loved. And when we know we are loved for *who we are,* we desire to change in order to please the one who loves us. That's why John writes, "We love Him, because He first loved us."⁶

Unconditional Desire

People of faith (empowered by the Spirit) are to mirror the unconditional *desire* modeled by God toward their marriage partner. This is no easy task. And it requires a work of God in the human heart, which means we must be open to him moving *in* our hearts, not just *on* our marriage. Something formative happens in *us,* as well as in our relationships, when we choose to value our spouses and develop *unconditional* desire for them no matter *how* they act. Eventually they will feel confident that they are loved and will want to change in order to please us.

As believers, we must fight to maintain our *desire* for our spouses *while* they are still acting offensively toward us. It is ineffective to pray, "God, change my wife so I can get along with her." You can pray for change, but you can't pray for change because you can't stand your husband the way he is. If there is no *desire* to be in a relationship with our spouses irrespective of how they act, our prayers will be worthless. We must start by asking God to fill us with desire to be in a relationship with our spouses *before* they change, and watch what God does!

What does that mean? It means we must trust God to help us look past the faults of our spouses—past the things that would make us shun them or write them off. We must value our spouses as God values us. People instinctively know whether or not they are being valued and *desired,* or just being manipulated to act in a different way.

Our *desire* to be in a relationship with our spouses shouldn't be grounded in their performance, or by what we may personally gain from the relationship. As people of faith, we have a vast reservoir of love and power available to us through our relationship with God. We need to shunt those resources into our human relationships. We receive love, kindness, and goodness from our connection with God, and we need to use those relationship-building powers to connect with those in relationships with us.

How Desire Takes Flight

In order to keep desire alive in a marriage, we must understand how it takes flight. At the beginning of every marriage there is a high level of *desire.* But desire begins to erode when things such as *disappointment, offense,* or *lack of attention* prevail in the relationship.

First, let's talk about *disappointment.* Couples generally don't enter a marriage thinking, *This marriage is going to be pretty mundane or maybe mediocre at best.* No way. They think, *Our love is different. It's going to be beautiful. It's going to be great!* Then the daily grind starts to grind away, and she assumes he will_____, and he assumes she will_____, and she feels he was inconsiderate to_____, and he feels she was expecting too much when she_____; and there they sit—*disappointed.*

The Scripture says, "Hope deferred makes the heart sick."[7]

When our expectations are not met, our hearts get sick. Since we can't endure that for very long, we begin to *harden our hearts* and begin to lose interest in the relationship. *Desire retreats.*

The only way to deal with disappointment is to reorient our expectations. Sometimes life surprises us and holds *more* joy than expected (becoming a grandparent did that for me), and sometimes life hurts. When life does not always turn out as we had hoped, we need to rethink our expectations.

Another way desire leaves is through *offense*. Every relationship of intimacy experiences *offense*. It seems the closer we get to a person, the easier it is to "let it all hang out" and "dump" on him or her. Jesus claimed that "offenses come" in all relationships.[8] When we get offended it breeds hurt and unforgiveness. If we don't let the offense go, our hearts grow cold and we lose the desire to keep the relationship alive.

Desire leaves most subtly through the *lack of attention*. The less attention you give to the people in your world, the less you will desire to share your life with them. Jesus taught a kind of *law of attention*: "For where your treasure is, there will your heart be also."[9] He is saying that anything you "treasure," or *pay attention to,* your heart will run after—you will *desire* it. Understanding this principle will radically change your life.

Let me give you an example: Did you ever go for months without even thinking about purchasing a new car and then happen by a new car lot? You step into the showroom and sit in one of the shiny new vehicles. Everything is new and perfect. That *new-car smell* fills your nostrils. You grip the new steering wheel and your heart begins to race at the thought of owning this wonder machine. Suddenly, leaping from within you comes this *desire*—this *burden*: *Buy this new car!*

But don't be fooled. Your heart simply follows whatever you *focus on* (or pay attention to). If your focus is on God and the kingdom of God, *His* desires will become *yours.* If you focus on something forbidden, you will desire that thing.

In temptation, Satan tries to get a believer's attention. Why? If he can get our *attention,* he has a shot at our hearts. Did you ever wonder why the God of the Bible made miracles? Miracles made people turn their heads; it got their attention. When God got someone's *attention,* He had a shot at his or her heart.

Because of the importance of our attention, Paul tells us, "Finally, brethren, whatever is true, whatever is honorable, whatever is right, whatever is pure, whatever is lovely, whatever is of good repute, if there is any excellence and if anything is worthy of praise, let your mind dwell on these things."[10]

This principle of *attention* works in our relationships with one another. Once we get to know people, we often quit paying attention to them. It is not unusual to go to a restaurant and observe a couple who won't even talk to each other during their whole meal. When we take each other for granted, we lose the desire to keep the relationship fresh and lose the energy necessary to work out our differences when they arise. The reason many relationships die is simply that no attention is given to them and desire is washed away.

Our spouses are valuable and precious, and we need to treasure them—to attend to them. When we attend to those we love, a *desire* rises within us to do anything we can to build our relationships with them. This is one of the reasons my weekend seminars are so impacting: We get couples paying attention to each other again—and desire reemerges! *Refocusing* on someone we have lost desire for may be all that is needed to restore that desire. But as you refocus, make sure you hone in on the right things. Refuse to focus on your husband's bad points, or on how your wife has offended you in the past. That is the wrong *focus*; it will kill desire. Focus on the positive things about your spouse, even if you have to organize a search party to find some.

Jesus had the *law of attention* in mind when He told us to pray for our enemies.[11] He knew if we attend to an enemy in prayer, they wouldn't be an enemy much longer. Prayer, like any other focused attention, breeds intimacy between you and the other person. It is a *"desire steroid."*

Here are some simple "attention" samplers: When you see your spouse, practice thinking, *There you are!* instead of *Here I am!* Learn to physically turn toward, intently listen to, and look directly at your spouse. Anyone can be nice to the people they see once in a while. Any businessperson can communicate "worth" to a potential client. But to consistently celebrate and value someone as close to you as a husband or wife—that has power. Don't let your spouse think everyone else is more important to you than he or she is.

We all appreciate it when someone looks upon us with approval. We feel special and accepted, and we open ourselves to those kinds of people. If you will learn the art of focused attention toward your spouse, you will heal old wounds and make him or her feel important and valuable. When you make your spouse feel that way, you foster a new openness and freshness in your relationship.

I will often spend time gazing at my bride, Debbie. I watch her work around the house. I look at her while she is sleeping. When we go to the mall, instead of looking at all the other people, I usually walk a little distance from her and just look her over from different angles. I've discovered that my *desire* for her rises in direct proportion to the amount of *attention* I give her.

This stuff really works!

The Hard Heart

In dealing with people, I have discovered you can leave a relationship without actually leaving it physically. In the case I described earlier with Michael and Janet, Michael's lack of desire caused him to leave Janet. He had not yet left her physically; they were still living together. But he left her by abandoning his diligence and courage to work through and fight for their relationship. They were actually living like "married singles." The seed for divorce had already been sown because divorce eventually follows places where *desire* wanes.

Jesus claimed the only reason divorce occurs in a relationship is due to a *hard heart*. To have a *heart* for something is to have a *desire* for it; to have a *hard heart* is to have a *lack of desire*. Jesus said, " 'What therefore God has joined together, let no man separate!' They said to Him, 'Why then did Moses command to give her a certificate and divorce her?' He said to them, 'Because of your hardness of heart, Moses permitted you to divorce your wives; but from the beginning it has not been this way.' "[12]

When your heart becomes hard, you will no longer desire your marriage and you start the process of divorce. Jesus mentioned adultery later in this text as one of the main reasons for divorce. This is true because adultery is one of the most difficult offenses for a spouse to work through without hardening his or her heart.

So what about those of you who have *no* desire remaining—no spark, and you feel dead inside about your spouse. There is still hope for you. Remember, God is a God who *raises the dead*. He raises "dead" marriages, too. I see it all the time. There is always hope for you.

10

Law Number Seven:
The Law of Love

"I love you!"

What exactly did you mean when you said that? The word "love" is used so often and in so many contexts, it is difficult to tell what people really mean. We say, "I love my wife," "I love ice cream," "I love my dog," "I love God," "I love that song," "I love Mom." Hopefully, you don't love your mom the way you love your dog, or love God like you do ice cream.

Marriage is a potpourri of loves: *affectionate love, friendship love, sexual love,* and *committed love.* Let's talk about those, and then about how *divine love* can join in the mix of human relationships and empower these various forms of human love.

Affectionate Love

Affectionate love is the warm feeling of tenderness for another person. It is usually the reaction you have when you see an innocent little child, meet a kind older person, or unexpectedly bump into an old friend. It is a momentary sense of endearment that you have in response to the innocence or sweetness of another. Though this love is momentary and fleeting, it is still a rich and wonderful love that should be cultivated in your relationships—your marriage relationship in particular. Focusing on good memories and the characteristics that made you fall in love with your spouse will cause this kind of love to reemerge again and again.

Friendship Love

Friendship love emerges in us when we share the same likes and dislikes with another person. Some friendships blossom easily, but with a little work, you can learn to become friends with just about anyone. Friendship in marriage is an important factor for its success. Work hard to build a friendship with your spouse. Simply paying attention to each other; giving each other compliments or showing appreciation for what the other one does; letting your spouse know how you feel or showing interest in how they feel; giving gifts (especially small, unexpected ones); noticing them and validating them for being in your life; listening to them; giving lots of nonsexual hugs, touches, and holds; and publicly affirming them will all cause you both to light up with *friendship love.*

Sexual Love

Though we will address sexual love in detail later in this book, it is important to note that this expression of love is crucial to a healthy marriage and provides a kind of "cleansing" for the relationship. A couple must fight to stay "wild" about each other— if you don't, this love *will* die. And though things may look normal to everyone on the outside looking in, you will know and recognize (if you dare to be honest) that your marriage is slowly dying.

Committed Love

God wants us to be *committed* to ironing out our relational wrinkles in marriage. The Scripture says, "If possible, so far as it depends on you, be at peace with others."[1] He is telling us to commit ourselves to doing all we can to keep peace in our relationships.

One of the words translated to "commit" in the original Greek text of Scripture (*paratithemi*) is a compound word that basically describes the act of *depositing* something—like depositing money in a bank. We deposit money in a bank and leave it there until we need to withdraw it to meet a financial obligation. To *commit* in the context of a marriage relationship is to decide to continually *make deposits* into the life of the person we are married to. However, that becomes very difficult if the spouse receiving the deposits of love and kindness refuses to *give anything back*.

Imagine going to a bank over a period of time making deposit after deposit. Then, when a financial need arises, you go back to your bank to withdraw some funds but the bank informs you that they only take deposits and never allow any withdrawals. Had you known that from the beginning, you would have never made your first deposit! Then imagine them adding insult to injury by offering to continue doing business with you in the future. Chances are you would change banks.

Many people are just like this. They have *"Deposits Only, No Returns"* stamped on their relational foreheads. They gladly accept emotional deposit after emotional deposit, but when you need them to give some "care" *back*, they don't seem to be willing to give *any* in return. With a spouse like that, our natural response is to want to "change banks." To get rid of that spouse. To look for someone else to marry.

The Limits of Human Love

Note that these *human* loves (*affectionate love, friendship love, sexual love,* and *committed love*) find inspiration *in the people* being loved—as we focus on *them,* something about *them* elicits the love. If a person is cute and sweet, he gives rise to *affectionate love.* If someone likes what you like, *friendship love* is a cinch. If a sexy, good-looking individual catches your eye, *sexual love* interest surfaces.

But problems start when the person being loved *changes:* A child's cuteness is aborted by adolescence, a husband's sexiness gives way to a beer belly or old age, a wife starts to enjoy and spend lots of time with an interest her husband finds boring. This is when human love starts to cave in. Natural human love is a kind of *contractual agreement:* You act a certain way, look a certain way, like certain things, and you will be loved for it. However, if you change, you may discover that the love is no longer there for you. Human love is *conditional.*

Divine Love

Then there is *divine* love. The significant difference between divine love and natural human love is that divine love is based upon a *covenant,* not a *contract.* A *covenant* is like a last will and testament. When a person writes a will, it outlines the gifts he will leave to his loved ones *after his death.* He is obviously not giving in order to get something in return, because he will be gone *before* the gifts are dispersed. It is *unconditional.*

Once the person has died, his gifts are offered. He has *no guarantee* that the people will "receive" his gifts or that they will "return" his love with fond memories or kind words about him. Even if the "predestined" recipients display hatred for their benefactor and reject his gifts, the dead man cannot reclaim his gifts—he is gone. He was totally committed to them before the act of kindness was offered.

This is an example of *love based upon a will,* and it gives us a snapshot of God's covenant dealings with humankind. God's kindness to us, His love toward us, has always had a *covenant* base. "Covenant" is a difficult concept for those of us in the Western world to grasp because we are so contract-oriented. Covenants cannot be broken like contracts can. Once a man dies, he cannot change his will. Once a covenant is put in force, it cannot be altered. Covenants are *not* a fifty-fifty proposition. It takes only *one* to establish a covenant because he gives the full 100 percent. The recipient of the covenant agreement is just that—*a recipient*. He or she has only to *respond* to experience the benefits of the covenant. Get this: *God's love for us is based upon a covenant, not a contract.*

"For God so loved the world, that He gave his only be-gotten Son."[2] This was done before God had any guarantees that anyone would respond to his giving. He gave His all at Calvary—his 100 percent. Remember the night Jesus was be-trayed? "The Lord Jesus, on the night He was betrayed, took bread, and when He had given thanks, He broke it and said, 'This is my body, which is for you; do this in remembrance of Me.' In the same way, after supper he took the cup, saying, 'This cup is the new covenant in My blood; do this, whenever you drink it, in remembrance of Me.' "[3]

He was referring to his death. He was saying that His broken body and shed blood would open the door for a "new covenant" to be enacted. This was Jesus' last will and testa-ment. This is why Jesus *died*. Every act of kindness that God has ever bestowed on the human race was based upon the covenant-inaugurating death of Jesus Christ. His love was re-leased toward us in an irreversible way, and it will never be rescinded.

Incarnational Love

When Jesus claimed that God promised to "join" a couple together in marriage,[4] He was pointing to how God gets all *tangled up* in the human soul. Paul said believers actually become the "temple of the Holy Spirit."[5] That means there is an intermingling of God's spirit with the human heart—a kind of *incarnation* of God's presence in the believing heart. "Incarnation" refers to the way God expresses himself in the world through human beings. This is why Paul says that "the love of God has been shed abroad *in our hearts,* by the Holy Spirit."[6] If you are a believer in Jesus Christ, you are filled with the very same love God has for the world. Jesus prayed to the Father, saying, "The love you have for me may be in them and that I myself may be in them."[7] These verses point to the unyielding conclusion that the kind of love with which God loves is *within* the followers of Christ. Learning to release this quality of love into our marriage is paramount if we are going to experience God's help to "join" us together.

You and I are supposed to love our spouses with God's love—unconditionally! Our acts of kindness and love are not to be dependent on whether our spouses respond the way we would like or not. That would be *contractual* love—fifty-fifty love. The love we are called to give is to be based upon *covenant,* not *contract.* Though covenant love longs for a response, it is given without any guarantee of one. Obviously this is a scary enterprise and creates the potential for people to use us, but this is sacrificial love.

Mere human love can't do this. It gives a bit and then waits for a response. If there is none, it stops giving. All the forms of human love we discussed—*affectionate love, friendship love, sexual love,* and *committed love*—are simply *responses* to an outside stimulus. They are not loves that act independently of the one being loved. We find a person of the opposite sex attractive; the potential for sexual love is birthed. We see someone's innocence or kindness, and the potential for affectionate love blossoms—no sacrificial effort is required on our part. We share mutual likes and dislikes with another, and we react in friendship love. Easy stuff. But these loves fade when the person being loved ceases to act in a way that initiated the love to begin with. To love when there is nothing in the person fostering that reaction requires sacrifice. Sacrifice is essential for covenant love.

For covenant love to be enacted, there must be a death. Jesus did that for our relationship with God; guess who gets to do so in our relationships with others? You and I, of course. A *will*, or covenant, is powerless until death occurs. If you are going to have a relationship with God—a relationship that has a *covenant* as its foundation—you are going to have to learn to *die* to self, specifically, to give up *selfishness*. The great apostle Paul said, "I die daily,"[8] and he wasn't even a married guy! Some married folks will have to die every quarter hour or so to keep selfishness at bay.

Before you perform an act of kindness for anyone, make sure you have died to selfishness—that you are not just fishing for a response. That's what *contractual* love does. If you have "died," you won't care if there is a response or not.

God Wants to Kill You (Not Physically, Of Course)

It is amazing how often Jesus spoke of our need to die to our selfish nature: *"Pick up your cross . . ."* *"Lay down your life . . ."* *"If you lose your life for my sake, you'll find it . . ."* He

127

even gave us a simple parable about it: *"I tell you the truth, unless a kernel of wheat falls to the ground and dies, it remains only a single seed. But if it dies, it produces many seeds."*[9] Jesus taught that the one way we could guarantee we would be alone is to refuse to die to our selfish nature, but if we willingly set selfishness aside, we would experience new life.

He Will Lift You Up

God promises to bless those who give their lives away like this. When Jesus refused to assert His rights and chose instead to die on the cross, it looked as if He was the loser. But it was this self-abnegation that paved the way for God to make His life significant: "Therefore [because of Jesus' sacrifice] God highly exalted Him."[10] The feeling that you are being exploited or taken advantage of when you let the selfishness within you die is not uncommon. But just the opposite will occur: If you do this as a kind of prayer, God will lift you up and you will not be exploited.

When you refuse to act selfishly and choose instead to give to another, you are releasing God's power to "join" the two of you in the relationship. Scripture promises, "All of you, clothe yourselves with humility toward one another, for GOD IS OPPOSED TO THE PROUD, BUT GIVES GRACE TO THE HUMBLE. Therefore humble yourselves, under the mighty hand of God, that *He may exalt you* at the proper time."[11]

If you have had lots of conflict, this is one of the most powerful things you can do to move your marriage relationship toward success. If you want God to get involved in your marriage, there must be a *dying to self,* or a commitment to living a life of self*less*ness.

The good news is, it takes only *one* to put a marriage on

the footing of a covenant marriage. Don't ask God to change someone so that they will treat you better. Ask God to help you to accept your death, and then it won't matter how the other person treats you. Divine love keeps giving no matter how people change or act. Divine love gives it all—lock, stock, and barrel. A dead man can't take anything with him—he gives it all. To love without condition is to love as God loves.

If you cry, "I can't do that!" you are right. But God never intended us to do this by our own human power. Christianity is not so much our responsibility as it is our response to God's ability. What He commands, He enables—He energizes us to do. He promises to "equip you in every good thing to do His will, working in us that which is pleasing in His sight."[12] Paul asserted, "[I]t is God, Who is all the while effectually at work in you [energizing and creating in you the power and desire] both to will and to work for His good pleasure and satisfaction and delight."[13] We may not be able to "commit" to love with unwavering tenacity in our own strength, but God promises to help us *if* we develop the habit of looking to Him instead of to ourselves when we unconditionally love others.

Law of Reciprocity

Though divine love is not *contractual* in nature and does not *demand* a response, it *anticipates* one, because it puts in motion the *law of reciprocity*. Newton's third law of motion states that *for every action there is an equal and opposite reaction*. This is the law of reciprocity. That is how, for example, the jet airplane works. A thrust of hot air out the back of the engine produces an equal and opposite push, hurling the plane forward.

Jesus showed us how this law works in our relationships with others: "Do not judge, and you will not be judged; and do not condemn, and you will not be condemned; pardon, and you will be pardoned. Give, and it will be given to you."[14]

Simply stated, "If you smile at someone, he most likely will smile back. If you strike someone, the chances are he will hit you back. If you express kindness, you are almost certain to have someone express kindness in return. If you are critical of everything and everyone, you can expect to receive critical judgment from others."[15]

If it is true that every action has an equal and opposite reaction, you can see the advantage of being the *first* to give. Your gift then becomes the action that demands an equal and opposite reaction. The farmer uses this law of reciprocity. He can either be the first to give to his field, predicting its destiny by what he plants in it, or he can wait to see what the field will give to him first, all by itself.

If you are *passive* in your relationships with others, you will give only an equal reaction to what *others* are doing to you. You will get along only with those who get along with you first. You will be nice only to those who are nice to you first. You'll not be able to choose your friendships because you will befriend only those who go out of their way to befriend you first. When you *respond* only to how others treat you first, you are *subject* to everyone else's mood swings and actions.

I believe Jesus claimed it "is more blessed to give than to receive"[16] because it affords you the advantage of control. When you understand the *law of reciprocity,* you can *put it to work* for you. You can "predict" the destiny of any relationship by being the first to give.

My younger brother Ed speaks of the way he won Gail as his wife: "At first, she was not interested in me or in a relationship with me. I was the interested party. But I did not wait for her to pay attention to me or be nice to me first. I just started attending to her with kindness, openness, honesty, and just plain ol' adoration. There was some initial resistance, but I wouldn't yield to that. I just ignored it. I wasn't a stalker, but I kept giving the kind of attention she responded to until I won her."

Whenever people don't receive the acts of kindness we give to them, we feel rejection and naturally want to retreat. But if you stick it out while you're being rejected or ignored, and refuse to respond to the *non*feedback or even negative feedback of others, your acts of kindness will eventually generate a favorable response from them.

Selfless giving allows you to stay on the action side of the action-reaction law of *reciprocity.* However, staying on the action side is more easily *said* than done, especially if you are in a relationship that has turned mean and nasty. Some people are so skilled at being jerks that it is extremely difficult to keep from reacting to them negatively. These people are committed to a *lifestyle* of suspicion, criticism, anger, rebellion, and complaining. If you are married to a person like this, you will feel the pressure to dole out to them the meanness they are doling out to you.

Sometimes we are too weak to stand up under the torrent of negativism. Many believers *don't even think* of using their faith in God to help them abort the harmful reactions that naturally arise in us when we are being treated negatively. The problem is that kindness, gentleness, caring, forgiveness, and selflessness are all Christian traits that are in various stages of development in us. For many, these traits have not become a *lifestyle* yet. Many are just getting out of kindness kindergarten, and we are facing men and women with Ph.D.s in meanness. Consequently, these *developing* believers start out pretty well being the "kind Christian" when *first* under attack, but they run out of steam pretty easily. Then they revert back to the same kind of defensive actions and attitudes that permeated their lives before they came to Christ. The sad thing is that the unbeliever then thinks the acts of kindness, which were so swiftly replaced by good ol' selfishness and anger, were just hypocritical *put-ons*.

But even though we are not perfect, God promises we can overcome evil with good."[17] We do not have to be losers in our struggles with evil people. The evil behind their horrible attitudes and actions will eventually be overcome, if we keep coming back to the divine love that has been placed in our hearts by the Holy Spirit. Scripture gives us the promise: "Let us not lose heart in doing good, for in due time we will reap if we do not grow weary."[18]

It takes endurance to stay free from the wrong end of the action-reaction cycle. While you are sowing acts of kindness, the person skilled in evil will be sowing acts of evil. While you are refusing to respond to the acts of evil, they will be refusing to respond to your acts of kindness. What's worse is that your acts of kindness will usually inspire the evil person to be meaner—it's a struggle for *control*. The question is, what will win? The good flowing from you or the evil flowing from them? Good always wins if it is sown consistently for a sufficient length of time. How long is that? It mostly depends on how hardened the person is whom you love. Some people are really tough, and it may take some time for them to come around.

The Anatomy of Divine Love

Let's zero in and take a closer look at the characteristics of divine love. How do you know what it is? What does it look like and how does it act?

Divine love is more than *affectionate love* or *friendship love*; it bypasses *sexual love* and *committed love*. The Greek word that denotes divine love in Scripture is *"agape."* It basically means a love where the higher lifts the lower, an active love that benefits others. *"Agape"* is the Greek word for God's *covenant love*. Biblically, it is a selfless, giving love that is dependent *not* upon the person being loved, but on the one who is doing the loving. It is an initiating love, not just a responding one.

The dynamics of *agape* are best seen in the famous "love chapter" from 1 Corinthians, chapter 13:

> *Love endures long and is patient and kind; love never is envious nor boils over with jealousy; is not boastful or vainglorious, does not display itself haughtily. It is not conceited—arrogant and inflated with pride; it is not rude (unmannerly), and does not act unbecomingly. Love {God's love in us} does not insist on its own rights or its own way, for it is not self-seeking; it is not touchy or fretful or resentful; it takes no account of the evil done to it—it pays no attention to a suffered wrong. It does not rejoice at injustice and unrighteousness, but rejoices when right and truth prevail. Love bears up under anything and everything that comes, is ever ready to believe the best of every person, its hopes are fadeless under all circumstances, and it endures everything {without weakening}. Love never fails. . . ."[19]*

Let's take a closer look at this exposé on love:

"Love endures long . . ."

To endure means you refuse to change your disposition toward another even when you experience pressure to do so. You keep your commitment to another even if it means you suffer because of it. You remain durable and faithful.

"(Love) is patient . . ."

To be patient with someone is to bear the pains or trials they may inflict upon you, calmly and without complaint. That's a big bite to chew! It means you manifest forbearance even while being provoked or while under strain. It means you are not hasty or impetuous to react to what others do or fail to do; that you are steadfast despite opposition, difficulty, or adversity; that you are able and willing to bear with the inconsiderateness, rudeness, and inconsistencies of another. *Agape* love does this. You can readily see how this kind of love could help relationships stay together.

"(Love) is kind . . ."

Everyone loves kindness, and we are all drawn to kind people. To be kind to another means you are affectionate and loving to them. It means that you are of a sympathetic nature; disposed to be helpful and solicitous (solicitous means there is an eagerness in you to do favors for others). To be kind is to be of a forbearing nature; it means you are gentle—one who is committed to bringing relief or pleasure to another. This kindness has been deposited in us by the Holy Spirit.

"Love never is envious . . ."

When you are envious, you have a painful or resentful awareness of an advantage being enjoyed by another, joined with a desire to possess the same advantage. Divine love does not envy what another has.

"Nor boils over with jealousy . . ."

Even though envy and jealousy are often called synonyms, they are different in that envy refers *only* to the goods possessed by another and jealousy refers more to the sense of rivalry between two people for those possessions. Jealousy often makes a person intensely zealous to get things just to outdo someone else. With jealousy there are often strong implications of distrust, suspicion, and even anger between the two parties. *Agape* love does not boil over with jealousy.

"(Love) is not boastful or vainglorious, does not display itself haughtily . . ."

To be boastful or vainglorious is to puff one's self up and to shower yourself with praise. The ancient Hebrew proverb instructs us: "Let another praise you, and not your own mouth; someone else, and not your own lips."[20] Boasting is calling attention to some accomplishment you have made or item you possess in order to make yourself look better than others around you. Boasting is usually an exaggeration of trivial success and it is often done to gain more credibility in the eyes of others. It is also used to put others down. People who practice *agape* do not call attention to themselves; they make the person they love feel most important.

"(Love) is not conceited—arrogant and inflated with pride . . ."

To be conceited is to have an excessive appreciation of one's own worth or virtue. It usually breeds intolerance for others, their thoughts and wishes. People who are conceited quickly consider themselves the only ones, to be right and refuse to deal with any relational conflict because they believe they had nothing to do with creating it to begin with (pride).

"(Love) is not rude (unmannerly), and does not act unbecomingly . . ."

When you are rude, you are inconsiderate of how your actions affect those around you. You are rough and unfinished—

crude. A rude person has not undergone the discipline of becoming courteous and refined toward others—they are too full of themselves. Consequently, they are often offensive and uncouth in manner or action. Rude people may even feel that their abruptness is a strength based upon honesty and frankness. But love is not coarse or vulgar, it is not forceful or abrupt. It places enough value on others to become sensitive, courteous, and skilled in dealing with them.

"Love {God's love in us} does not insist on its own rights or its own way, for it is not self-seeking . . ."

Even though this statement is clear, ponder it for a while. Most people fight for their rights and their way, no matter who gets hurt in the process. But *agape* love isn't like that.

"(Love) is not touchy . . ."

Many people are touchy because they have incredibly low self-esteem. Touchy people are ready to take offense at the slightest provocation. They are acutely sensitive and often become irritable over what others would normally overlook. A touchy person puts everyone around them on edge and they must use extra tact, care, and caution when dealing with them and can never really be honest whenever conflict arises. Divine love aborts touchiness.

"(Love is not) fretful . . ."

The word "fret" meant to "devour" during the Middle English period. Today it is used to mean the condition of the mind whereby you mentally strain over some incident or person until you actually "eat away" your emotional strength. Fretful individuals agitate over an incident, a word that was spoken, a look that was given, an unfulfilled promise, until they become vexed and disturbed. There are people who fret and fret until it eats away their health.

"(Love is not) resentful . . ."

To be resentful is to maintain an indignant displeasure or persistent ill will over something that is considered to be a wrong, an insult, or an injury. Resentful people never forget what you did to them. These people give offense a permanent and safe harbor in their minds.

"(Love) takes no account of the evil done to it—pays no attention to a suffered wrong."

Here is one of the best ways that you can gauge whether or not you are walking in *agape* love. When you begin to take into account the wrong that people have done to you, or how they have failed you, *you are not walking in divine love.* Before coming to faith in Christ, you and I were once the enemies of what God wanted. But God chose to not take our offenses into account. Jesus took our place, so God did not charge us with the wrong we deserved. When you stay full of the Holy Spirit, you are filled with this *agape* love and you don't notice how others fail you.

"(Love) does not rejoice at injustice and unrighteousness, but rejoices when right and truth prevail . . ."

Do you realize how many people rejoice when evil prevails and causes harm to others? *They got their just due.* The love of God does not talk like that. It rejoices only when God's right and truth come forth in a person's life, not when they experience the judgment of their wrong.

"Love bears up under anything and everything that comes . . ."

You've heard folks say, *"I can't take it anymore."* Love can! *"I just can't stand my spouse any longer."* Love can! Instead of caving in to our natural human responses, we must learn to yield to this love that can take "anything and everything that comes."

"(Love) is ever ready to believe the best of every person . . ."

Human nature tends to believe the worst of every person. (Keep this in mind next time someone has a bit of juicy gossip about a Christian leader or someone else.) Even when it refers to those closest to us—spouse, children, or fellow Christians—we tend to believe the worst about what they say or do. Often we judge others by their performance, and if we see the slightest flaw, we are quick to condemn. But God's love helps us believe the best of everyone.

Believing the best of people somehow releases them to become as great as they can be. Children should be brought up in this kind of loving environment. If you focus only on the negative qualities of your children and never show that you believe in them, they will often grow up confused and never amount to much. If you don't believe in them, they won't believe in themselves; and if they don't believe in themselves, they will lose in life's fight.

It is interesting to note that God sees us "in Christ."[21] I believe that if He focused on us *as we are,* in our inconsistencies and foolishness, we could never grow. But He sees us as we can be—so *we can be.* Divine love expects the best of every person.

"(Love's) hopes are fadeless under all circumstances
and it endures everything {without weakening} . . ."

To have hope is to cherish a desire with expectation of fulfillment. This aspect of divine love makes you expectant for
positive change in your relationships with others, no matter
what the circumstances are. In contrast, natural human love
quits after being disappointed a few times.

"Love never fails . . ."

When divine love is applied in a relationship, it never
fails—you always win with divine love. The actions of *agape*
love are not of weakness but of great strength. Can you imagine
the success of a home filled with this kind of love? What if the
Church were filled with it? Paul said, "For the love of Christ
controls us."[22] It is one thing to have *agape* love in you as a result of being a believer in Christ, but it is an entirely different
matter to yield to it until it flows through you and "controls"
you. If we practice these expressions of divine love, looking to
God for strength, it will bring a zero failure rate into our relationships with others. Love never fails.

That doesn't mean everything will be perfect and those
close to us will never abort a relationship with us. That isn't
the case. Lots of folks abandon God, but that isn't because
God's love failed. The love description given in 1 Corinthians
chapter 13 is a description of God's attitude and perspective toward us. It is also the description of *how* we are to view our
spouses, if we want God to "join" us in holy matrimony.

Part

3

Sex, Lies,
and the Internet

11

What's Sex Got to Do with It?

LET him kiss me with the kisses of his mouth—
for your love is more delightful than wine.
        —Song of Solomon 1:2

FIRST of all, I'd like to welcome all the men who have decided to read this book. If you are like most guys, this is the first chapter you turned to.

Before we begin, I must mention that there are two groups of people who take issue with my approach to this subject. The first are those representing academia. I get in trouble with this group because I come across as more sophomoric than academic when I talk about sex. I prefer not to talk about sex as though it were something done in a lab or a sterile operating room. I don't use terms like "male genitalia" or "breasts"; I much prefer the nomenclature *wieners* and *boobs*. I don't refer to how some men are particularly fond of a woman's posterior; I will say some men start the launch sequence the moment they see their wife's butt. It's not that I am trying to be tawdry or crude (though I have frequently been accused of being so), it's that I think God created sex to be *fun*, so talking about this enterprise in a way that makes people giggle seems completely appropriate to me. Besides, I am not an academic and have never claimed to be.

The other group I seem to offend is the radically prudish religious crowd. I have greatly looked forward to writing on this subject, particularly as a pastor. Most ministers are scared to death to talk about sex. I had one pastor's wife who was getting ready to interview me for a radio broadcast ask, "You're not going to use the '*s*' word, are you?" At first I wasn't sure what she was talking about. In fact, the first '*s*' word that popped into my mind had *four* letters, not three. Then it dawned on me she meant the word *sex*.

Holy cow! There are some so uptight about this subject that they refuse to even *say* the word "sex"! Most pastors prefer to use the word *"intimacy."* I've often wondered if it's not this Pollyanna approach that is most responsible for such statistics as 50 percent of Christian men are involved in pornography; Christian teenagers having sex and getting pregnant with as much frequency as those outside the Church; adultery between Church members becoming an everyday occurrence; or sexually transmitted diseases pouring into Christian families. Maybe this is happening with greater frequency *because* we can't say "sex"!

There is such a fear of this subject in some religious circles that you don't even have to *say* it to be censored. I had one Christian radio station in Tulsa, Oklahoma, cancel one of my radio spots because I *spelled* the word sex! That's right—I did not say it, I said s-e-x. They told us they felt the spot was "too controversial." (Apparently, people don't have sex in Oklahoma. That's why I live in Green Bay; it's too cold *not* to have sex!)

Often I get static from other ministers because I am so open and direct about sexual issues. I suppose they reason the *holy* thing to do is to be indirect (I'll address the *holy* issue in a moment), dance around the issues and speak in some ridiculous religious code. But God is not embarrassed about sexual issues and He does not speak in "intimacy code." In fact, there are portions of scripture that are so direct, even *I* blush. When the nation of Israel was being unfaithful to God, look at the analogy the Almighty uses to make his point:

> *Yet she became more and more promiscuous as she recalled the days of her youth, when she was a prostitute in Egypt. There she lusted after her lovers, whose genitals were like those of donkeys and whose emission was like that of horses. So you longed for the lewdness of your youth, when in Egypt your bosom was caressed and your young breasts fondled.*
>
> —Ezekiel 23:19–21

Holy cow! I think *I* would have used the analogy of a puppy that keeps running away from home. But not God. He uses some pretty graphic sexual references as an analogy of Israel's unfaithfulness. Don't tell *me* God is embarassed about sex.

I find it interesting that when God decided to mark the children of Israel as His special people, He went straight for the penis. I am referring of course, to circumcision. How bizarre is *that*. I have no idea what God's reasoning behind that was, but you've got to admit, He sure knew how to get a guy's attention. Can you imagine Abraham selling this new plan to all the guys?

"Hey guys. Come here!"

"Yeah Abe. What's up?"

"I got some really good news. God has decided that we will be His special people."

"Alright!! That rocks!"

"Yeah . . . and guess what?! He's giving us a special sign that nobody else will have!"

"Really . . . what is it, a tattoo?"

"Noooo . . . it's not a tattoo . . ."

"A special haircut?"

"Noooo . . . it's not a haircut . . ."

"Well . . . what is it?"

"Well . . . God wants us . . . uh . . . He wants us to . . . uh . . ."

"Good heavens man! What is the sign?!"

"Well . . . God wants us to cut off the end of our wieners."

"*Say What*?!!"

This whole idea of circumcision was a major point of contention in the early church. Not a lot of people are aware of this, but virtually all the early Christians were Jews. In fact, they did not believe a non-Jew could even become a Christian. Eventually, more and more non-Jews started becoming Christians so they decided that it was OK for a non-Jew to become a Christian—as long as you *became* a Jew. In other words, they insisted you had to be circumcised. Talk abut getting bogged down in religious details. To them, the condition of one's wiener was essential to determine the condition of one's heart. Other's felt that one's wiener had nothing to do with one's heart. This led to some pretty intense fights. Check out what the Apostle Paul said when he got in a fight over this issue:

> *As for those agitators, I wish they would go the whole way and emasculate themselves!* [i.e. just cut the whole thing off!]
> —Galatians 5:10–12

Wow! Pretty intense for an Apostle, don't you think? He got so mad at these guys for "trimming" their wienies that he wished they'd just cut their wienies off altogether!

The Apostles and church leaders eventually had a big meeting in Jerusalem to debate the issue. Finally they decided that you did *not* have to become circumcised to be a Christian. Praise the Lord for that! It's hard enough to get people to come to church.

And about this *holy* thing: for the love of heaven, Christians need to stop calling sex *holy*! Look, the Father is holy. Jesus is holy. The Spirit is holy (hence the name *Holy Spirit*). But my penis never has been, nor will it ever be *holy*. Oh, I know what they are trying to say, that marriage is a special bond that was instituted by God, and so on, but knock it off with the *holy* nonsense. I believe preachers like using such terminology because it lets them off the hook so they don't have to talk to their congregations about sex. After all, one must be very careful when discussing that which is *hooooly*. The result is a church that is tragically silent about a very important issue.

Let me say that I *do* understand that many are reticent to even bring up the subject of sex (much less do it, frankly) because of the way sexuality has been abused in our culture. Many have been and continue to be sexually exploited. To be sure, we are living in an *over-the-top,* sex-crazed culture, and much evil is done in this area. However, that is *precisely* why I think the Church needs to address the issue openly and frankly.

In the creation narrative, *original sin* had to do (at least in part) with the issue of education. Adam and Eve were invited by Satan to discover the knowledge of *good and evil.* Obviously God knew what the difference was, because after this first couple partook of the forbidden tree He said, "The man has now become like one of us, knowing good and evil."[1] Since God knew what good and evil were, Adam and Eve could have asked him about it instead of learning it from a *forbidden* place. *Where* you learn things influences *what* you learn. I'm convinced that if Adam and Eve had learned about good and evil from God, *good* would have prevailed. Since they learned about it from a forbidden place, *evil* prevailed. The same holds true about sexual matters. If people learn about sex from a context where sex is forbidden (in the context of lust or immorality), *evil* prevails. Contrariwise, if people learn about sex from God's perspective (contextualized in the marriage union), *good* prevails.

This is the tragedy of the Church's silence on the subject. We are forcing people to get their sex education from sources other than God and the Scriptures. Hence, the men, women, and teenagers in our congregations are being educated about sex by the apostles of absurdity in our secular culture. Just turn on your cable TV after 11 P.M. and you will be inundated by sexual *mis*information. And these educators have *no* problem saying anything they want in their promotion of sexual promiscuity, couched exclusively in the context of lust and immorality.

Church members hear this destructive sexual misinformation all the time. And when they turn to the Church for answers, they are met with either a deafening silence or some sterilized, irrelevant explanation that communicates about as much as the deafening silence. How in the world can the Church present the truth and override the false information being heralded by all the media sources in our culture, if we allow only the other side to talk? We are trying to win a war where we are content with the other side having all the bullets. Why? Because we believe the subject of sex is something that should not be openly discussed in the Church.

Even faith-based marriage seminars treat sex as something that should be discussed only in secret. Many Christian marriage seminars *separate* the men and the women during the sex talk. *Where are we? In junior high school?*

The truth is, sex was *God's* idea. And God always has great ideas. He is the one who created our bodies to feel the way they feel when they are touched and caressed. He is the one who created the potential for orgasm—that almost out-of-body experience. Sex is a divine gift.

A Little History, If You Please

The early Christian Church was composed exclusively of Jews. Over time, however, those outside of Judaism (the Gentiles) outnumbered the Jews and the Church became predominantly *non*-Jewish. As the Church moved forward without their Jewish brothers, we lost something truly vital to understanding God's plan and meaning for marriage: we lost thousands of years of Jewish tradition in which sex was viewed as something wonderful in God's sight.

As heathens turned from their pagan ways and joined the Church, they knew sex only from the perspective of lust, debauchery, perversion, selfishness, and even violence! Heathens used sex in every sickening way of which they could conceive. When people openly repented of their sins and were baptized, sexual sins were the ones most frequently confessed. Viewing sex as something wonderful stayed with the Jews, however, and the Christian Church struggled with that concept for *centuries*.

History shows that the early leaders of the Church—priests and even popes—were married and had children. Early on, marriage and physical love were viewed as good. But as time passed and the Church moved further and further away from her Jewish roots, she began to view sex as something pagan and dirty. Married priests began to be told not to have sex if they were going to celebrate Mass. Soon sex for the clergy was forbidden altogether. Eventually priests and nuns were required to take vows of celibacy so they could stay pure from the pollution brought on by sexual contact. Some religious orders would punish the men if they so much as spoke to a woman—even if that woman was their mother.

Theologians began teaching that sex was a perversion of God's original plan, that the sin of Adam and Eve caused people to turn to this vile act. They believed God had originally planned to use some form of pollination for procreation. Eventually these fanatical views began to spread to the laity. Married couples were encouraged to avoid sex on Friday out of respect for Christ's death; then on Saturday out of respect for the Virgin Mary; then on Sunday out of respect for Christ's resurrection; then on Monday out of respect for lost souls . . . Well, you get the idea. There were even folks who tried marriage *without* sex. (Can you imagine the tension in *those* homes?)

It wasn't until after the Reformation that Martin Luther decided to abolish the celibacy requirement for clergy and married a former nun himself. However, he was so shocked at the powerful impact of orgasm that he was convinced the Holy Spirit left the room when a man and woman copulated. He had no idea that sex was such a powerful thing.

The negative view of sex that has percolated during most of Christian history was *never* part of Jewish thought. In his book *Kosher Sex,* Rabbi Shmuley Boteach writes of how Orthodox Jews view sexuality. He asserts that rabbis have always taken the responsibility to sit down and teach young men the specifics of how to bring their wives to orgasm: "The rabbis made female orgasm an obligation on every Jewish husband. No man was allowed to use a woman merely for his own gratification."[2]

Can you imagine having that conversation with *your* pastor? Not likely. Most preachers would rather die than utter the words *"penis"* or *"vagina"* (much less mutual *orgasm!*) in front of another person. Consequently, most young couples getting married in the Church have no idea that sex isn't just for personal gratification—with each of them only focusing on his or her own quest for pleasure. The idea that sex is to be used to *serve* certainly takes it out of the arena of lust and perversion and makes it congruent with Christian thought. But the modern Church can't seem to stop reacting to the perversions of paganism and almost completely ignores sexual matters.

A Kind of Parable

When the Apostle Paul spoke of sexuality in marriage, he said it was a "mystery." Paul writes, "For this reason a man will leave his father and mother and be united to his wife, and the two will become one flesh. This is a profound mystery—but I am talking about Christ and the church."[3] Comparing marriage with Christ and the Church suggests that something in the relationship we are called to have with Christ—something in the relationship of husband and wife—gives us a snapshot of what our relationship with Jesus Christ is supposed to be like. This makes marriage a kind of parable.

But notice Paul's blunt mention of sex in this text. The phrase "one flesh" is a direct reference to the sexual act. Paul is claiming that the actual act of becoming "one flesh" is a metaphorical act. Why would God use sex as a metaphor for Christ and the Church if it were a filthy or naughty thing? Why would God use this metaphor at all? Precisely because of the power of sexuality. Though there is nothing physical about the Christ-Church relationship, sex models the necessary vulnerability and openness that is required within the human soul when one cultivates a relationship with Jesus Christ and His lordship.

Obviously, marriage is more than sexual love. It is a potpourri of loves: friendship love, affectionate love, committed love. But sexual love is peculiar to this human bond. For God to use "sex" symbolically in reference to the Christ-Church relationship proves there is no question that he sees sex as pure, innocent, and void of corruption—no matter how fallen human beings have perverted it. The mystery of attraction, the power of the emotion, the openness and ecstasy of sexuality, the natural ebb and flow of physical interest in relationships, the flirting and playfulness, were all designed by God to be a beautiful rhythm of love and commitment—never the kind of hedonistic, self-centered depravity many have made it.

How Important Is Sex in Marriage?

Not only does Rabbi Boteach claim that Jews have always viewed sex in marriage as a gift from God and *never* as something dirty, he also points out that Jewish thought sees sex as more than a side issue in marriage. It is *the* central issue! It is this kind of love that makes a marriage a marriage. Why? Because sex is the only form of love that is exclusive to marriage. All other kinds of love can be shared with others outside the marriage bond.

For example, though husband and wife share friendship, you can be friends with lots and lots of people without being married to them. Similarly, marriage should have loads of faithfulness and devotion, but you can be a faithful and devoted person to *whomever* you know. Certainly, married partners experience attraction for each other, but even attraction is not unique to marriage—many different people may appear *attractive* to us.

Sexual love, by contrast, *is* exclusive to marriage—at least that's the way God intended it. This kind of union between a man and a woman was designed by God to be shared by *one* man and *one* woman, together, alone, for life. Stripping marriage of carnal love is to domesticate it, to make the relationship *common*.

The problem is, many couples have so much misinformation about sex, it gets confusing and muddled, eventually causing more trouble for them than they think it's worth. Either they overromanticize it or they believe it must be fueled by a ravenous, lust-filled passion they lost somewhere, some time ago.

Listen again to Rabbi Boteach on this point:

> The culprit in all this is the Western romantic ideal, which says that ideally love leads to sex. Through sharing experiences, showing each other consideration, genteelness, and warmth, would-be lovers slowly fall in love. And then, after love has ensued, it leads on to the sexual climax, the apogee of the relationship. Every great classical love story involves these stages: the sexual act is, in the Western romantic view, the consummation of love. And the operative word really is to "consummate." Sex is the summit of man/female relationships. Love would be incomplete without it. Before the act there is *love,* but only sex can elevate it to the next level: *making love.*
>
> To Jews this is completely unintelligible. The Bible says about the first human coupling: "Adam came to know his wife Eve." Prior to their physical coupling, they may have known each other but they were only acquaintances. There was no love. No one within the Jewish community would so degrade love as to claim that it can be possibly formed first, in so short a period of time, and secondly, without direct physical contact. Love came only through physical intimacy.[4]

Wow. What would marriages look like if they used *sex* to help them *build love* instead of thinking sex was the culmination of it? The modern idea is that after we find *that perfect someone,* love will ensue. Then our culture tells us we should date (for years in order to do an adequate "test drive") and only then should marriage be considered. First comes romantic love, usually some sex, and then comes marriage. This is the reason many couples (particularly women) believe that sex is no big deal—that marriage is more about *romantic feelings* and finding the "right one." The very idea that *sex* should be considered the *glue* of marriage and that it has the power to build, cleanse, and fuel romantic love seems completely backward to us forward-thinking moderns. To claim that sex is to be front and center in marriage seems odd enough to us today, but the idea that sex is a central *reason* for getting married seems completely offensive and ridiculous.

None of this means that the purpose of marriage is sex! Not at all. It means sex is central to marriage—that sexual love is central to *building* romantic love and intimacy.

The New Testament supports the idea that sex is central to marriage. Paul actually claimed sexual desire was a "gift" from God and was the primary indicator as to whether a person should marry or not.[5] Sexual drive is certainly not the only issue to assess when considering marriage, but Scripture claims it is where you start—it is *primary.* If you don't have much of a sexual drive, or very little interest in it, you may have a *gift* for celibacy and you shouldn't get married. If you *have* a sexual drive, you should interpret that as a *gift* for marriage, and go for it!

"But shouldn't this be about love and romance and not *sex?*" the ladies, in particular, cry.

Ah, yes, *romance* . . . the *new* reason behind marriage. It sounds lovely and mystical and like the stuff dreams are made of, but it's not what the Bible teaches as a *reason* for marriage. Yet, instead of pastors teaching the scriptural reason for marriage, they actually add fuel to the romantic fantasy by spiritualizing it—saying believers should be careful not only to *fall in love,* but to "find that perfect person that God made just for you." Spiritualizing misinformation is a pretty effective strategy for destroying lives.

I am not saying people should avoid falling in love or recoil from romantic *"you-seem-like-the-one"* feelings; those things are fun, but they are just feelings that ebb and flow within a lifelong relationship—to base marriage on something so *seasonal* is not wise. As subversive as it sounds to the typical man and woman of today, romantic feelings are nowhere near central to, or critical for, a happy marriage. We have *got* to get out of the ridiculous, destructive, romantic fantasyland we have created.

No one within the Jewish community would degrade the centrality and power of sexual love as a foundation for marital love (versus romance and soul-mate searching). Check out how Hasidic Jews go about the dating process:

> First, a man and a woman meet. They do not necessarily know how attractive they will prove to each other. However, assuming that they meet and everything goes well, they continue to see each other for a period of time, say a few weeks or even a few months and then they decide on marriage.
>
> Do they love each other? Probably not. They might feel very attracted to, and have strong feelings for, each other. But on their wedding night it all happens, aided and abetted by sex. They unite in carnal knowledge for the first time. And it is the potency and the power of this physical act, which they are both discovering for the first time, that are truly explo-

sive and engender a pleasurable love appropriate to marriage, bridging the chasm that once separated them.[6]

Now, before you have a cow or claim this is a bunch of bull, consider this for a moment: For thousands and thousands of years, apart from a casual meeting or two in public, men and women didn't know each other before their wedding night. Their real introduction to each other was *having sex*. Relationships thrived and divorce was rare. Now fast-forward to today. We are *so* much smarter, much more romantic and now greatly enlightened; yet our relationships crumble and divorce rates are reaching epidemic proportions. Perhaps we are not as smart as we think we are.

Though it seems far-fetched to the modern mind, biblical teaching promotes the idea that people are to grow in love *after* they get married; they don't need to fall in love *before* they get married. And the Bible views sex as such a powerful tool that, if used appropriately after marriage, it will weld two souls together, forever.

When Adam saw Eve, he named her "woman"—literally, "man with a *womb.*" In other words, he immediately noticed she had different parts that were intensely *interesting* to him. There is no indication that they started dating or that they tried to see if they were compatible by living together for a couple of years. The text says Adam got so excited at first glance that he started to predict, "A man will leave his mother and father over one of these. And they will become one flesh— they will have *sex!*"[7] And Adam and Eve did it. Right in the Garden. Completely without shame.

What does all this mean? For one thing, it means the Church, and Christian people in general, must stop avoiding the subject of sex. We need to talk about the power sex holds to "weld" two souls together as one. We must remind ourselves and prepare our children to understand (in age-appropriate ways) that when a husband and wife engage in sexual love, they leave themselves in a trajectory of ecstasy—to a place where they are no longer in control of themselves. In this act, a couple becomes completely vulnerable, open, and yielded to each other. In this act of ecstasy, they lose themselves in each other in a way they would never dare to do in any other setting. And it culminates in an experience that the Bible says is "as strong as death."[8] Theologians have said the sexual act is a kind of *little death*—it is *that* powerful.

With purposefulness, we need to remind each other and warn our children that sex is *not* to be trivialized or participated in outside the bonds of marriage. To do so confuses and hamstrings our souls. Though God is greater than and able to heal the mistakes of our past, our sexually loose culture has ravaged and butchered the souls of many (more on this later). We must urge everyone to steer clear of lust, perversion, and the selfish hedonism that pervades our culture, which means we have to *talk about it.*

The power inherent in sexuality is the very reason there are so many prohibitions given to us about sex in the Bible. Sex *must* be kept in the context of marriage in order to be safe—in order for its power to be used to build and not destroy. And each of us needs to learn how to keep our sexual impulses within the context of marriage. Sex is a rich, cleansing, love-enriching act that will add joy and fun to life *if* it is corralled within the bonds of matrimony. It will destroy when it is not. Paul wrote, "God wants you to be holy, so you should keep clear of all sexual sin. Then each of you will control your body and live in holiness and honor—not in lustful passion as the pagans do, in their ignorance of God and His ways."[9]

Husbands and wives need to be challenged to learn about sex, to practice it, to celebrate it, to trust God to bind them together through it, to allow it to cleanse and purify their relationship, and to lose themselves in the sheer ecstasy of it. That would be the Christian thing to do. When a husband and wife understand the *why* of sex from God's point of view, they stop limiting it to unreasonable romance or the level of desire produced by hormones that come and go at various times. Sex based on romance and hormones is purely selfish; sex based on servanthood, sacrifice, faith, and hope is *amazing*.

Paul had this kind of sexuality in mind when he penned: "The husband should not deprive his wife of sexual intimacy, which is her right as a married woman, nor should the wife deprive her husband. The wife gives authority over her body to her husband, and the husband also gives authority over his body to his wife. So do not deprive each other of sexual relations."[10]

Sex is a servant. Sex is a cleanser in the marriage relationship. Sex is a way to lose one's self in another, not in one's self. All this is unheard-of in a secular culture, but it is what makes *real* sex, sex. Wonderful. Beautiful. God-ordained fun.

Sadly, instead of couples really loving sex, it has become more of a battleground than anything else for them.

12

Sex Wars

MEN want sex; women want love. In order for sexual desire to ignite within a woman for her man, he must make her feel loved, adored, and significant. In order for a man to feel sexual desire dawning in him for his woman, she just needs to show up.

Men are pretty simple and straightforward when it comes to sexual issues: They basically have an on/off switch and it's a pretty easy switch to throw. A woman's sexual controls, on the other hand, look more like the control panel for a 747 jet—lots of lights, buttons, and levers. And the control panel is pretty complex and a bit disorienting to the novice.

Not only do men and women function different sexually, *why* we want sex differs dramatically. For women, sex is a fueling station for the soul, a loading dock for intimacy, feelings of closeness, and warmth. When a woman has had a hard day or is facing problems or prolonged stress, she feels empty. She needs attention, care, commitment, a listening ear, and tender warmth from her husband to *fill* her soul. The emotional attention of being adored and cared for is what sets her up for great sex.

Men are completely the opposite. A man is looking to empty his soul through sex, not fill it. When a man has had a hard day or is under extreme emotional duress over the loss of a job or some other difficult situation, he doesn't feel empty. He feels totally jammed and overwhelmed. Tests have shown that men with pent-up tension have difficulty thinking, hearing, and doing things requiring mental and physical coordination (for example, driving). Men under stress also suffer from a kind of time distortion where five minutes feels like twenty to them. Sex for a man is a great release, a way to reset his emotional and physical meter. It enables him to think and feel differently about his life. If a woman sees her man in a befuddled state, under great stress from problems at work, or under the strain of too many unpaid bills, she should consider having sex with him. Men express physically what they can't express emotionally. Sex *really does* cleanse and clear up a man's brain.

Because of the different ways men and women approach sexuality, women often believe that men want just sex, not love and intimacy. But that is not true. Men *do* long for love; they want intimacy and closeness, and they want to show love and adoration for their wives. The problem is, men need sex in order to love—men *feel* intimacy and closeness *through* sex. This is why a man's primary interest in a woman *is* sex—it is the only path to intimacy he understands. This disgusts many women. For them, marriage should not be about sex; it should be about companionship, faithfulness, and sharing. I teasingly tell women that if their husbands wanted companionship, faithfulness, and sharing, they'd buy a golden retriever.

Truth be told, men want to give their hearts to their brides. The problem is, women have been given misinformation. When I was growing up, they used to tell girls that the way to a man's heart was through his stomach. Sadly, they were about six inches too high.

When a man has sex, his softer side emerges. It is this

"after-sex" sensitivity that women find amazingly seductive. But this is precisely the challenge.

When you have one member in the relationship who needs love, closeness, and intimacy *before* wanting sex, and another member in the relationship who can't really feel love, closeness, and intimacy until *after* sex, you have a problem. One can't help but wonder if the whole sex thing isn't some kind of cosmic joke. Yet, what if God designed this to be so on purpose? What if instead of arguing with each other and judging each other as perverts or frigid prudes, we worked at understanding and accommodating each other? This would mean we would have to view sex as a way to *serve* the one we love.

When sex is viewed as a way to love and serve each other in marriage, it brings a whole new order to human sexuality. Imagine a husband who cares enough to remember to practice those typical after-sex soft, caring feelings *before* sex in order to trigger sexual desire in his wife. Or envision a wife who gives herself freely to her husband because she *gets* that he navigates to intimacy *through* sexuality. (Ladies, the good news is, if you want to see that "softer side" more often in your man, there is a sure-fire way to get it!)

Though there is always the danger of manipulation and abuse in any relationship as intimate as marriage, and though it may take a while to figure out how to do it, a wholesome rhythm will emerge if each partner commits to creating an atmosphere where the sexual needs of the other are met. At any given moment it may not seem fair, but if you continue to work on it honestly and openly, you will look back over time and see relational ebb and flow that ultimately brings sexual satisfaction to *both* in the marriage union.

The key to getting what you want is to give your spouse what he or she wants. If you are concerned only about what you want, then you will most likely find yourself among the couples we call "married and miserable."

In her book The Sex-Starved Marriage, author Michele Weiner Davis captures the insanity of holding out on each other sexually:

> Sex-starved men wait for wives to become sexier, more flirtatious, and receptive to their sexual advances before putting energy into their relationships. They shut down emotionally. They end up watching inordinate amounts of television. They leave their soda cans in the family room. They forget they have children. They clam up. This makes women feel communication starved. Communication-starved women feel depressed, short-changed, and resentful. They develop panic attacks, cry, overeat or under-eat, lose sleep, take up residence in their less-than-attractive sweat suits, nag, criticize, and, last, but not least, shut the door on intimacy. They simply lose desire. When men tune out, women turn off. And when women turn off, men tune out."[1]

Guys, if you want more sex, you are going to have to meet more of the emotional needs of your spouse. Gals, if you desire more of your emotional needs to be met by your husbands, you are going to have to meet more of his sexual needs.

Let's Get Physical

There are wagonloads of evidence that says sex is great for a person's health. In fact, having sex an average of three times a week is equivalent to running eighty miles a year. Sex increases good hormone production, strengthens bones, improves muscle tone, and loads your system with good cholesterol. Endorphin release, which is nature's aspirin for pain, happens during sex, and makes it a great management tool for the general aches and pains that present themselves in our bodies.

The hormone DHEA (dehydroepiandrosterone), produced by the adrenal glands, is also released just before orgasm. DHEA improves mental awareness, boosts the immune system, inhibits the growth of tumors in the body, and builds bone tissue. In a woman, oxytocin (the "love and cuddle" chemical) is released in huge doses during sex. A woman's estrogen level also increases. Estrogen gives a woman an overall feeling of contentment and calm, aides in memory retention, and affords her a healthier cardiovascular system.

Husbands and wives need to have sex. It's healthy for you. In this regard, the counsel of the Nike corporation is the best there is: *Just do it.*

Hey . . . You Awake?

Why is it that some people want to have sex more than others? (And believe it or not, it's not *always* the guy.) Despite what novelists and poets claim, sexual drive is not the stuff of romance; it is the result of our hormones raging. The drive for lovemaking is the aftereffect of a hormone cocktail released in the brain, causing chemical and electrical reactions that make us hungry for sex. If you "up" the hormone level in a person, you up their sex drive. It's as simple as that.

Testosterone is the hormone that most directly impacts the sex drive in both men and women. Most men receive a testosterone rush very early in the morning. With no thought at all, a man is suddenly awakened with a formidable erection. That is when most men reach over and whisper those three words every woman loves to hear: "Hey . . . you awake?"

Testosterone also affects a woman's sex drive. Some time ago, I had a woman come to my office asking if she could talk with me about something. As we sat down she described how she, though happily married, had lost all interest in sex. She said she still loved her husband and everything was fine at home, but her interest in sex had vanished. She had mentioned it to her doctor and he decided to run some tests. They determined that her testosterone levels were very low, so he prescribed a testosterone supplement designed specifically for women.

"I took it for one week and . . . nothing. I took it for a second week and . . . still nothing. I took it for the third week and suddenly—" she leaned forward and blurted, "I felt like a man! I can't leave my husband alone sexually. I attack him whenever I get the chance." Then she said, looking a bit concerned, "What do you think of that?"

I sat there for a moment in silence and then asked, "Where can *I* get some of that stuff?!"

Testosterone levels are the *why* behind the disparity in sexual drive between men and women. Testosterone in teenage boys is fifteen to twenty times higher than in teenage girls. It isn't until a woman hits her late thirties that she is for her gender what a nineteen-year-old boy is for his. If you compare the sex drives of men and women, you find that men maintain a stronger interest in sex from their teen years until they hit forty to forty-five. Then the shoe is switched to the other foot and women begin to show a greater interest in sex than men. At this point, women generally outpace men in sex drive until they both get close to their sixties. After that age, both genders pace about the same for the rest of their lives. Old love is sweet love because there is less conflict about sexual issues.

Though sexual drive is governed by testosterone, the psychological environment can either help or hinder the release of this sexual hormone cocktail into the brain, particularly in women. Women recognize that factors like closeness, trust, and a sense of being "treasured" help them "feel" sexual attraction. However, this is only because these feelings create an atmosphere in the brain for the testosterone to be released. Though some psychological factors can affect a man's sexual drive, men, for the most part, seem to be in a constant state of *readiness* for the release of testosterone. This ease of arousal for the male gender is no small frustration in most marriage relationships. Many marital wars have been fought over sexual issues.

Sexual Equilibrium

Very few relationships find themselves equally matched when it comes to sexual desire. This is one of the supporting arguments for those who believe couples should have sex before they are married. They believe sex before marriage helps a couple determine if they are compatible sexually. But premarital sex is rarely an accurate indicator of sexual desire. Early in a relationship, whether a couple is living together or in the honeymoon period in marriage, many forces are at work that influence people's true sexual desire.

A chemical deception is at play during premarital and early marriage sexual relationships. Weiner Davis writes:

> "During [early sex], with the help of PEA [phenethylamine], dopamine, and norepinephrine, the person with the low sex drive experiences a surge in sexual desire. While under the influence of the love cocktail, the low [sex drive] person thinks, feels, and acts like a high [sex drive] person. This individual, who ordinarily has little interest in sex, who is not easily aroused and doesn't think about sex, experiences just the

165

opposite. On any given day, sexual fantasies, love play, and sexual initiation all become part of the [early sex] behavior of the low [sex drive] lover, who is now believing, 'I have finally found someone who turns me on.' Meanwhile, the high [sex drive] person is thinking, 'I have died and gone to heaven. I have finally found someone who enjoys sex as much as I do.' "[2]

After this "love cocktail" subsides (and it *always* does) the low-desire spouses go back to their normal state and the high-desire spouses are left with the shock and horror that they have married someone who does not have the same sex drive as they do. The problems now begin to build. The high-drive person cries out, "You don't *want* me anymore!" The low-drive person replies, "You don't want me; you just want sex!" This precipitates many arguments, which can begin to tear the relationship apart.

The fact that one partner in a marriage has a lower sex drive than the other doesn't mean there is anything wrong with that person's sex drive. There are all kinds of factors that influence a person's sex drive: biological, physiological, psychological, relational, et cetera. Virtually every marriage on the planet features one person with a stronger sex drive than the other. Sadly, all the sex information out there assumes that a normal and healthy couple will have an equal amount of sexual desire, but this is just not true.

And just about every book on sex gives couples this formula:

Desire → Arousal → Intercourse

Desire leads to arousal which leads to intercourse. Sounds good, but the problem is that it is not true for *many* people. There are lots of people who seem to demonstrate little to no desire up front, yet seem to enjoy intercourse immensely once they are into it. These people don't feel like doing it until they start doing it. And then they *really* get into it. Plus, the more sex couples have, the more testosterone their bodies produce. That means couples not having enough sex should simply focus on having more sex, not on trying to boost their *desire* for sex.

But couples are not hearing that message. What they are hearing is: If you don't have desire up front, *there is something wrong with you.* As a result, the high-desire spouse feels insulted while the low-desire spouse feels minimized. High-desire spouses may withdraw and stop asking for sex since they feel so rejected, and low-desire spouses may put out a "closed for business" sign because they are constantly reminded that there is something wrong with them. The expectation that desire should be there *before* engaging in sexual behavior actually creates false expectations that wind up damaging the relationship.

Imagine if couples learned the truth: that people with low desire can actually make some of the greatest lovers in the world. High-desire spouses would begin to cherish what they have and would no longer feel rejected by their partners' lack of exhibited desire. Low-desire spouses would no longer feel broken, in fact, they would begin to feel very comfortable about who they are sexually. When people discover this, it liberates them, and they can enjoy who they are.

That being said, high-desire people need to learn how to control their sexual drive and be respectful of their low-desire spouses. They shouldn't ask for sex *every time* they feel a little pressure in their loins. Just as people who eat every time they think about food end up fat and unhealthy, people who demand sex whenever they feel an urge end up being unhealthy as well.

Special Equipment

I have heard many women say, "Sex is just a male thing. It is pushed so men can have fun." But nothing could be further from the truth. God intended sex to be pleasurable for both men and women. Physically speaking, a woman is a masterpiece of sexuality. God even gave women their own organ dedicated to sexual pleasure; it's called a clitoris. (If your husband isn't quite sure where that is, you may want to point it out to him.)

Wow! Your own organ dedicated for only one purpose—sexual pleasure. Men don't have that. Ours is a multifunctional thing. It's enough to make a guy jealous. Though, I suppose it's a good thing that God did not give us our own organ dedicated to nothing but sexual pleasure. We'd probably never leave it alone.

13

The Five Keys to Great Sex

HAVING established that sex is significant for a happy marriage, I want to give you what I believe to be the top five keys for great sex in a marriage (and I want to give it to you in "Top Ten," David Letterman fashion). To do an effective job, however, I must spend the bulk of my time explaining what it takes for a *woman* to experience great sex. Why the focus on the woman? Because sexually, men are easy. All a man needs for great sex is for the woman to show up.

Key Number Five: Romance

HIS left arm is under my head and his right arm embraces me.
—Song of Solomon 2:6

I often hear men complain that their wives are not interested in sex, but they could not be more wrong. A woman is a virtual storehouse of sexual energy. Men just don't recognize it because a woman's sexual drive is not on the surface like it is for them. The only foreplay most men really need is *oxygen*. As long as there is air to be had, he is ready. Not so for his wife. Hence, using himself as the standard, he often wrongly concludes that since she is not ready like him, she must be devoid of sexual desire.

Even in our supposedly sexually enlightened society, it still appears that men need to be educated about female sexuality. They need to understand that a woman's sexuality tends to hibernate more than a man's does. Additionally, once her sexuality begins to awaken, her sexual passion emerges at quite a different pace than a man's. Sexually speaking, a man is more like a light switch and a woman is more like an iron: She just isn't as instant as he is, and she requires a bit more electricity. A husband needs to be aware of this and must take responsibility to awaken the sexual desire in his wife. If he does, he will smile more often.

For a woman to experience sexual arousal, she needs her husband to be a *lover* to her. She needs *romance.* Men are not *against* romance; they just have no idea how important it is to a woman. Men tend to *do things,* such as wash the car or go to work to earn resources for the family, in an attempt to show how much they love their wives. Truth be told, most men have never had any one model what it is to be *romantic.*

Romance is about *sensuality,* not just sexuality. Sensuality involves holding hands, hugging, cuddling, sweet whispers, feeling the roughness of a beard or the silkiness of hair, putting your cheeks together and smelling your partner, walking hand in hand on a lonely beach, dimming the lights and lighting a fire in the fireplace—all things that help us connect emotionally with the moment. Sensuality doesn't set a goal for "sex," because it isn't goal-oriented at all. Neither is it always sexually explicit; it's really about doing things that reflect your feelings and attraction toward each other.

Married couples get in trouble when they don't discern the differences between sensuality and sexuality. Men particularly find the distinction difficult. But making the distinction is crucial. Here is what is important: Wonderful *sexuality* is the result of wonderful *sensuality*. When couples are newlyweds, they naturally spend lots of time holding hands, hugging, kissing, and so forth. But over time couples tend to bypass the sensual and move, in a more goal-oriented way, directly to sex, especially after children. Less time is afforded flirting, being playful, and sharing intimate contacts that were once so delightful. When intimate behaviors are abandoned, we begin to feel we are drifting apart. If we are not careful, sex itself ends up being more an issue of performance than an outworking of intimacy. When sensuality falls away, couples become interested in sex only for the sake of sex.

We must realize that gazing at each other, talking, listening, touching, and holding hands are as important to couples married for years as they are to newlyweds. Husbands and wives who run right to sexual intercourse, without including the stages of intimacy that should have preceded it, end up leaving their partners feeling empty and sometimes used (women in particular). You need to think of sex as a gourmet feast. Now I'm not suggesting that every sexual encounter *has* to be a six course meal—sometimes peanut butter and jelly sandwiches hit the spot. There's certainly nothing wrong with a quickie "meal" now and then. Just be sure you don't live in Quickieville all the time.

Interestingly, when couples first begin to *connect* romantically with each other, hormone cocktails light up their brains! A number of powerful brain chemicals are released when this happens. These chemicals create intense feelings of elation: *dopamine* gives a feeling of well-being; *phenylethylamine* increases one's capacity for excitement; *serotonin* causes the sense of emotional stability; and *norepinephrine* engenders a kind of "high" that makes you feel like you can do anything. The problem is that this early romantic connection, which is more infatuation than true love, is temporary, lasting on average from three to twelve months. If couples aren't careful, they will not move through infatuation to the next level, *marital bonding*. This is the emotional link between a man and woman that makes them intensely valuable to each other.

This is where romance comes in. It helps them revisit the infatuation stage to transition them into building and improving *marital bonding*. When a man purposely reflects his feelings of value for his wife by doing little romantic things—opening a car door, bringing home some flowers, taking her out for a romantic dinner, turning down the lights for some nonsexual cuddling, taking a weekend getaway together, or attending one of my Laugh Your Way to a Better Marriage® seminars (shameless plug)—he re-creates the conditions of the couple's early relationship. This literally "tricks" their bodies into releasing the hormone cocktail that made them feel "high on love" in the first place. There is no way to make these feelings of infatuation stay permanently, but a couple can ensure they get an occasional hormonal "hit" by doing some good planning. This kind of activity will reignite both their romantic feelings and sexual drive. Romance actually repositions the couple emotionally to enhance their marital bonding.

According to research done by Dr. Desmond Morris, couples are most likely to bond when they move systematically and slowly through twelve steps of progressing physical intimacy. When couples go through these steps *in sequence,* it makes their relationship intensely personal and fosters a deep love and commitment that lasts for a lifetime.

The following stages represent the progression of physical intimacy from which a permanent commitment often evolves (the first nine are *sensual* and the last three are explicitly *sexual*): 1) Eye to body. 2) Eye to eye. 3) Voice to voice. 4) Hand to hand. 5) Hand to shoulder. 6) Hand to waist. 7) Face to face. 8) Hand to head. 9) Hand to body. 10) Mouth to breast. 11) Touching below the waist. 12) Intercourse.[1] The good news is, even if a couple has a tired, patterned sex life, walking through these twelve steps regularly and in sequence will reinvigorate a couple's sensuality and restore gusto to their sex life.

Men need to work on being romantic. They need to understand that for romance to work *in* the bedroom, there has to be romance *outside* the bedroom. For a lot of men, the only time they pay attention to or touch their wives is when they want sex. The second he lays a hand on her, she knows what's coming. It is too predictable.

Listen, gentlemen, learn how to pay attention to your wife, learn how to kiss her and intimately touch her *without* the expectation of a sexual payoff. Learn how to step to the plate and swing for a single—for *first base.* Do you know what happens to players who always swing for home runs? They strike out most of time. And that is what will happen to you if you try to "score" with your wife every time you touch her. She will begin to resent your touch.

Be romantic! Kiss her without the expectation of sex. Touch her without the expectation of sex. Get with the Desmond twelve-step program. Spend time with her. Do things with her. Take her shopping. Compliment her. Be nice to her. Work hard at keeping her happy—no man has ever received great sex from a woman who was mad at him!

"But I don't wanna," you might complain.

Then you ain't gettin' any. It's just that simple.

Here's a great romantic suggestion: Pray with your wife. Hold her hand, and while she is listening to you, tell God how wonderful she is and how much you appreciate everything she does for you. You will be pleasantly surprised.

The Anti-Romance

One of the problems I have with pornography is how it has pushed men from being lovers of women with all their complexity to using them as props for selfish sexual gratification. Porn contributes to women becoming sexual objects. When women are just objects, men try to coerce them into playing roles that stimulate their selfish impulses. This gets men off the hook of caring for anyone but themselves. Sex, for pornography junkies, is no longer about how a man can satisfy a woman; it's about women being expected to do whatever they need to do to please men.

When this happens, husbands unfairly demand that their wives "service" them wherever, whenever, and however the man chooses. I recently had a gorgeous young lady come to see me in my office. She told me of how her husband was no longer interested in having sex with her. In fact, he had not requested vaginal sex from her in over a year. Instead he demanded that she do a number of perverted sexual things to him—things she did not feel comfortable doing, things that in no way contributed to *her* having a fulfilling sexual experience. Now *there's* a real Romeo! Rather than making love to his beautiful wife, he was more interested in her pleasing him by making her do weird things *to* him.

These are the kinds of stupid things men do when they are no longer lovers of women. If women let them, men become sexual *takers,* which turns them into sexual pigs.

If a man is a true lover, his first priority is to awaken and then satisfy the sexual desire of his wife. Then, and only then, does he allow himself to reach his sexual peak. *That* is a lover. Sadly, many men today are much more interested in being serviced by their wives or masturbating while ogling women on the Internet, instead of being lovers.

It used to be that men took pride in being lovers of women. Men would talk to each other about how to most effectively win a woman's heart. Consider this article found in an 1896 Farmer's Almanac, entitled "The Art of Kissing":

Don't peck a woman on the forehead or the end of the nose, or jerk at her bonnet strings in haste to get through. Do take the left hand of the young lady in your right; let go of your hat, just let it drop. Throw your left hand over the lady's shoulder and let it fall down to her waist. Draw her gently and lovingly to your heart. Don't be in a hurry. Her left hand is in your right . . . clasp it firmly, gently, and with thought and respect. Don't be in a hurry. Her head lies on your shoulder. Look into her half-closed eyes. Lean forward with your head, not your body. Take good aim . . . the lips meet . . . the eyes close . . . the heart opens . . . (don't be in a hurry) . . . the heart forgets all bitterness, and the incomparable art of kissing is learned.[2]

These were farmers! I don't mean to insult anyone, but if you make a list of the most romantic professions, farmers don't really cut it. These nineteenth century farmers may not have been the most sophisticated people in the world, but they sure knew how to make a woman want to be with them. If we men want our wives to be more interested in sex, we are going to have to learn to be real lovers again.

Key Number Four: Foreplay

"I will climb the palm tree; I will take hold of its fruit."
—Song of Solomon 7:8

Foreplay is about deepening *sensuality*. You need to practice romance all the time, but there is a point when you should go for a particular goal: the goal of making love. There are a number of passages in the Song of Solomon that capture the rhythm, canter, and dance of the romantic relationship between a man and a woman that lead to sex. Solomon writes about his bride, "Your stature is like that of the palm, and your breasts like clusters of fruit. I said, 'I will climb the palm tree; I will take hold of its fruit.' "[3]

Ah *yes,* climbing the palm tree, a lover's delight. Sadly, most men don't want to take the time to "climb" the palm tree—takes too long, involves too much effort. They just want to hop in a cherry picker, swing into place, and *grab the coconuts.* But guys, if you just reach over and "grab" your wife's "fruit" without taking the time to "climb the palm tree," you are no lover.

Foreplay is all about climbing the palm tree. But you need to climb the palm a step at a time. The first steps involve the romance we described earlier: gazing at her, stroking her arms, rubbing her back, touching and kissing her face, caressing her hair. But foreplay also involves emotionally touching your wife in ways that show her you care about *more* than just sex with her: take out the garbage, tell her to lie down while you take the kids for a while, cook dinner (without being told), grab the vacuum, pick up the house, and so on.

But at appropriate times, foreplay starts hinting toward sexuality. This is best expressed through *flirting.* To flirt is to be playfully romantic with sexual overtures. Happy couples do this all the time. It's in the tone of their voices as they talk with each other; it's in the love names they call each other; it's in the passing touch; it's present in the lingering stare from across the room; it's in those teasing whispers. Flirting adds joy and playfulness to human sexuality.

Flirting is all about the chase. Flirting builds *anticipation.* When it becomes obvious that the couple is approaching physical love, they begin to shudder with anticipation. The bride in the Song of Solomon declares, "Listen! My lover! Look! Here he comes, leaping across the mountains, bounding over the hills."[4] My lover thrust his hand through the latch-opening; my heart began to pound for him. I arose to open for my lover, and my hands dripped with myrrh, my fingers with flowing myrrh, on the handles of the lock.[5]

At some point it dawns on us that this is going somewhere. The *other* is coming. We are no longer going to be alone. There will be touch; there will be contact; there will be connection. This is the *real* deal. But men, in particular, must beware. Just grabbing your wife's "fruit" probably won't work. You have to dance *around* the fruit *first*—this will awaken the sexual desire in your woman.

It's important for men to learn where erogenous zones are and how to touch them. As I said, guys are pretty easy. There is basically one spot we like you to touch and you can do it all day as far as we are concerned. But it's not like that for women. A woman's moods shift and what she finds sexually stimulating can vary from time to time. (It is helpful to learn more about the physiology of sex from such books as *Intended for Pleasure,* by Ed and Gaye Wheat.)

One of the most important secrets a man needs to know about sex is that this *slowness* will actually enhance his sexual experience. Our Farmer's Almanac article said don't be in a hurry three times. Lust is *fast*. Most porn depicts sex as *fast*. But lovemaking transcends lust. And men need not fear that they will not get as much out of the event—going slowly will *not* leave them unfulfilled. When men approach their wives in a slow, methodical way, their sexual desire intensifies. Men who sustain an erection longer than twenty minutes before ejaculation are amazed at the intensity of their orgasm.

There is no such thing as easy sex—at least not the kind of sex that satisfies. Some men get married thinking that marriage is their ticket to "easy sex," only to be shocked that even in marriage, sex requires effort on their part. Pornography always portrays easy sex, but it is an illusion. Then there is the promise of easy sex from an adulterous affair. The adulteress drips with the promise of easy sex, but it is a mirage. The truth is, even the adulteress ultimately wants the same thing your wife wants—for you to be a lover to her.

So guys, here's a question for you: Do you want *really* great sex? Try making foreplay a twenty-four-hour process. I call it "slow roasting your woman." Touch her, then leave her alone. Kiss her, then leave her alone. Rub her back without trying to score. Flirt with her. Take your time. Don't always be in such a hurry. I promise you, you'll be headed for some of the best sex of your life.

Key Number Three: Endurance

> *UNTIL the dawn breaks . . .*
> —Song of Solomon 4:6

Okay. You've been romantic; you've engaged in foreplay; you've danced the Desmond twelve-step, and you've hit step twelve. You have come together in intercourse and you are beginning to get lost in each other. It's all good . . . until . . . oh no! *Premature ejaculation!* While I understand that this is a very sensitive subject, a large part of the male population suffers from this problem. We need to talk about it.

I was with my wife at a hospital in Milwaukee, Wisconsin, as she was going through treatments for cancer. (She's 100 percent clean today, years later. God is wonderful!) We were flipping through channels on the TV when we happened upon a woman saying, "Today we are going to discuss why so many women have a difficult time achieving orgasm."

"Okay, I'm in," I said. And we started watching the program.

They had a panel made up of women doctors and psychiatrists who theorized all the possible reasons that some women struggle in this area. Each time they went to commercial they would use a teaser question designed to keep you tuned in till they returned. At one point right before the commercial break, they posed this question: "What is the average length of a man's sexual experience?" There were three possible answers: a) two minutes, b) ten minutes, or c) twenty minutes.

As they broke to the commercial I turned to Debbie and asked with a smile, "Do you know what the answer is?"

"No," she replied.

"Two minutes," I quipped.

"No it's not!" she snapped with a look of shock.

"Just wait and see," I said calmly.

After the commercial the answer appeared: a) two minutes.

What is *really* sad is that two minutes is the *average.* That means at least half of them don't even get to *two minutes*! So let's do the math: If a woman needs anywhere from *seven* to *fifteen* minutes, and the man is finished in just *two* minutes, well, you definitely have yourself a math problem.

I have had women come up to me and say, "Pastor Mark, I have not been able to have an orgasm. What is wrong with me?"

I always reply with, "Let me ask you a question. When your husband makes love to you, is he done in two minutes or less?"

They always look a bit surprised and answer, "Yeah . . . how did *you* know?"

Look, when a man is making love to a woman, he wants her to be able to lose control. When a woman loses control, she releases all the sexual energy she has in her. That moment is what makes for really great sex. However, for her to be able to *lose* control, you must be able to stay *in* control *until* she loses control. It is not likely she will be able to lose control if you lose it in two minutes or less.

Now, ladies, *you* can help with the premature ejaculation issue. One of the ways a man becomes a skillful lover and is able to maintain control is for him to experience regular, consistent sex. If you make love with him only twice a month (or *less*), it is not likely he will *ever* be able to maintain the kind of control you want in a lover. The good news is, there are lots of good books on how to overcome the "two-minute drill." Many offer great practical advice and exercises couples can do together. (I'm not big on exercising, but this stuff even I would sign up for!)

Bottom line: Great sex requires *endurance.* Solomon said of his lover, "Until the dawn breaks and the shadows flee, I will go to the mountain of myrrh and to the hill of incense."[6] Ahhh . . . Myrrh Mountain and the Hill of Incense. You may ask, "Where exactly are the Mountain of Myrrh and the Hill of Incense?" Well, think it through. In this text he has just talked about his bride's hair, her eyes, her lips, her neck, her breasts—and then winds up at Myrrh Mountain. Where do *you* think it is? That's right! He's talking about her vagina. And the amazing thing is that he says he will be there "Until the dawn breaks and the shadows flee." In other words, *all night long*! Now, that's *endurance,* baby.

Key Number Two: Privacy

> *"LET us go early to the vineyads . . .*
> *there I will give you my love."*
> —Song of Solomon 7:12

It is difficult for most women to feel very sexual if your lovemaking is not safe and private. That means she probably won't be interested in doing the "wild thing" if you have dinner guests waiting in the next room. To a lot of men it would make little difference, but in order for a woman to lose control to you as her lover, you are going to have to make her feel safe enough to do it.

This issue of privacy can reveal itself in a variety of ways:

• If she doesn't feel that you value her enough to protect her from ridicule or harm, she won't feel very sexual.

• If she doesn't feel that you are providing a safe financial environment, she may not feel very sexual.

• If she doesn't feel you are providing a safe environment for her children (safe in both physical *and* emotional ways), she will not feel very sexual.

• If you don't provide privacy *from* your children, she will not feel it is "safe" to make love to you. Many women get overly concerned that the children may perceive that mommy and daddy are doing something bad. There is a simple solution to this problem. Buy a lock.

Privacy and safety are essential to a great sex life. Sadly, just having children around can make it pretty difficult to maintain much privacy.

The Maternal Caveat

Having children can really mess with a woman's perception of and even her desire for sex. *Everything* changes after childbirth. A woman is not the same emotionally or physically. For example, her seductive breasts are suddenly transformed from erogenous zones into public utilities. And guys, realize that things are going to be different for her for a while. She is being touched and grabbed and pulled on *all day long* by that little creature you caused her to have. Don't be shocked when you come home if the *last* thing she wants is to have you touch her or put *your* mouth on her! Often sex goes from being spontaneous to you needing to call to make an appointment. But go ahead and make the appointment, it'll be worth it, and it's important for your marriage.

Men need to remember that small children are exhausting. If you don't believe it, just take *one day* and do everything that she does and you *will* believe it. Just a few hours with my grandchildren by myself can cause me to want to self-medicate, and I love my grandchildren more than life itself. I just find it physically and emotionally draining to care for a very small child. Most men do.

I do need to say this to the moms, however. Ladies, you cannot use motherhood as an excuse to neglect the sexual needs of your husband. I know a lot has happened to you, but you need to remember that *nothing* has happened to him. He is the same sexual *wild man* you married. You cannot allow yourself to become so engrossed in your children that you forget to be a lover to your husband.

"But little Johnny *needs* me!" you might protest.

I'll tell you what little Johnny needs: *a father.* If you neglect the sexual needs of your husband, chances are pretty high that little Johnny will grow up *without* one.

I cannot stress this enough. Early childhood years can be *very* stressful on a marriage. This is why so many marriages fail just five to seven years after they say their I do's. Don't let this happen to you. Yes, things are going to be different with kids. And yes, sex won't come as easily or as naturally as it once did for many of you. But you need to appropriately address and manage the sexual area of your relationship. You need to make adjustments and be patient with each other.

One of the most helpful things a man can do to maintain a normal sex life during the stressful child-rearing years is to share in the responsibilities of child rearing and domestic chores.

USA Today did a survey. The number one need for men: sex. Number two: food. Number three: sleep. They did the same survey with women. Number one: sleep. (Probably why it's not a good idea to awaken your wife in the dead of sleep with "Hey—you awake?") Number two: food. (Dude, she's trading you in for a cheeseburger!) And finally: sex.

Guys, why don't you take the kids for a while and let them peel *your* brain like a banana and let your wife take a rest? Then, why don't you make dinner for her or take her out? Look, if you deal with numbers one and two, it will help you get to her number three a lot easier.

Even though things are very different with small children, the good news is, things *will* go back to the way they were. The *really* good news is, those little rug rats eventually grow up and you get your house back! Lots of people fear the empty nest because they have so neglected their marriage in favor of their children that when the children are gone, they find themselves staring at a stranger across the dinner table.

Not us! We were happy when our kids left home. We were happy for them to launch out into their lives and into all the possibilities life affords. And we were happy for us. Man, we are having the time of our lives. We have each other all to ourselves again. We have enjoyed life with the kids, and now we are enjoying life after the kids. There really is life after children. And if you work at it, you can look forward to the empty nest season of life as well.

Key Number One: Exclusivity

Exclusivity. Sexual love is *privileged* love. This kind of love is fulfilling only when there is a desire for the couple to be emotionally and physically separate from other people. In friendship love, if a person wanted you to be his or her *only* friend and no one else's, that would be a signal of some kind of weirdness. We should have many friends. But not with sexual love. Sexual love is exclusive love. Only two should be in on this—that defines normal.

I love this verse:

> *I am my lover's and my lover is mine.*
> —Song of Solomon 6:3

A couple's desire should be for each other, alone. *That,* my friends, is the number one key to incredible sex—when *one* man focuses exclusively on *one* woman, and vice versa. Naomi Wolf captures the power of this when she writes,

> I will never forget a visit I made to Ilana, an old friend who had become an Orthodox Jew in Jerusalem. When I saw her again, she had abandoned her jeans and T-shirts for long

skirts and a headscarf. I could not get over it. Ilana has waist-length, wild and curly golden-blonde hair. "Can't I even see your hair?" I asked, trying to find my old friend in there. "No," she demurred quietly. "Only my husband," she said with a calm sexual confidence, "ever gets to see my hair."

When she showed me her little house in a settlement on a hill, and I saw the bedroom, draped in Middle Eastern embroideries, that she shares only with her husband—the kids are not allowed—the sexual intensity in the air was archaic, overwhelming. It was private. It was a feeling of erotic intensity deeper than any I have ever picked up between secular couples in the liberated West. And I thought: Our husbands see naked women all day—in Times Square if not on the net. Her husband never even sees another woman's hair.

She must feel, I thought, so hot.[7]

Something extremely powerful takes place when one man makes one woman his sole source of sexual input. However, this flies in the face of what our culture teaches us. Sexual gurus say the key to great sex is *lust*. The experts of our day preach that the more you fantasize, role-play, view pornography, masturbate, or imagine yourself having sex with someone else, the better your sex life will be.

I can't decide if they are blatantly lying to us or if they are just that incredibly stupid, but trust me when I tell you that lust will destroy your sex life.

14

Lust in the Dust

*WHY be captivated, my son, by an adulteress? Why embrace
the bosom of another man's wife?*

—Proverbs 5:20

SEX and lust have become synonymous in our culture. Many
experts claim that lust is essential for a healthy sexual relationship—that lust is what keeps the "spark" alive in human sexuality. Certainly the media have bought into this idea. But is
lust *really* good?

Lust is *uncontrolled desire.* It is aroused when one participates
in the *forbidden.* Saying that lust is essential for good sexuality is
to claim that marital love requires a husband and wife to find
ways to make what they do sexually, forbidden in some way.
Going after the *forbidden* empowers uncontrolled desire: *lust.*

The Scriptures reject the idea that lust is good for *anything.* Remember the tree that got the first couple in trouble?
It was forbidden. The apostle John warns: "The world is passing away, and the lust of it; but he who does the will of God
abides forever."[1] Remember that sex was God's idea. Is it really
conceivable that what God created should be fueled by *lust?*

The apostle Paul speaks of "passions" that are "aroused" by the forbidden,[2] but he also refers to a new kind of energy that is afforded us by doing what is right—a "new way" of living.[3] What if there is an energy that is available for a great sex life based on the fact that you are doing what is *right*? What if sex gets jammed with energy when it is pure, innocent, private, and exclusive? What if the deluge of sex in magazines, on billboards, on TV, in movies, on the Internet, and in song lyrics is more destructive than it is helpful to our sexual lives?

Young men and women in our country today think our culture has always been flooded with a free-flow of hot babes on the Internet and X-rated videos in the family video store. They don't *get* that the popular culture in America has not always encouraged masturbation, voyeurism, multiple partners, and an anything-goes attitude. They have no idea that during their grandparents' time, sexuality was considered a private enterprise charged with mystery and sacredness. So where did the idea that lust is good come from? A short history lesson will explain the slippery slope of sexuality and just how we have fallen so far.

The lesson begins with a man named Alfred Kinsey. Kinsey was a Harvard-educated zoologist who is referred to as the father of the sexual revolution. In 1948 Kinsey irrevocably changed American culture and created a media sensation with his book *Sexual Behavior in the Human Male,* and the subsequent release in 1953 of *Sexual Behavior in the Human Female.* Using the technique of his own famous sex interviews, he urged people to break through shame, fear, and guilt, and speak freely about their sexual histories. Kinsey's work shocked society at the time with statistics of what people were supposedly doing—everything from premarital and extramarital sex to masturbation and same-gender sex was reported to be common and "normal." When Kinsey published his research, the press compared its impact to that of the atom bomb.

The response from Americans was dramatic. While shocked by Kinsey's revelations, people began shifting their behaviors to line up with what was reportedly going on in bedrooms across the country. Because an "expert" said it was so, it *must* be so. Hence, the 1960s brought us the *"sexual revolution"*—a revolution that was supposed to improve people's sex lives and bring them to a new level of sexual liberty. Hugh Hefner, inspired by Kinsey and believing he was fulfilling a need, began *Playboy* magazine to encourage sexual openness and freedom.

Kinsey's work went unquestioned for nearly forty years. But in the early 1990s, those in the psychological community began to question Kinsey's methodology. Thanks to the work of Dr. Judith Reisman, Kinsey's "junk-science" has been well documented. In her book *Kinsey, Sex and Fraud,* Reisman exposes the flaws in Kinsey's work.[4]

In reaction to his very strict repressive upbringing, Kinsey purposefully selected the most degenerate people in American society for his research interviews, and presented *their* practices as normative. His research participants were not typical Americans; they were prisoners, ex-cons, rapists, pedophiles, homosexuals, prostitutes, and even thirty-one women who said they had copulated with animals! This group was hardly a swath from mainstream America.

Kinsey's biased research made normal Americans feel stupid and repressed for having their sexuality tethered to the safety of marriage and monogamy. Lust, immorality, and perversion became *en vogue* and began to be considered normal sexual behavior. New sexual boundaries emerged: *whatever, whenever,* with *whomever.* And all the experts began to parrot this view. Kinsey's fraud was so influential that it affected the *Lawrence v. Texas* Supreme Court decision to legalize sodomy, as well as changes in other laws across the United States concerning sex crimes.

Most of the West has walked the path of open sexuality for nearly sixty years based on Kinsey's research. And we are definitely still reaping the effects of the seeds of his misinformation. The *sexual revolution* has promulgated one of the greatest lies ever thrust on modern culture, and it is this: *Lust leads to great sex.*

Fantasy

The belief that *fantasy* is essential for a healthy sex life explains why sex experts encourage couples to view pornography. The claim is this: The more you fantasize, the more you view pornography, the more you check out all the "hotties" around you, the greater your sexual energy will be. The problem is, the idea doesn't hold true in real life. Lusting is like eating junk food all day long. The result is that you won't be hungry for a *real meal* later. Your mama was right; snacking *ruins* your appetite. Lust has the same affect on your sex life: It will ruin the *real* thing.

Concerning men and pornography, Naomi Wolf writes:

> "A whole generation of men are less able to connect erotically to women—and ultimately less libidinous. The reason to turn off the porn might become, to thoughtful people, not a moral one, but in a way, a physical-and-emotional-health one; you might want to rethink your constant access to porn in the same way that, if you want to be an athlete, you rethink your smoking. The evidence is in: Greater supply of the stimulant equals diminished capacity."[5]

You want a really great meal tonight? Don't eat anything else for the rest of the day. By the time your evening meal comes, you will cherish every morsel. Guys, you want *really* great sex? Don't view pornography or ogle the women who pass by you. In fact, refuse to allow yourself to think of any other woman but the one in your life. Let your wife be your *only* source of sexual stimulation, and I *guarantee* that your desire for her will rise dramatically, resulting in the best sex of your life! That is why *exclusivity* is the number one key to incredible sex.

This is the claim of the ancient Hebrew proverb: "May your fountain be blessed, and may you rejoice in the wife of your youth. A loving doe, a graceful deer—may her breasts satisfy you always, may you ever be captivated by her love."[6] The best cookin' is home cookin'.

But no, the "experts" say men and women should *fantasize*. Husbands and wives are supposed to ignore their *real* partners and fantasize about someone else. What is wrong with that picture? Many of the sex experts insist that pornography *feeds* desire, but they are wrong. What pornography does, is feed discontent with what you have at home.

In November 2004, while giving testimony to the U.S. Senate, Dr. Mary Anne Layden called pornography a "toxin" that damages the viewers, their spouses, and their children, creating a *mis*education about sex and relationships. She said her research showed that the more porn a person consumes, the more damaging it is to both the person's beliefs and behaviors. Dr. Layden spoke of a "pornography distortion" that *warps* a person's beliefs and attitudes concerning what constitutes a healthy sexual relationship. Layden's studies revealed that beliefs about sexuality are altered as pornographic images are sent to their brains and people are aroused. Then these beliefs become reinforced by orgasms associated with porn. She pointed out how pornography takes sexuality out of the context of intimacy, procreation, or marriage and makes it about body parts, entertainment, self-gratification, strangers, and even being predatory (involving violence, children, animals, and so on).[7]

Sociologist Diana Russell, who has written several books on the subject, says, "Pornography is affecting people at an increasingly young age and unfortunately for many kids growing up today, pornography is the only sex education they'll get." In his book *Men Confront Pornography,* Michael Kimmel states that pornography is one of the major sources of information that young males have about sexuality and is key to the development of their sexuality. Other research says the same is true for young girls. Imagine that! Much of what our young people think as fact about what sex is supposed to be like—what it looks like, feels like, sounds like, everything it's about—is learned from porn. How disturbing and destructive is that?

Dr. Layden, who works as the director of the Sexual Trauma and Psychopathology Program at the University of Pennsylvania, reported how her clinical practice proved that pornography doesn't enhance, but rather *damages* the sexual performance of those who view it. Men have problems with premature ejaculation and erectile dysfunction because they have "spent so much time in unnatural sexual experiences with paper, celluloid and cyberspace, they seem to find it difficult to have sex with a real human being." She further claims, "Pornography has raised their expectation and demand for types and amounts of sexual experiences at the same time it is reducing their ability to have sex."

Dr. Layden also testified that there are *no* studies and *no* data that indicate a benefit from pornography use. It is only the propagandists who spread this lie. In Dr. Layden's words, "If there were a benefit, then pornography users, pornography performers, their spouses and their children would show the most benefit. Just the opposite is true. The society is awash in pornography. If pornography made us healthy, we would be by now."[8]

Additionally, there is an addictive nature to pornography. Porn is very much like a narcotic: You will need a bigger and bigger dose to get the same buzz. Research indicates that even non-sex addicts, while viewing pornography, will show brain reactions on PET scans similar to those of people taking cocaine. Pornography is potent, addictive, and permanently implanted in the brain. Even minimal users of pornography show signs of significant negative impact. In a series of studies, researchers observed numerous and significant changes in people exposed to porn for just six one-hour sessions a week. Imagine what is happening to those men and women who are indulging for twelve, twenty, or more hours weekly.

I met a man at one of my seminars who told me he had been an alcoholic, drug addict, and porn user, claiming he was now clean of all three. Impressed by his story, I asked him, "Of the three—alcohol, drugs, and porn—which one was the hardest to kick?" In a split second he replied, "Without question, the porn." Wow! Harder to kick than alcohol and drugs.

One of the common reports I hear is about men who, while making love to their wives, insist on having a pornographic magazine open next to her so he can look at the magazine while having sex with her. (You can imagine just how wonderful that makes her feel.) Why would a man do such an obviously stupid thing? Because his addiction has brought him to the point that unless he looks at those pictures, he cannot maintain an erection. Good grief—this is supposed to produce great sex?

Dr. Layden's clinical experiences show that spouses of porn users are often depressed, and are more likely to have eating disorders, body image disorders, and low self-esteem. The wives can't function in the fake sexual world in which their husbands live and they may try to please their spouses by engaging in sexual behaviors that they find degrading. Wives may think that they can increase the sexual energy in the relationship and satisfy their husbands if they view the porn with them; but in Dr. Layden's experience, the wife will often "get a short-lived boost in sexual activity but soon she notices that when her husband is having sex with her, he is turning around to watch the porn on the TV screen. She then realizes that he isn't having sex with her at all. He's masturbating inside her body while having sex with the women on the screen."[9] Another example of the *supposed* great sex lust fosters.

Many men need greater and greater doses of porn to achieve an erection, and eventually get to a place where no matter what they see, they *cannot* achieve an erection at all. According to the book *Media, Children, and the Family: Social Scientific, Psychodynamic, and Clinical Perspectives,* research has shown that sexual arousal and excitement diminish with repeated exposure to sexual scenes, and because the viewer of the porn is left relatively unexcited, he or she is likely to seek out the more bizarre.[10]

I get so irritated when I read of "sex experts" suggesting that pornographic magazines and movies can actually *improve* your sex life. It's a lie that is destroying marriages. Here's an e-mail I received from a woman who attended one of my seminars:

> In my first marriage, my husband was very eager to use pornog-
> raphy to spice up things between us and keep from having to deal

with the changes in my body after having two children. He seemed so much more eager to be with me when using magazines and movies, that at first I thought it would be a good thing. I also read that couples were encouraged to do this, so I thought it was normal. However, deep down, I was very hurt and longed for him to give me all his attention. As time went on, it took more and more for him to get aroused and fulfilled. I thought every step down would be as far as I would allow things to go, and each time I ached again to be enough for my husband. Ironically, the more things we added into our private world, the less fulfilled we both were. We had sex less than ever, and the bond between us was very strained. The marriage is now over.

Porn didn't seem to help that marriage. Here's another:

My husband and I used to watch a video to help us get in the mood, or while we were making love we would have the tape playing in the background. I think we always thought it was turning the other person on and we were doing it for them. We never really addressed the issue until I found out my husband was addicted to internet porn sites. We stopped with the tapes during lovemaking. We discovered it wasn't turning either of us on, it was only making us feel worse. We decided to spend time enjoying each other, learn about our bodies or explore what gifts God gave us in each other. With the videos, we were focused on others instead of each other. Since getting rid of the porn, our sex life is better than ever! Now we are completely in tune with each other and have found a new sense of real closeness. It is amazing how this has improved our lives. Learning to look into each other's eyes has made a huge difference. Seeing your spouse as your only sexual source (as opposed to using porn) has made love making so much more intimate.

And here's yet another:

> *At nineteen I married a young man who was into porn, drugs, and alcohol. I didn't know there was a different way of life. After four years we divorced. I felt used, abused, and unloved compared to those other women in his fantasies. I felt my life was the pits.*
>
> *My new husband has always been patient with me and never looks at porn and consciously works at keeping his thoughts and eyes focused on me. I feel loved and cherished and special. I never knew sex could be so enjoyable as it is now after twenty-two years. Your teaching about this has been very encouraging.*

These are not isolated stories. I hear this repeated over and over again by the thousands of couples that attend my seminars. I really think the proponents of pornography who tell couples that lust improves their marriage bed are getting their information from an alternate universe.

Mark Schwartz, director of the Masters and Johnson clinic in St. Louis, Missouri, said:

> "Porn not only causes men to objectify women—seeing them as an assemblage of breasts, legs and buttocks—but also leads to a dependency on visual imagery for arousal. Men become like computers, unable to be stimulated by the human beings beside them. The image of a lonely, isolated man masturbating to his computer is the Willy Loman metaphor of our decade."[11]

(Willy Loman is the insecure, self-deluded traveling salesman in *Death of a Salesman*.)

The truth is, lust is *not* improving or enhancing human sexuality, regardless of what the purveyors of this garbage are saying. At the 2003 meeting of the American Academy of Matrimonial Lawyers, two-thirds of the three hundred and fifty divorce lawyers said the Internet played a significant role in divorces in the past year, with excessive interest in online porn contributing to more than half of such cases.[12]

And here is a tasty tidbit of info: Those most likely to be into pornography and all forms of sexual experimentation—everything from anal sex to wife-swapping and masturbation to S&M—tend to be white, educated, upper-class liberals. If, therefore, porn and unfettered sexual experimentation and lust are truly the keys to great sex, then it only stands to reason that white, educated, upper-class liberals would report having the best sex. To the contrary, however, sexual surveys have shown that the people who report having the best sex—experiencing orgasms most or every time during sex—are married, conservative Protestants![13] If married, conservative, religious people—a group most unlikely to use porn and lust—report having the best sex, how in the name of heaven does the media keep pushing porn and unfettered sexual experimentation as the key to great sex? The answer is simple: White, educated, upper-class liberals overwhelmingly dominate the media.

Please understand that while I address most of my comments toward *men* in this section, I do know that there are women out there totally wrapped up and held in the bondage of fantasy, pornography, and lust. All of these same rules and principles apply to them as well. Women are just as damaged by the use of pornography, and their sex lives are ruined just as much; however, research indicates that it is by far a greater problem for men.

The Anti-Kinsey Report

Contradictory to the culture-altering lies perpetrated by Alfred Kinsey in the 1950s, researchers at the University of Chicago did a more reliable scientific survey in 1994. The study, released in the book *Sex in America,* paints a much more conservative picture of what "normal" is in our country.[14] Yet the media and the experts are still on the loose portraying America as a bunch of sex-crazed wackos. In Kinsey-*esque* fashion, they propagate lust as the sure way to sexual bliss.

We have a multibillion-dollar sex industry that feeds us all the lust we can handle. But despite people gorging themselves on an endless, *all-you-can-eat* buffet of sexual lust, their sex lives are losing steam. Despite unfettered access to sexual information of every kind and despite increasing social acceptance of virtually any sexual expression (no matter how bizarre), today we have a nation of sexually frustrated people.

Rather than couples enjoying new heights of sexual ecstasy, people are constantly in search of sexual fulfillment, turning to pornography, affairs, or even sex with prostitutes. We continue to read more and more reports on the rising number of "sexless" marriages. For people who should be sexually liberated, we find ourselves increasingly in a culture of the sexually frustrated.

15

Don't Be Yankin'

I have had a number of sex experts get upset over my assertion that men and women should save their sexual energy for each other and not waste it *masturbating.*

Fifty years ago people said if you masturbated you would go blind. Of course, that was a lie. But now we have turned the tide so far, we are almost saying if people *don't* masturbate they will go blind. Thomas Szasz claimed, "In the nineteenth century [masturbation] was a disease; in the twentieth, it's a cure."[1]

Few subjects irritate me more than the idea that masturbation is *good* for your sex life. I am truly amazed at the passion with which the proponents of masturbation defend it. I really don't get it. It seems to me there are two choices: a) have sex with a *real* human being, or b) pull on your wiener or rub on yourself. How is this a tough call?

Hey, you wanna yank and rub—go ahead, I really don't care. But what I *do* care about is the misunderstanding that masturbating actually improves your sex life, that masturbating puts you "in touch with your body," that masturbating is an adequate substitution for *real* sex. Masturbation is not even close to real sex; it is in a category all by itself.

Stuart Brody of the University of Paisley, UK, and Till-mann Krüger of the Swiss Federal Institute of Technology in Zurich measured blood prolactin levels in male and female volunteers who achieved orgasm while engaging in masturbation versus sexual intercourse in the laboratory. (Boy, you have to wonder what kind of person would volunteer to masturbate or have sex in a lab?) To the researchers' surprise, the increase in blood prolactin levels was four hundred percent times higher in both sexes after orgasm from sexual intercourse compared with orgasm from masturbation.[2] "This explains why orgasm from intercourse is more satisfying than masturbation," says Brody.[3]

Masturbating is *not* real sex; it carries one-fourth the impact of real sex. A real orgasm occurs when your body reaches a sexual peak and endorphins are released into your bloodstream and every cell in your body stands up, grabs the hand of the cell next to it, and shouts, "Hallelujah!" The narcotic-like buzz of a orgasm can last for hours. *That* is an orgasm. During masturbation all you experience is a hollow sexual release.

Sex experts, psychologists, and even preachers, however, have gone out of their way to try to convince people they do not have to feel bad about masturbating. My response to that is: You may be able to fool your mind into *not* feeling bad after masturbating, but you will *never* be able to fool your body into an actual orgasm. All you will experience is a hollow release that is not equivalent to an *orgasm.* That is why those who masturbate often report engaging in the activity three, five, even seven times a day—or more. The masturbator must repeat the deed again and again to satisfy his or her sexual need.

Foolishly, serial masturbators are deluded into thinking that multiple ejaculations are a sign of their sexual virility, but they are not. Their bodies know that what is going on is not sex, and if the masturbators ignore their body and continue this activity, they will ultimately pay the price as they condition their bodies to an alternate and inferior form of stimulation.

In his book *When Good Men Are Tempted,* author Bill Perkins writes:

> During a counseling session a woman blurted out, "Bill, Shawn never wants to have sex with me anymore. When we first got married, that was all he wanted to do. Now we only have sex once a month, and that's when I beg him." While meeting alone with me, Shawn told me, "It's just easier to read pornography and masturbate. I've done that for years. It saves me the hassle of dealing with my wife."
>
> I wish I could say Shawn's behavior is unusual. It isn't. Men often prefer sexual gratification without intimacy and self-sacrifice. Obviously, when masturbation drains a person of sexual energy, their spouse will suffer the consequences.[4]

Men and women may think that having lots of hot, lusty, sexually charged masturbatory events centered on fantasy and self-indulgence is a great idea, but the reality does not live up to the promise. I ask guys who are always checking out other women, looking at pornography on the Internet, and sitting around in the dark masturbating (what I lovingly refer to as *"yanking on your wanger"*), "How's that working for you? Is your sex life pretty good?"

They quickly admit that their sex life stinks.

The Danger

A man at one of my conferences said he could have sex for hours on end but nothing ever happened. No matter what, he could not achieve an orgasm. He had conditioned his penis through masturbation so that it would not respond to a woman's vagina.

Men and women can actually condition their genitals through masturbation so that they will no longer respond to their spouse's body as they should. Think about it: If since a boy is thirteen years of age he stimulates his penis (sometimes multiple times a day) by grabbing it with his hand and rubbing back and forth as fast and as hard as he can, there is no way this activity does not condition his penis to his hand rather than to the softness of a woman's vagina. It is this very tight stimulation that causes many men to prefer oral sex or even anal sex to vaginal sex, since greater pressure can be applied to the penis.

Here is a quote from a report by the Andromeda Andrology Center:

> A very common reason for delayed ejaculation is this: Most men have their first orgasm through masturbation. Many men go on to have quite a few more orgasms by continuing to "take matters into their own hands." And, many men exert much more pressure with their hands than they are likely to experience during intercourse. In doing so, they essentially train themselves to sexually respond to lots of pressure. In its most severe manifestation, delayed ejaculation takes the form of ejaculatory incompetence, a condition where the man can never ejaculate inside the vagina.[5]

Women can suffer the same consequences. I know of many women who find it virtually impossible to respond to a man's penis because they have spent years and years training themselves to respond to their own hands or a vibrator. Women who use vibrators to gratify themselves *apart* from their husbands need to understand that their husbands will *never* be able to recreate the sensation that the battery-powered vibrator does.

Appropriate Play

Let me be clear: I do not have a problem with couples learning about each other's bodies by stimulating each other. I do not have a problem with couples who are separated from each other for extended periods of time talking sexually on the phone or communicating via the Internet and touching themselves as they interact with each other. (Still, not as great as the real thing though.)

My objection is tying masturbation to pornography and to fantasies that create distructive addictions. My objection with masturbation is when it is a solo endeavor, practiced in an imaginary world of unrealistic sexual fantasy. My objection is with men and women who, while living in a home with a *real* person, choose to ignore that person and "take matters into their own hands." My objection is with lying to teenagers and encouraging them to engage in an activity that is peddled as "good and natural," when it holds the potential to damage their sex lives (we will go into more detail on this shortly). Masturbation is not real sex. It is not great sex. It is not fulfilling sex. It is a counterfeit experience that can rob you of the joy of *real* sex. A man should be a lover to his wife, skillfully captivating her heart so she willingly gives her body to him and he can make passionate love to her. A woman should be a lover to her husband, skillfully capturing his heart in passionate love.

Many women's books and magazines will tell you women need to masturbate to learn what feels good to them and to understand their bodies. But you don't have to do that *alone*. Husbands and wives should be exploring each others's bodies *together* to learn what feels good, not going off on a solo adventure. Sex should be a team sport, not an individual competition. Know that just as there are experts out there promoting vibrators and masturbation for women, there are also experts saying that these things will make it *more* difficult for a woman to achieve orgasm and satisfaction when actually making love with her husband.

Masturbation is the lazy coward's way out. Instead of being a lover to his or her spouse, the masturbator becomes a lover of self.

The Masturbation Generation

"But doesn't everyone masturbate?" you might argue.

The answer is, no. Everyone does *not* masturbate. But thanks to the sexual misinformation they are being fed today, I dare say *most* end up masturbating—simply because they feel they should. Once I was interviewed by a writer for a popular woman's magazine. She was a very attractive woman who was white, educated, upper-class, and by her own admission, very liberal. When I spoke to her about the destructive effects of porn and masturbation, she looked at me as if I had dropped in from outer space. She was shocked that anyone would even challenge the "benefits" of porn and masturbation. She claimed it was a scientific fact that people *must* masturbate.

"Didn't *you* masturbate when you were a teenager?" you ask me.

No, I didn't. I was in my early twenties before I ever masturbated. I decided to give it a go, thanks to the encouragement of some other pastors I worked with. Go figure. I gotta tell you, after your first sexual experiences have been with a vagina, masturbation is not that big of a thrill. I had a hard time making it work. I even spoke to a doctor about it, assuming that there was something wrong with me since I was having a difficult time. Finally I achieved success (if you can call it that). I remember thinking, *This is supposed to replace a vagina?* I ejaculated all right, but I did not achieve an orgasm. That was when I began to challenge people to make the distinction between the two.

Here's an idea: Instead of teaching our kids that they are no different from animals and have no control over their sex drives, let's teach them that they *do* have control over themselves and that life is about more than instant gratification. Let's teach them that waiting for a *real* sexual experience is so much better than creating a false one. We must warn them about the addictive nature of masturbation and pornography and how they can negatively affect them for the rest of their lives. Kids aren't stupid. Many will choose great real sex over artificial sex, but not when you, their teachers, MTV, and even their youth pastors tell them that masturbating is fine. They need to embrace the discipline of learning how to delay gratification so that they can have wonderful sex the *rest of their life.*

Condoms

This brings us to the crowning jewel of the proponents of lust: the condom. Here is where I am convinced that the modern sex experts have completely lost their minds. Wrap my most sensitive sex organ in plastic? Good grief! To me, having sex with a condom is like trying to eat an ice cream cone with a sock on your tongue.

Every time I see someone in a movie or on television use the words "great sex" and "condom" in the same sentence, I just shake my head in disbelief. Man, if you cannot tell the difference between sex without a condom and sex with a condom, we should have a telethon to raise money for you! To say that sex with a condom is just like sex without a condom is like saying you can't tell the difference between filet mignon and a slice of Spam.

But what about sexually transmitted diseases?! For the record I would like to say the following: If you are going to have sex outside of marriage, by all means, wear a condom. If I were you, I'd wear two or three (kind of like double-bagging at the grocery store.) Just don't delude yourselves into thinking this is great sex. It is not. You want great sex? Get married. One of the great things about being married is *you don't have to wear a stupid condom!*

Some may wonder, *What about birth control?* Look, if you want to practice birth control there are many, many options available to you. I always discourage condoms because I believe they interfere with real intimacy.

Of course, there are women who prefer condom use because it is less *messy*. But girls, you want your husband feeling the incredible sensation of his most sensitive flesh touching yours. It helps the guy to connect with and bond to you in a way that is just not possible with a flesh-numbing condom.

And here's a little known fact: Semen improves the emotional state in women. Gordon Gallup, a psychologist at the State University of New York led a study that concluded that women who used condoms were more depressed than those who did not.[6] After considering all potential causes, researchers could only offer the following conclusion: Semen acts as an antidepressant in women. A pretty positive outcome from such a *messy* endeavor!

The Best Possible Sex

For all you academics, I have created a scientific formula for what I consider to be the basis for the *best possible sex* (BPS) a couple can achieve. In my formula, BPS can be achieved only when both the man and the woman are feeling very sexual or turned on. If you believe that great sex can be achieved with just one partner being turned on, then we truly have differing ideas of great sex. In my formula, "a" equals a turned-on man (☺♂) and "b" equals a turned-on woman (☺♀). So, if:

$$a = ☺♂ \text{ and } b = ☺♀$$

then our formula is:

$$a + b = BPS$$

At every seminar I do across the country, I pose the following question to the women: *If you knew your man had just been viewing pornography and then wanted to use you for sex while he was fantasizing about those women he had just viewed, how many of you would feel sexual or turned on?*

After a very careful tally and a subsequent and thorough recount (to eliminate for even the remotest possibility of a "hanging chad" in the midst), the number of hands that go up is *always* zero. I have surveyed thousands upon thousands of women at my seminars and have never, ever had a single hand go up. And even if a few ever do, it cannot begin to compare to the amount of women who are flatly turned off by porn.

Think about this. If women are turned off to the idea of their husbands viewing any porn, then how in the name of heaven can these so-called experts believe that porn can lead to great sex?

Some have said to me, "You can't ask women a question like that in public! No woman would ever raise her hand to admit in public that she gets turned on!"

Oh *really?* Because I then go on to ask the following question: *If you knew your man considered you his only sexual source, that he only thought about you and treated you like you were the only woman in the world, how many of you would feel sexual or turned on by that?*

Virtually every female hand in the room goes up. (Apparently women do *not* have a problem raising their hands and admitting to being turned on.)

So we know that the answer to the porn question equals zero. For our scientific purposes we will simply refer to the answer to the second question as "lots." So, even the most brilliant mathematical minds available to us would agree with our deduction that "lots" is much bigger than "zero." In staying in step with our formulaic approach, this would look something like:

$$\text{Lots} > 0$$
(Lots is greater than zero.)

This means that a porn-watching husband produces an unhappy woman, or:

$$\textbf{Porn} = \text{☹}♀$$

We have also seen that studies show that repeated porn exposure (RPE) results in diminished male sexual response. So, if the sign for a normal male is ♂, then the sign for a diminished one must be Hence:

$$\textbf{RPE} = \text{◯}^{\vee}$$

Furthermore (now stay with me), if:

$$a + b = BPS$$

and,

$$Porn = \otimes\female + \male$$

Then

$$\smiley\female + \smiley\male - Porn = BPS$$

Translation for all you nonmathematicians: If a turned-on man and a turned-on woman results in the best possible sex, and porn results in an unhappy woman, with repeat porn exposure resulting in a diminished male, then a man and a woman without porn logically results in the best possible sex.

Ergo, the "experts" who claim that porn and lust lead to greater sex are lying to you. Their conclusions are obviously based on broken science (BS), which then leads to our final (rather self-explanatory) formula:

$$Experts = BS$$

Which is what I've been trying to say all along.

The Emperor Has No Clothes

There is a children's story called *The Emperor's New Clothes,* written by Hans Christian Andersen. In the story, all the adults in the kingdom did not want to admit the emperor was naked. They wanted to be thought of as wise and educated by those who were telling the lie. Finally a child spoke up and told the truth. The crowd broke out into laughter and the emperor was embarrassed. I feel like that child.

The "experts" believe the answer is for us to listen to *more* of their twisted wisdom and insights, but I say it is high time that we start challenging what these experts say. Porn does *not* improve sex and masturbating does *not* help men's and women's sex lives.

The emperor is naked.

16

The Power of Imprinting

Not everyone who has unprotected sex gets pregnant. Not everyone who has unprotected sex gets AIDS or some other sexually transmitted disease. Yet enough do that we take great lengths to warn people of the potential dangers. Sadly, little has been said of the danger of premarital sex and how it can negatively affect people for the rest of their lives.

The Potential Damage

Some years ago, while doing some videotaping of cranes in the wild from a helicopter, I learned of how these birds *imprint* when they are first born. Whatever creature it is they first interact with after birth, they assume is their mother, even if it is a human. I immediately thought of what first-time sex does to a man. This overwhelming new experience *imprints* on him, and he connects the context with the experience. Those who have their first sexual experience outside of marriage tend to imprint on the lust of illicit sex. Those who have their first sexual experience in the context of marriage tend to imprint on the girl.

Consider scenario A:

Boy gets girl to let him fondle her in the backseat of a car. Soon he is undressing her. His heart is pounding as it becomes clear that she will allow him to have sex with her. The windows are steamed, he is now in a major hurry lest she change her mind or someone catch them. He experiences an adrenalin rush not unlike what a thief experiences when he first steals or what a thrill seeker gets when jumping from an airplane. He then enters her body and experiences his first sexual experience with a woman.

This incredible encounter leaves a major imprint on him. Now he is likely to view sex in the context of lust and naughtiness. This is the man who will constantly be pushing his wife to try some outrageous new behavior, take sexual risks, or constantly role-play—all in an attempt to *relive* the experience that has had such a profound impact on his psyche. This is the guy who prefers to do it in an elevator, the backyard, or in some semipublic place. This is the guy who needs his wife to pretend she is a cheerleader or a naughty nurse before he can get excited as he tries to re-create his sexual imprinting. He is not so much interested in the girl; he is interested in the sex. For some, the woman becomes *interchangeable:* any woman willing to have sex with him will suffice. Many of these men later turn to illicit affairs or porn, fantasies, and masturbation in a pathetic attempt to revisit the experience upon which they have imprinted.

Now consider scenario B:

A man falls in love with a woman and asks her to marry him. His friends approve, his family approves, his coworkers approve. They all join in a concerted effort to make the event a success and celebrate their approval of who he has chosen. With the approval of the minister, they commit themselves before God and are off for what arguably will be the biggest party of their life.

Then, with the joyous approval of every important person in his life, he takes his bride to their honeymoon suite and for the first time—without the rush or fear of a backseat encounter—he experiences the most wonderful sensation of his life as he enters his bride's body and reaches his sexual peak.

He now ties *everything* I just mentioned to that one girl: all the approval of his family, friends and coworkers, the Church, the celebration, and most important, the incredible sensation he has just felt. All these elements join together and he *imprints* on the girl, for it is because of her and only her that he has just experienced the most wonderful day of his life. Nothing impacts a man like his *first* sexual experience.

What About the Woman?

A woman also receives a great deal of damage from being sexually promiscuous, and her damage is both psychological and physiological. First the psychological damage:

When a woman experiences sex without commitment, she soon learns (falsely) that sex means little to nothing. Why? Because nothing happens as a result. No meaningful relationship ensues and he may never even call her or talk to her again. She has inaccurately learned that sex means nothing. Because of this, many married women view sex as an unimportant side issue in marriage, when it is, as we have already discussed, a key and central issue to a successful marriage.

As for the physiological damage, science shows us that when a woman has sex with a man, a chemical called oxytocin is released into her system. Oxytocin is a neuropeptide most commonly associated with pregnancy and breast-feeding. It seems to act as a human superglue and helps a woman bond with her infant. This chemical also helps a woman bond with her lover during sex. New scientific studies, however, suggest that if a woman has multiple sexual partners, this will lower her levels of oxytocin, which in turn can inhibit her ability to bond to her husband. According to an article by Drs. John Diggs and Eric Keroack, "People who have misused their sexual faculty and become bonded to multiple persons will diminish the power of oxytocin to maintain a permanent bond with an individual."[1]

It is like taking a piece of strong packing tape and applying it to a box. Leave it alone, and it will hold that box together for decades and decades. Take it off and reapply it, and, well . . . it just doesn't hold as well anymore. Keep taking it off and applying it and taking it off and applying it and—I think you get the idea. This is what can happen to a woman who has multiple sex partners.

A few years ago, Robert Rector and Kirk Johnson, of the Heritage Foundation, did an analysis of the 1995 National Survey of Family Growth. They found that women 30 or older who had just one lifetime sexual partner (their husband) had a divorce rate of only 20 percent. Sleeping with just one extra partner prior to marriage increased that probability to 46 percent. Two extra partners boosted the number to 56 percent. Amazingly, the price of sleeping with just one extra partner leads to a divorce rate of almost 50 percent.[2]

The Boys Are the Biggest Losers

When I was growing up, boys were told to marry a virgin because the other girls were "damaged goods." It may well turn out, however, that it is the girls who should be the most careful to marry a virgin. Even though women also suffer negative consequences from promiscuity, I believe that the biggest losers tend to be the boys. Why? Because a previously sexually active woman, despite lowered levels of oxytocin and a less-than-positive attitude toward sex in general, still is internally wired to want to connect with her husband. Indeed, that desire is so strong, it causes her to fight through many of the negative side effects of her previous sexual experiences. A man, however, has no such natural wiring. If he fails to properly imprint and bond to the wife of his youth, he may spend the rest of his life in a disconnected state from her—indeed, from *any* woman. What he may do is attempt to reconnect with what he imprinted on so many years earlier and foolishly turn to porn, affairs, or lust. All of which can have severe negative consequences to his marriage.

Overcoming Sexual Damage

The degree of sexual damage people receive largely depends on the degree to which people become sexually involved before marriage, particularly if there are numerous sexual partners. It also can vary from person to person. For some who have had just a few consensual experiences, they may seem to carry little residual effects; while for others, even just one consensual experience before marriage can cause them to struggle for years in their marriage. You can imagine the result if a person's sexual experiences were *not* consensual. In cases of rape or incest, it is likely that much more damage will have occurred.

The question, of course, is: Can a person who has been damaged have a meaningful sex life? Thankfully, the answer is yes, *any* person can have a *wonderful* sex life, but it will likely come more easily to those who have waited until marriage. Those who have not may find they will have to work at it a lot harder.

Here's an analogy I like to use: There are people who can seemingly eat anything they want and never gain any weight.

Then there are those who allow themselves the slightest indulgence and they will gain a couple of pounds. What is the difference? One has a very different metabolism from the other.

So it is with those who did not wait till marriage for sex. Their "sexual metabolism" may be very different from those who did wait. Evidence shows that couples who wait until marriage report more satisfying sex lives than those who do not wait. And since sex is so important to the bonding of the couple, couples who marry as virgins have a *much* lower divorce rate than those who did not wait. A couple whose only sexual experience has been with each other in the context of marriage is likely to experience a natural bonding. Those who engage in premarital sex with one or more partners may find they will need to be much more intentional and deliberate in their approach to sex in order to bond with their spouses.

Be Transformed

In the New Testament, the apostle Paul gives us some very powerful advice that can help us overcome the negative effects of sexual damage: *"Do not conform any longer to the pattern of this world, but be transformed by the renewing of your mind."*[3]

So here we have the answer to the big question, *How can I make things different?* The answer is, *Change the way you think!* Quit thinking in the destructive patterns of our lust-driven culture, and be *transformed.* Transformed, not by special prayer or through being anointed with holy oil, holy water, or by being touched by some holy preacher, but by the *renewing of your mind.* In other words, you need to change the way you *think* about sex.

If you have imprinted on lust and find yourself constantly thinking in that way when you have sex with your spouse, you need to *stop* it. You need to *reimprint* on the girl you are married to. You need to key off of her and her alone.

You may find, however, that retraining the way you think can be extremely difficult. You may even find that your sexual performance may get worse initially as you refuse to think those lustful thoughts that drove your desire in the past. But if you persevere, you will find your sexual energy will come roaring back and now without the need for lustful thoughts that take you back to your early sexual encounters. You will find that your wife will be all you need in order for you to be sexually fulfilled. And you will find that the sex you experience *without* lust is way more fun, exciting, and fulfilling than the kind of sex you try to replay in your mind.

And for you women who have falsely learned that sex doesn't mean anything, you too must *renew* the way *you* think about sex. Sex is the key to a man's heart and you need to view it that way. You need to go out of your way to notice the small ways your sexual interaction with your husband energizes and motivates him to want to connect with you in ways that are not sexual.

But do not kid yourselves: Renewing your mind may prove to be one of the most difficult things you have ever undertaken. Ask God for His help and make a definitive decision that you will no longer live under the lies of your lust-driven past and that you *will be transformed* by thinking differently. Trust me when I tell you that the payoff is amazing and worth the effort.

Virtually *anyone* can experience a *wonderful* sex life regardless of their past. But let's stop pretending that sex before marriage is no big deal and start telling people the truth—for two reasons: One, so that our kids can avoid the problem in the first place; and two, so those who *have* been negatively affected can learn how they can still succeed by changing the way they think about sex.

Always remember, God is not a prude. He does not tell us to avoid sexual promiscuity because He is somehow embarrassed about sex. He just knows how we are wired and wants us to experience the very best.

Part

4

Till Death
Do Us Part

17

Fighting Fair

NOT long ago, I was listening to a TV preacher who was teaching about how to have a successful married life. He did a great job setting up his list of things to do to ensure success. Then he gave step number one: *Avoid confrontation.* I was taken aback. *Avoid confrontation?* I thought to myself of all the situations I've been privy to, avoiding conflict and confrontation is one of the *worst* things a couple can do. Couples who avoid confrontation shelve critical issues that should be addressed. Besides, there is really no way to avoid conflict, even if you put all your disagreements on the shelf. Over time the shelf gets really, really full, and then, eventually, it breaks.

The truth is, confrontation needs to be embraced. It is a key to real intimacy. Confrontation helps us come to know each other and exposes how we both feel about various situations. Even though it is often rough and thorny (and we need to learn how to fight fairly), conflict is absolutely essential for any husband and wife who want to draw closer to each other.

Jesus commanded, "If a brother sins against you, go to him privately and confront him with his fault."[1] He is telling us it's a good thing to talk to each other about uncomfortable things. But lots of folks wrongly steer away from confrontation, and it ends up being destructive in their relationships.

Bill Hybels writes:

> Tenderhearted people will go to unbelievable lengths to avoid any kind of turmoil, unrest, or upheaval in a relationship. If there's a little tension in the marriage and one partner asks the other, "What's wrong?" the tender one will answer, "Nothing." What he or she is really saying is this: "Something's wrong, but I don't want to make a scene." In choosing peace keeping over truth telling, these people think they are being noble, but in reality they are making a bad choice. Whatever caused the tension will come back. The peace will get harder and harder to keep. A spirit of disappointment will start to flow through the peacekeeper's veins, leading first to anger, then to bitterness and finally to hatred. Relationships can die while everything looks peaceful on the surface!
>
> Peace at any price is a form of deception from the pit of hell. When you know you need to tell the truth, the evil one whispers in your ear, "Don't do it. He won't listen. She won't take it. It will make things worse. It's not worth it." If you believe those lies, there is a high probability that you will kill your relationship sooner or later.[2]

Make friends with confrontation (we'll talk more about *how* later). Through confrontation we discover that not everyone thinks like us, not everyone has the same perspective we have, and not everyone has the same emotional and spiritual needs we feel. People are different from each other. What's weird is, at first we view our differences as attractive and interesting, but over time we start to get mad at each other *because* we're different. How crazy is that? Unfortunately, we tend to dislike people who are different from us, and marriage does not inoculate us from that tendency.

Marital Ambivalence

When a man and woman first fall in love, they naturally overlook things that could drive a wedge between them. They tend to overlook an irritating laugh or the way the other orders off a menu, treats other people, or argues a point. *It's okay,* they reason. The one they love is *too* wonderful for those little irritations to be a problem. Love is blind to those things; it suppresses those negatives. They are not remembered and, therefore, need no response.

It was Shakespeare in *The Merchant of Venice* who first coined the saying, "Love is blind." What's interesting is that recent research, conducted by University College in London, has found that feelings of love lead to a suppression of activity in the areas of the brain controlling critical thought. The research suggests that once we get close to someone, our brains ignore the need to assess the character and personality of that person. The study also showed that the areas of the brain responsible for producing negative emotions and judgments had reduced levels of activity in regard to a "special someone." In other words, when we get in the *love mood,* it causes a temporary insanity that sabotages normally clear-thinking brains.[3] We really do go *blind.*

Love *is* blind, but that's not really the problem. The problem is, *so is hate.* No couple goes to the altar thinking, *In just a few years our love will be a pale memory of what we are feeling right now.* Most couples believe their relationship is special and that their love will last a lifetime. But life isn't fair. There are cycles of highs and lows. Relational storm systems move in and we experience hurt and hostility. There are thunderous outbursts, followed by empty silences. There are tears and ultimatums. But then comes brokenness—the storm cloud passes and the sun begins to shine; hope and romance reappear like rainbows in the sky. There are apologies and promises of renewed love, followed by good days.

But the good days don't last. And over time the once-isolated thunderstorm begins to look more like a strong line of severe thunderstorms—bigger, more severe, and definitely more destructive. Irritation rules the day and isolation rules the night. Once couples go through disappointment after disappointment, unmet need after unmet need, and hurt after hurt, they arrive at the place where they focus only on the negative things about the other person, *just as they used to focus only on the positive.* And just as they were once blinded to the bad of their partner in their early days of love, they become blinded to anything good about their spouse. It is not unusual to hear deeply conflicted husbands and wives say they are unable to remember *anything* good about each other *or* their marriage.

This is *marital ambivalence.* The term is descriptive of the way we can love our spouses for a season, and then flip over to feel great rage or hatred for them. A love-*to*-hate relationship often occurs when people have completely lost the intimacy within a previously loving relationship. The couple may still feel a sense of obligation or may even retain some passion for each other sexually, but there is an irreconcilable storm of angst growing within them fostered by the disappointments of the past. If unresolved, it will blow their marriage apart.

Knocking Down the Barriers

Communicating is not an easy thing. Lots of barriers show up to keep us confused, preventing us from understanding each other. These barriers make us come across to each other like we are speaking completely different languages.

Let's address four common barriers that try to preempt good communication (there are many more). These barriers must be broken through if the two of you are going to really understand each other. They are *distractions, beliefs and expectations, differences in style,* and *self-protection mechanisms.*

Distractions

When you open up a conversation with your spouse, watch to see whether you have his or her *attention*. It is important that you don't just start talking when *you* want to, but that you take time to observe whether the *time* and the *place* are appropriate for communication to actually occur. Our lives are filled with distractions. We have environmental noise, which includes everything from the TV blaring to the kids screaming to the cell phone ringing . . . Then there are internal noises, which include being in a bad mood, being pressed by a deadline at work, feeling ill, or having to process through a bad day.

If you want to communicate about something important, find out if *now* is okay before you start talking. If he or she seems distracted, ask if talking later would work better. This shows respect and honor for your spouse, and it will be appreciated. The Bible says there is a time to plant and a time not to plant.[4] Just as a farmer waits for the right season and finds the best *places* to plant seeds, you must be sensitive to both time and place when sowing your seeds of communication. A farmer would never run out to the field to plant during a thunderstorm—don't try to discuss important things if your spouse is having an emotional thunderstorm.

Don't hit a touchy issue if your spouse just got home for the day and their mind is still reeling from issues at work. Don't try to talk about an important decision with your wife while she is cooking dinner or dealing with the children. The only contribution she wants from you right then is you rolling up your sleeves and helping her out. Late at night, when you are both tired, is not a good time either. Set aside a special time and a quiet place to be together: at home before the kids arrive from school, going on a walk, eating at a favorite restaurant, and so on.

Beliefs and Expectations

Studies from various fields (medicine, psychology, law) have shown that people tend to see what they expect to see when they look at people and situations. We look for and hear in others what we are expecting to see and hear. This causes some real trouble in the area of communication. We seldom perceive what is *really* going on, unless we are suspicious of our own biases. Being suspicious of one's analysis and judgment of a situation takes some real humility—not something that comes naturally.

If you believe your spouse is always mad at you, you will see only the things that support that belief. Any evidence that would suggest something to the contrary is simply filtered out. If you believe your husband doesn't like to do the things you like to do, you will interpret any hesitation on his part toward doing something you enjoy (which may be him simply considering his schedule) as a confirmation of your bias that he doesn't like to do anything with you. If you believe your wife thinks you are incompetent, you will process life's events through that filter. Even a simple "Honey, will you pass the salt" can be interpreted into "I knew it. She doesn't think I do anything right!" In other words, your beliefs and expectations become *self-fulfilling prophecies.*

Our beliefs and expectations therefore influence the actual *behavior* of those around us. A psychology class at University of California, Berkeley, decided to conduct an experiment on their professor without his knowledge. The class was instructed to listen intently, take careful notes, and look interested whenever the professor lectured near the radiator in the room. Whenever he wandered from it, the whole class was to subtly act bored and uninterested. By the end of the week the professor was lecturing while sitting on the radiator! Whether you realize it or not, how we view people affects them.

Oftentimes, when young people leave home and enter adulthood, they begin to experiment with different behaviors. It seems whenever we get away from those close to us, change comes more easily. I guess that's because those who know us well aren't around to look at us strangely when we try something we haven't tried before. As these young adults add a new behavior in their life, the new crowd around them has no clue that they are just practicing the new behavior. If they like it, they can make the practice a habit and assimilate it into their personality.

However, when they return home for Thanksgiving or Christmas, they may notice that it won't take long before they start acting like they did when they were kids. It will be as if they had *never* changed. This can happen for one very simple reason: We tend to naturally act the way people *expect* us to act. People's expectations influence us. This certainly holds true in marriage; each partner's beliefs and expectations of the other will either liberate us to be able to change or lock us into the changeless past.

We need to be careful here because the truth of the matter is that our beliefs about each other are often wrong. But being suspicious of one's *own* beliefs is very difficult—*we believe what we believe.* However, we must work hard at busting up our presuppositions and biases if we want a shot at understanding each other. We must recognize that the assumptions we make about our partner's motives are never appropriate. We need to ask more questions and avoid judgment. We need to learn to listen for the *why* behind the actions we see, instead of living in the presumption that we already know the *why* behind those actions.

Differences in Style

Some of us are expressive; some of us are more reserved. Some of us grew up in homes where we had to yell in order to secure food at the family dinner table; some of us grew up in homes where no one *ever* yelled unless they were about to go postal. When two people live together under the same roof and have completely different experiences with communication styles and rules, they have to work hard at *understanding*—not what they think is going on, but what is actually going on. Obviously, these differences can distort the communication process.

Self-Protection Mechanisms

If, while entering into dialogue with a spouse, either partner feels threatened or fears rejection, he or she will either shut down or start fighting. It's the old "fight or flight" response. Rejection is painful, *literally.* Naomi Eisenberger and Matthew Lieberman at the University of California, Los Angeles, have shown through brain scans that rejection actually registers in one of the areas of the brain that responds to physical pain.

Unless you communicate *safety* before you communicate anything else, you will never communicate effectively. Safety doesn't mean you never fight or argue, it just means that you are careful to lay the ground rules. Start your conversation by *affirming your commitment to the relationship.* Everyone is listening for the "bottom line." Affirming your commitment helps your spouse to see that you are interested in resolving a problem, not in attacking or rejecting him or her.

Duking It Out

Getting rid of these barriers to communication helps us enter a "ring" that every married couple must enter—the *fighting ring.* That's right. Successful marriages are ones that *duke it out* in order to establish the rules of the relationship and to set up meaningful, mutually respected boundaries. If you refuse to fight, you are basically surrendering to having only one of you in the relationship dominate the entire marriage. Then needs will go unmet. And somewhere down the road, the last straw *will* break the camel's back and someone is going to bolt. Keeping the peace at any cost will eventually cost you your marriage.

So you have to learn how to fight (nonviolently, of course). No one is exempt—not if you want to have a real marriage. But you need to "fight fair." Here are some rules for *fair fighting* that will help you to not hit each other *below the belt:*

Clarify the Issue
Before you actually start fighting (or confronting—the term *"fighting"* scares some), make sure you deal with yourself first. Start by *clarifying the issue.* Is it really something important, or are you just being touchy or picky? Is it something

that will resolve itself after your spouse gains more experience, or is it a permanent issue that pervades the way you both live?

This is an important point. Couples tend to fight over some of the *stupidest* things imaginable! To this day, after more than thirty years of marriage, my wife and I *still* feel obligated to debate the finer details of the most banal and meaningless subjects. I usually have to blurt out, "For the love of heaven, woman, does it *really* matter?!" Of course, being a redheaded woman of German descent, she is quick to assure me that it does, in fact, matter greatly. But it doesn't. She is just being stubborn. And if we don't start laughing at the absurdity of our discussion, we will be headed for a big argument about absolutely nothing.

Step Carefully

Paul writes, "Brothers, if someone is caught in a sin, you who are spiritual should restore him gently. But watch yourself, or you also may be tempted."[5] Paul is saying we need to watch ourselves so we do not succumb to the temptation to jump on our spouse in a judging or criticizing fashion. He says we need to be "gentle" in the process. If you feel angry or restless (*anti*gentle emotions) and you want to deal with the issue immediately, be watchful—you can hurt more easily than help if you are in an emotional tizzy.

Sadly, many of us feel the most motivated to discuss issues when we are the most upset. The trick is to be smarter than your emotions. When your emotions are screaming the loudest is probably not the best time to be debating the finer details of life. It has been my experience that there is a time to teach and a time not to teach. If you are in a moment of strain and the air is charged with negative emotion, any attempt to "teach" your point of view will be perceived as judgment and rejection.

Ironically, when we are *not* upset, we let things slide since we figure we are not that angry. So it is usually during a state of irritation that we are most likely to feel the time is right to enter the battle. Just be careful.

Time and Place

Third, it is important to pick the right time and place for the confrontation. But as I just pointed out, we often let our emotions determine the appropriate time and place to share the "seeds" of confrontation, and that usually leads to very poor results.

Clarifying the issues, doing your best to minimize your emotions, and selecting the right time and place for a fight are a big part of fighting fair. The next step is to approach your spouse with honesty, care, and vulnerability.

The Conversation

Everyone listens for the bottom line when confrontation happens. *What is it that you want? Are you threatening your spouse with an ultimatum? Affirming your commitment* helps your wife or husband to see that you are interested in resolving a problem, not in getting your own way in a situation. Tell your husband how much you love and need him and that your marriage is the most important thing in the world to you. Tell your wife you really value her love and friendship.

Next, *carefully state the issue without placing blame on anyone.* Avoid broad-brushed statements like *You always . . .* or *You never . . .* The moment you say something like that, the other person's defense mechanisms turn on and he or she no longer hears what you are saying. It is easy to brush off such absolute statements. Stick with saying, I *feel* alone. I *feel* that you are blocking me out, that I don't matter. I *feel* as if nothing I say has any bearing on where we are headed. I *feel* confused. The *I feel* phrases will get you a lot farther than the blaming, *you*, phrases ever will.

Last, *encourage and invite dialogue*. After you have gotten the issue on the table, ask, "What do you think? Am I all wet on this? Do you see any validity in what I am saying?" Honestly long for and value your spouse's perspectives. Your spouse may initially try to write you off, or go into shock because of being confronted. But he or she may surprise you and open up, immediately repent, and ask you to forgive them. No matter what the result, it is always better to confront the situation than to sweep it under the rug.

Teamwork

How in-sync you feel as a couple is connected to how well you work together as a team to resolve conflict. This means you must learn how to process conflict by working *together*. Working together as a team implies you have an atmosphere of mutual respect and acceptance. This means you take the time to discuss the problem with the goal of understanding the *other person's view* of the situation, to brainstorm possible solutions, to find a win/win arrangement (which means finding agreement and compromise), and to have follow-up discussions on whether the win/win is actually working.

The worst thing a couple can do is default to a *no-holds-barred, every-man-for-himself* approach to fighting. This causes fights to escalate and causes couples to use fighting techniques that are not fair.

Unfair Fighting

One of the best ways to love someone is to act in his or her best interest. This often means you must leave the comfort level of the relationship and confront your loved one about an issue that needs to be addressed. This is not easy to do. Confronting people is often very frightening. When a person you love emotionally wounds you, you *must* talk with him or her about it.

However, there are some things you *don't* want to do when you confront your spouse—things that are unfair and will add to, not resolve, relational strife. Here are some classic unfair fighting techniques:

The Kitchen Sink Technique

This is where one of you throws everything into the argument. This fighting technique avoids sticking to the issue at hand; you want to bring up every other incident that has ever bugged you, and every statement that has ever hurt you. This technique demands you bring up past issues and unresolved injustices; that you reference all the shortcomings and failings you've observed, along with the defects in your partner's character; then there are the unresolved points from your last argument; yadda yadda yadda. Fighting like this will cause your spouse to shut down, simply because there is no way to cover all the points referenced.

Mind Ambush

Here is where you never allow the other person to be right—you even challenge their personal preferences, feelings, thoughts, and experiences. If your spouse says, "You make me so angry when you do that," you respond by saying (in a condescending tone), "Now, sweetheart, you might be a little *frus-*

233

trated, but you are not *angry.*" It is hard to be understood when the person you are trying to communicate with dismisses your thoughts and feelings.

Mean Clowning

When a clown acts evil, it makes for a scary movie. The unfair technique of "mean clowning" is about one spouse being sarcastic and making devastating remarks about the other, claiming it is all done in fun. And if the person being teased gets defensive, you can accuse him or her of being too sensitive. This kind of fighting is great in public because it makes the offending spouse look like a fun-loving person, while the other one looks like a spoilsport. But it is just unfair fighting.

Play Psychologist

Everyone likes to play psychologist, to analyze those around us. But when you use this technique to fight, you quickly "peg" your spouse using psychobabble terms: *You are an egomaniac; you have a mother complex; you say that because you are basically an insecure person; you can't face the truth because you have an inferiority complex.* Labeling people is quite effective.

Leo Buscaglia writes,

"Black man," "Chicano," "Protestants," "Catholics," "Jews." All you have to do is hear a label and you think you know everything about them. No one ever bothers to say, "Does he cry? Does he feel? Does he understand? Does he have hopes? Does he love his kids?"

If you want to know about me, you've got to get into my head, and if I want to know about you, I can't say, "She is fat. She is thin. She is a Jew. She is a Catholic." She is more than that. She is more than *labels*. The loving individual frees himself from labels.[6]

This fighting technique is *really* unfair and *very* dismissive.

Help to Death

This group wrestles with things that bother them by trying to help their spouses to the point of *nausea*. Of course it is good to be helpful, but if you are constantly trying to help by taking over responsibilities, dominating conversations, and giving unceasing, unsolicited advice when no one has asked your opinion—you will only communicate that you think your spouse is inept. People who fight with this technique usually claim they are simply "helping" for the good of the other person and that their spouse should be thankful and open to their "constructive criticism," but in reality they are fighting in an unfair way.

Collecting Injustice

This is where you make collecting injustices a hobby. These folks are not interested in dealing with "anger before the sun goes down," as Scripture commands. No way. They like to stew over hurt, inequity, and failed promises, so they can explode later. At some point, when they have had enough, they shout, scream, throw things—even hit people—all while feeling totally justified. Lots of folks love the "rush" they get after they *get things off* their chest. The problem is, this kind of fighting destroys. Here's a news flash: If you don't deal with your relational "poo," the poo is going to fly; and it will eventually hit the fan.

Talk to Win

Many folks have learned how to win arguments even when they are not right. They just know a style of arguing that makes them unbeatable. Some do so by *monopolizing the conversation.* If you are one of these, your mate can't get a word in edgewise. If he tries to talk, you will either ignore him or accuse him of cutting you off before you are finished. Others talk to win by *refusing to listen* while their spouse is talking. While your wife is talking, you are preparing how you are going to hammer your point more thoroughly, completely ignoring any points of concern she may have. Still others *wander.* You wanderers just wax on and on making molehills into mountains, talking about things unrelated to the point, and never, under any circumstances, come to the point. All these tactics exasperate your spouse, who will eventually put up a white flag and you will get your way. Pretty effective stuff, but still fighting dirty.

Power Plays

This tactic ensures a win by a grab for all the marbles— all the *power.* Sometimes power is secured by *one-upping* the other person through threatening or coercing them overtly— beating them into submission, as it were. Other times a kind of *anti*power power play is exerted in the classic *one-down* fashion. This is where you purposely refuse to win, but in the back of your mind you know the apparent winner will pay, and pay very soon. This is where you make life so miserable for the other one in the marriage that he or she finally gives up. Passive-aggressive behavior is really a *power play.* Effective tactics include using guilt, saying things that hurt the other person, or just saying things that get under the skin of your mate while you smile to yourself.

Role-Playing

Role-playing is a great way to avoid the real issues. Role-playing is about doing one's "job," not about getting to know the other person. Many husbands and wives don't really know or understand each other. He is the husband; she is the wife. In many Evangelical circles this means the husband is the boss and the wife is the servant. It is true that Scripture teaches us that men are the "head" of the home, but that has more to do with respecting the husband than empowering him to lord over his wife. More significantly, it calls men to love their wives as Christ loved the Church and gave himself for it.[7] Roles in the home were never supposed to be strategies for avoiding conflict. The truth is, knowing and understanding each other is much harder than playing a role.

When the Going Gets Tough, the Tough Get Going

This is the number-one unfair way to fight of all—you threaten to bail on the relationship if you don't get your own way. Maybe you talk of divorce, or separation, or "going crazy," or committing suicide. These kinds of threats certainly get people's attention. And that's the point: This tactic is used to completely disassemble *any* argument—you can usually win with this one, but not forever. At some point your spouse is likely to ignore your "cry for wolf" and things could get out of hand very quickly.

Getting Burned

Physical skin burns and fighting have common ground: *pain,* plus they come in first, second, and third degrees.

First-Degree Fighters

Couples who argue at the *first degree* generally talk about problems of recent origin and are more issue focused, rather than pattern focused (coming back to old arguing patterns that have been well ensconced over time). If you are here, you will easily benefit from some communication training. Just decide to work at understanding each other early and you won't have to break up bad patterns of communication.

Second-Degree Fighters

Couples who argue at the *second degree* are pretty serious fighters. Their arguments revolve around well-entrenched disagreements that deal more with *power rules* of the relationship than with any issues they face. The overall atmosphere in the home of second-degree fighters can be charged with anger and conflict. Fights can be vicious, loud, and long. A couple at this stage cannot move to resolve quickly. These couples will require more than a few simple new communication skills. They need to take some time to understand each other's real concerns and unearth the *why* behind the negative communication patterns they fall into as a couple.

Third-Degree Fighters

Couples who are fighting at a third-degree level are weary and despairing. When these couples fight, they really don't believe it will change anything; it's hopeless banter that is more habit than heartfelt. The entire household is in a funk and strife always lurks beneath the surface, ready to burst into fury at any moment. These couples frequently talk about divorce.

The more severe the fighting becomes and the longer it has been that way, the more difficult it is to see change in the marriage. However, severely conflicted marriages can emerge with real intimacy and joy. Again and again, I have seen couples in seemingly hopeless situations reconnect and grow in love together.

Just Relax!

Don't let everything bother you. Foster a realistic appreciation for each other. Flooding each other with criticism in the name of "honesty" and "openness" is guaranteed to put enormous strain on your relationship. The thinking among many marriage therapists for years has been that "being honest" with your feelings is the key to a healthy relationship, but this is a bad idea that continues to be repeated over and over again by supposedly educated people who seem to spend more time repeating what was told to them than actually thinking on their own. It is one of the reasons 80 percent of the people who go for marriage therapy end in divorce. I do not believe couples should "share" everything they feel in some foolish and plastic attempt at "honesty." One of the reasons I am still married to the same woman after thirty-plus years is that I *don't* share everything I think and feel, because sometimes what I think and feel is not very kind. If you are feeling something mean and nasty, it's best to keep your mouth shut.

Research supports the idea that it is not beneficial to share *all* of one's negative feelings.[8] One of a couple's communication goals should be to reduce the negative statements they make to each other. Researchers in social psychology have shown that making positive verbal statements—even when you do not totally agree with your own statement—helps you move toward deeper commitment in the relationship.[9] There are times when expressing a negative feeling is appropriate and necessary; however, you cannot allow the negative to overshadow the expression of positive and tender feelings you have or have had in the past. It is important to recall fond memories and to speak of the reasons you had for being drawn together in the first place. A positive trip down memory lane can bring great joy.

18

Cloth Diaper Marriages

WHEN my kids were babies, we had cloth diapers. Disposable diapers were available at the time; we just couldn't afford them. No, we did not indulge in those fancy throwaway diapers; we had the good ol' *mess 'em and clean 'em later* diapers. You put them in a diaper pail, a delightful little plastic container where a lovely, pungent brew of baby poopies would slowly stew until you got around to washing them so they could be reused. Now, don't misunderstand me, I do not miss cloth diapers. God bless the person who invented the disposable diaper! (I know, I know, they are bad for the environment—landfills and all that—but cloth diapers were bad for the environment *where I lived,* so I welcomed the invention of throwaway diapers.) But I *do* have a problem with throwaway marriages—relationships that are tossed aside because they get some "poo" in them.

We need to develop some *"cloth diaper" marriages*—marriages that you stick with no matter how crappy they get. Relationships that you hold on to—yes, you need to learn how to wash and dry them, and maybe use some fabric softener to make them nicer to touch and smell—but you don't toss them away. Sadly, what we have instead is a culture of quick, no-fault divorce that fosters throwaway marriages—*disposable love*. It's amazing, but some folks hold on to their underwear longer than their sacred vows of matrimony, and they didn't even pledge to the underwear, "Till death do us part."

We live in a *throwaway* world. We throw away everything. When I was growing up, repair shops were not hard to find. Shoe repair, television repair, appliance repair, and watch repair shops were commonplace. Today that isn't true. When was the last time you had a pair of shoes fixed? Who repairs torn socks anymore? Unless you have an expensive watch, you just throw away the one you have when it quits working. We throw away everything today—even the things that should *never* be thrown away, things that are designed to last for a lifetime, like marriages.

What contributes to throwaway marriages? I think it's bad thinking. Somewhere along the road, we need to ask ourselves: *What's the point? What should one expect out of marriage? Why should a person get married in the first place?* Our answer to these questions is critical.

Cats and Dogs

I had just finished doing an interview at an Iowa television station, smack in the heartland of America, when the attractive young lady who was giving us a tour of the station told me that she and her husband were getting a divorce.

"That is sad," I replied. "Why the divorce?"

In a tone that communicated the assumption that I would no doubt agree with her, she said, "Oh, we *wanted* the marriage to work. It's just that our pets don't get along."

Slightly stunned and not sure how one should respond to such a ludicrous statement, I maintained my smile and queried, "Your . . . pets don't get along?"

"No, it is sad though. . . ." And then as if to add a degree of credibility to her position, she squeaked out, "At least we're still friends!"

I don't know. Maybe it's just me. But I don't get how a person's pets are more important than their marriage. How does a commitment to an animal trump the vow they made to each other before Almighty God? I mean—we're talking *pets* here. A dog and a cat. This couple was so shallow in their commitment to each other and so relationally inept they couldn't navigate through the tension and complexity of a dispute over a cat and a dog. *Beaten by pets!*

Seriously, I think if I were going to divorce over such a reason I wouldn't admit it to anyone. But this woman, without even knowing me, freely shared her twisted logic, casually assuming it would be received as completely reasonable by all who heard it. It is bad enough when couples throw away their vows just because *they* aren't happy; apparently, there are couples who throw away their relationship if their parakeet is not happy.

Consume, Consume, Consume

In our consumerist society, we like to get things that make us feel better, make us look better, or promise to make us happier. Since the late 1940s, Madison Avenue advertising firms have been striving to get Americans to purchase items under the premise that a particular product or service will make our lives *bigger* and *better.*

And we believe them.

Before consumerism became so dominant, people generally acquired things because they *needed* them. And they bought things that were practical and durable and dependable. Today people tend to buy things, not so much because they need them, but because they *want* them. And they don't buy practical things to use; they buy things that project an image. Why? Because in a consumerist culture, the things people *possess* define who and what they are. Products are the stuff of *identity*.

The consumerist mind-set runs deep. If I run to the store to buy some simple dish soap, I can buy the inexpensive brand that sports the name "Dish Soap" on the front of the bottle. But just looking at the label Dish Soap makes me feel flat, empty, nondescript. So for some reason, I can't settle for that. As a consumer, *what* I buy defines *who* I am, and I have no idea who I am if I buy something labeled "Dish Soap." I need something *more*.

Then I see it! Right next to the unsophisticated Dish Soap is a product called "Dawn." My heart lights up—*now we're talking*. Who wants to wash their dishes with Dish Soap when you can wash them with morning-fresh, bright *sunshine*? Presumably with Dawn, a person can do the dishes *and* dispel the darkness in life *at the same time*.

But just before I make my all-important decision, I look to the other side of the *imagineless,* unfulfilling, *chore*-oriented Dish Soap. *Alas,* there is yet another amazing product possibility: "Joy." Wow. Who would have thought that a person could experience *joy* while doing the dishes? And couldn't all of us use just a little more joy?

The Joy has it, hands-down.

So what if it costs a little more, I muse. *After all, aren't I worth it?"*

Somehow I feel a bit more alive holding that bottle of Joy. I don't know how, but that little vessel of pleasure makes me feel *skinnier* and *smarter,* and I'm sure my wife, Debbie, will praise me when I return home—after all, I am bringing new *joy* into our home! Surely she will take one look at that bottle of Joy and gleefully respond, "Joy? O what waves of glory fill my soul! You went out for mere *dish soap,* but you, with your keen insight, have returned not with just soap, but with *Joy!*"

In reality, Debbie isn't nearly as controlled by consumerist thought as I am. She would actually say something more like, "Why didn't you get the cheaper generic one? It does the dishes as well as anything else."

Commodity Marriages

Whether we realize it or not, this consumerist expectation gets attached to just about everything we get involved in, including marriage. When you view marriage as a product or commodity, you are trying to make it define you in some way. You are saying, "I expect marriage to make me look better, to make me feel better, to make me happier, *right now.*" It ends up centering marriage on *me.*

The problem is, marriage is not a commodity, it is a relationship. And relationships often experience difficulty and demand sacrifice. At times a marriage may feel more like a liability than anything else. And if you believe marriage is only about making *you* happy, whenever there are more *cons* than *pros,* your mind will scream, *"Abandon ship!"* A consumerist mind-set can't work through a troubled marriage. It isn't governed by commitments or by values; *what's in it for me* rules the day. If the *what do I get out of it* isn't conspicuous, a person with this mind-set doesn't want anything more to do with the marriage. It ceases to be important whenever it no longer "does it" for them. And they feel totally justified in cashing out.

Everybody Wants to Go to Heaven, But Nobody Wants to Die

As I mentioned before, Jesus told his disciples, "Most assuredly, I say to you, unless a grain of wheat falls into the ground and dies, it remains alone; but if it dies, it produces much grain."[1] Another time he said, ""If anyone would come after me, he must deny himself and take up his cross and follow me."[2] And yet again, "If you try to hang on to your life, you will lose it. But if you give up your life for my sake, you will save it."[3]

As we discussed previously, God wants to kill you. . . . Not the physical you, but the *selfish* you. Jesus taught us that if we don't die to our selfish nature, we will never be able to experience all of the blessings that God wants to bestow on us. Talk about a paradox! Everyone wants to live, but Jesus taught us that the only way we can truly live is if we die. Well, if there was ever an institution designed to *kill* the selfish you, it's marriage. In fact, it is virtually *impossible* to succeed at marriage if you don't learn how to let the selfish part of you die.

It is not unusual for me to hear a frustrated spouse cry out, "I feel like I'm dying!" "Yep," I reply, "you probably are." The answer, however, is not to fight death to the self, but to embrace it. Remember, Jesus said if the grain of wheat fails to die, it remains alone, and that is precisely what we have today: millions of married people who refuse to die to self and become one with their spouse. The result is a state of profound loneliness. (Let me clarify once again that I am speaking of dying to *selfishness*. I am not advocating that one should die emotionally or physically due to neglect or abuse.)

It is hard to die to one's selfish nature under any circumstance, but this has been exacerbated in our consumerist culture, which screams at you, "You deserve it!" "You're worth it!"

"Reward yourself!" "Indulge yourself!" And the more selfish our world becomes, the higher the divorce rates climb.

You *must* understand that you will never be able to achieve a successful marriage if you stay focused on you and remain selfish. If, however, you are willing to surrender your selfishness, to *die* to yourself, then true life can begin to grow out of your marriage.

Sadly, since the 1960s, millions of children have been raised with no idea of how to *sacrifice* for other people. Our society has glorified the *do what you want* ideology to such an extreme that most don't even understand the *concept* of self*less*ness, much less *practice* it.

Marriage for the Christian is supposed to be on a completely different footing than the *what do I get out of this* mindset. We aren't supposed to be tossing difficult relationships away like some kind of disposable diaper. Consumerism, gimme monsters, and selfishness all contribute to bad marriages. But there is something much darker lurking. It has to do with American idols. . . .

19

American Idols

AMERICAN idols are everywhere, and I'm not talking about the singers. I'm talking about the pre-Simon, old-fashioned, evil kinds of idols. An idol is something we lift up above God Himself—something that carries more influence in our lives than God does. One can make an idol out of just about anything: food, entertainment, sex, ease, happiness, whatever. An idol is anything that answers the question *what's most important to you*, when the answer is something other than God Almighty. Idol worship sullies our faith, our individual lives, and our marriages.

Idol of Happiness

Many Christians have turned happiness into an idol. I'm not suggesting God is against us being happy. The Scriptures say, "Happy are the people whose God is the Lord."[1] God *does* want you to be happy—just as He wants you to be safe, fed, healthy, clothed, and housed. Wise Solomon wrote, "God gives any man wealth and possessions, and enables him to enjoy them, to accept his lot, and be happy in his work—this is a gift of God."[2] Clearly, God wants people to be happy. The Bible refers to it here as "a gift."

So when does happiness become an idol? It happens when we exalt our *concern* to be happy above the very concerns of God himself.

We live in a culture that says, "Above all else be happy; do what you want to do; satisfy yourself; look out for number one; do your own thing."

The Bible teaches that the husband should love his wife. We reason, *No problem—as long as it doesn't interfere with my golf game, my fishing time, or my hunting trip. Because I need that. After all, God wants me to be happy, right?*

Country singer Brad Paisley wrote a song about a woman who gave her husband an ultimatum. Verse one goes:

> *Well, I love her*
> *But I love to fish*
> *I spend all day out on this lake*
> *And hell is all I catch*
> *Today she met me at the door*
> *Said I would have to choose*
> *If I hit that fishin' hole today*
> *She'd be packin' all her things*
> *And she'd be gone by noon*

The music pauses for a moment and then he sings:

> *Well, I'm gonna miss her*
> *When I get home . . .*

Fishing made him happy.

The Bible teaches that wives should meet the sexual

needs of their husbands. But what if the wife is not happy with her husband? Shouldn't she reason, *God wouldn't ask me to do that, would He? Certainly, God wants me happy. That's most important, right?*

Need I drone on?

The point is, we willingly do "good" *up to a point.* We honor God, but only up to a point. We'll obey Jesus, but only to a certain point. And what is that point? Our personal happiness. There is no other place, no other area that so dramatically demonstrates this problem among Christians than in the way they approach their wedding vows. I know this will sound harsh to many, but the truth is, our wedding vows aren't really seen as vows anymore. A vow is a solemn promise, something that binds a person for life. Sadly, our marriage vows have been domesticated into pretty words spoken in a lovely ceremony, apparently more for show than for substance. For many people, they mean absolutely nothing. Pretty words are easily discarded when things get ugly and life is no longer pretty.

"For better or for worse," the vows say. But people don't mean it. I know because I have so many come and tell me they are getting a divorce because things are so ugly—worse than they ever imagined. I always look at them and ask, "So, when you said 'for better or for worse,' what exactly did you think *worse* meant?"

"Yeah," they say slowly as they try to overlook the shocking implications of my question. "But I didn't know it would be like this! I didn't know (s)he would make me so unhappy!"

Maybe we ministers should give folks an option to the traditional vows. Something like: *I take you for my husband/my wife, as long as you make me happy, because as soon as you stop making me happy, I reserve the right to break this vow that I'm swear-*

ing before Almighty God because the idol of happiness trumps the God of the universe.

I'm not trying to be mean, but doesn't it seem odd that those of us who claim to be followers of Christ, who believe we should be loving people, forgiving people, suffering to reach people, when it comes to our spouses, we say, "Oh, those things don't apply to my marriage. God knows my husband is a pig. God would never make me forgive him. He knows how unhappy I've been."

For many Christians, marriage has some kind of get-out-of-jail-free card attached to it. They seem to think the radical, difficult parts of Christianity (to love, to serve, to forgive, or to sacrifice) pertain only to those *outside* of one's marriage. Loving, suffering, turning the other cheek, forgiving are all wonderful Christian concepts, but one shouldn't have to do that in our own marriage. That would be *way* too much work. *Right?* And shouldn't marriage be the one place God *guarantees* happiness—as long as we find the *right one?*

"But stay in an unhappy marriage!?" you protest.

I've had people try to reason and argue with me about why they were bailing on their wives or husbands and justify it one way or the other based on the presupposition that God would not want them to suffer.

"Come on," they've said to me incredulously. *"Are you actually saying God would ask someone to stick in a marriage that makes them unhappy?"*

I grant you that the idea of staying in an unhappy marriage is a completely foreign concept to most folks, and it's one that is not readily received. (You may as well be speaking Swahili to *non*-Swahilis.) But have you ever considered that the reason the Scriptures call us to live by faith is to empower us to do what's right even *when it's hard to do*—whether or not we suffer while doing it? What if faith was designed by God to give us the courage to choose what's right though it makes us unhappy, though it means losing everything we have, though it means laying down our very lives?

Whoa, this sounds so—*Jesus*-like.

"So, you're saying we should just accept an unhappy marriage?" Absolutely not! In fact, my life is dedicated to showing couples how they can be happy together, how they can make marriage work, how needs don't have to go unmet, how they can succeed. I believe everyone can have a happy and successful marriage. But you can't secure a happy marriage if you're willing to discard an unhappy one.

Happiness dawns only when we are willing to sacrifice our personal happiness to do *what is right.* I'm not always happy. When things go badly around me, I'm not happy. When things I expected to happen, don't, I don't feel happiness. But I have learned a secret. When I do the right thing (though things around me are not right), things eventually change. And I have discovered that in the midst of unhappy situations, God is still there.

Jesus claimed, "In the world you will have tribulation; but be of good cheer, I have overcome the world."[3] You can "be of good cheer" or have *joy* when no one else seems to sense it but you and Jesus. The fact is, He loves you and cares for you no matter what is going on. Faith celebrates that.

A number of years ago archaeologists uncovered some letters written by martyrs during the first three centuries of the Church's formation. One martyr penned:

In a dark hole I have found cheerfulness; in a place of bitterness and death I have found rest. While others weep I have found laughter; where others fear I have found strength. Who would believe that in a state of misery I have had great pleasure; that in a lonely corner I have had glorious company, and in the hardest bonds perfect repose. All those things Jesus has granted me. He is with me, comforts me and fills me with joy. He drives bitterness from me and fills me with strength and consolation.[4]

This is the stuff the Bible talks about. And you can experience this same *joy* right in the middle of a troubled marriage. The Bible actually promises, "The joy of the Lord is your strength."[5] But you won't experience joy if you're serving the idol of happiness.

Jesus taught us that the only way to truly save your life is to lose it.[6] It is only when you and I are willing to do what's right, even if we suffer doing it, that we get to taste Christian *joy*. And this joy is present *before* you get God's answer to your problems. This is important to distinguish. The joy does not come from having the answer to your problem. It comes from being willing to suffer and still do what is right. But we must make the decision: *I will serve You, God. I will honor You, no matter what. I will do what's right. I don't care what it costs me. I don't care who it associates me with or who it separates me from, I choose to honor and serve You—regardless of whether or not it makes me happy at the time.*

Idol of Easy

In addition to the idol of happiness, we also worship the idol of *easy*. There are no *easy buttons* when it comes to accomplishing worthy endeavors, and this is especially true of relationships. Relationships like marriage take great courage and massive amounts of commitment. But this should cause no surprise; we know this makes sense. Nothing worthwhile happens without our working on it. From staying physically fit to getting an advanced degree to becoming a great cook—it all takes hard work.

There are often enormous challenges to overcome when we try to jam two lives into *one*. Just try to put two people into one pair of jeans, or two McDonald's milk shakes into one cup. The whole "two becoming one" thing implies some pressure, some give and take, some stretching. Marriage is all that and more. This is not work for the faint of heart—this takes guts, persistence, and faith.

Increasingly, people all over the world are becoming less oriented to governing their lives by things such as courage or commitment; many are prone to being controlled by feelings and are generally committed only to convenience and ease. For most, when the going gets tough, they just *quit* going.

However, being governed by feelings always produces problems in a relationship as complex as marriage. Why? Because our feelings are so fickle and wobbly. It's natural to have your feelings about your spouse shift from time to time. If you are controlled or governed by your fickle feelings, you are setting yourself up for a rough ride. The famous Hershey's candy bar commercial for Mounds and Almond Joy captures the gist of it: "Sometimes you feel like a nut, sometimes you don't." That is exactly how feelings work: Sometimes you feel like being nice, sometimes you don't; sometimes you feel like forgiving, sometimes you don't; sometimes you feel like you're in love, sometimes you don't. When you shun principles as cold and unromantic and refuse to be moved by anything other than *feelings* to sustain your marital commitment, you are saying you want life to be only cushy, convenient, and *easy*. We love *easy*; in fact, we worship it.

You marry to make life richer, better, easier—*right?* Wrong. The truth is, you usually hit annoyance and inconvenience by the second morning of your honeymoon. If you are accustomed to living by your feelings instead of your commitments, you will start thinking dark thoughts like, *Maybe this was a mistake.* Though one can usually suppress those thoughts early in the marriage, they tend to pile up under your relational carpet. If you don't keep it clean under there, it is pretty certain that you will trip and fall badly later on.

Disappointment

At the beginning of every relationship, there is a high level of hope and desire that causes it to run on autopilot. But over time hope and desire begin to erode when disappointment enters.

There are dozens of ways we can disappoint one another in a relationship as close and intimate as marriage. From *I thought it would be different* to actual differences in upbringing, values, habits about money, personality, motivation, work ethic, and sex drives, we have the makings of *marriage wars.* Sometimes people come across offensively because they are reacting to pain from the hurts that they have experienced in the past, and they are just trying to protect themselves from being injured again. Wounded animals do not act predictably when you approach them; neither do emotionally wounded humans.

When Jim and Laurie walked into my office, I was shocked to discover they were about to call it quits. From the outside, they looked like a great couple. Fun. Social. They were active in church. But secretly they were at war with each other. A lot of it had to do with the way each had grown up.

Jim grew up in a home where both his parents were quiet and seldom, if ever, raised their voices. In Jim's home, raising your voice meant you were extremely angry. Laurie, on the other hand, grew up in a larger family, where you had to yell or you lost your opportunity to get the food at the other end of the dinner table. The only time her family got quiet was when they were really, *really* mad.

When incidents that required discussion arose after Jim and Laurie married, Laurie would naturally begin to raise her voice. Jim would think, *Oh my! I'd better not say another word. She has lost her temper!*

Jim would walk silently out of the room, thinking he was helping the situation, while Laurie was thinking, *Why won't he talk to me? Why is he so angry? He must hate me.*

They totally misunderstood each other.

Thankfully, they had enough sense to come and talk with me about it. Many couples won't talk with anyone else about their struggles. Instead of working to understand each other or learning to navigate through their differences, they buy into the lie that differences are signs that they were not meant to be together.

We need to rethink how we respond to differences. We need to get smarter, to become more gracious, to learn how to value the unique way our spouse is *different* from us, even though that is pretty hard to do.

20

The Divorce Myth

THERE is a great joy to the early struggles of marriage. When people who "make it" talk about the early days of their marriage, they admit it was bittersweet but they say the sweet ended up outweighing the bitter. Researchers agree. In a recent study conducted by a team of leading family scholars headed by University of Chicago sociologist Linda Waite, researchers found that "two-thirds of unhappily married spouses who stayed married reported that their marriages were happy five years later. In addition, the most unhappy marriages reported the most dramatic turnarounds: Among those who rated their marriages as very unhappy, almost eight out of ten who avoided divorce were happily married five years later."[1]

The study went on to say that there is a kind of "divorce assumption" in America. People assume that they will either stay in a bad marriage and continue to be miserable or get a divorce and become happier. But the social science data challenge that assumption. Contrary to conventional wisdom, there is no evidence that unhappily married people who divorced were any happier than unhappily married people who stayed married! In no way does divorce reduce symptoms of depression, raise self-esteem, increase one's sense of mastery, or generally improve any of the twelve separate measures of psychological well-being. Even the unhappy spouses who divorced and remarried generally were no happier than the unhappy ones who stayed married. In fact, the evidence seems to suggest that unhappy people are unhappy, period—married or not.

Dr. Waite concluded, "Staying married is not just for the children's sake. . . . results like these suggest the benefits of divorce have been oversold." It may look as if you will gain ground by eliminating some stresses of a bad marriage, but divorce creates more stresses than people bargain for: the ugliness of a breakup between partners; the reactions of children; potential disappointments and aggravation about custody issues, child support, and visitation orders; new financial or health stresses for one or both parents; plus the brand new relationships or marriages that also fail to make one happy.

If you are expecting marriage to be nothing but *bliss*, you will be sorely disappointed. It's not that there is not bliss to be had—there is; it's that *bliss* comes only after *blisters*. Marital bliss is the result of marital blisters—lots of hard work, where you work till it hurts, sometimes till you bleed. Marriages get happy not because partners get along so grandly, but because they stubbornly outlast the ways they don't get along. There are all kinds of rough spots to work through when you step into life with another person: financial problems, job reversals, loss and its accompanying depression, child problems, and sometimes even infidelity. These things can destroy. But they don't have to.

I know there are millions of unhappily married people throughout the world today. Maybe you are one of them. But unhappy marriages are unhappy because most ignore (or are completely oblivious to) the mistakes they are making in their relationships. There *is* hope for troubled marriages—even if you have become heartbroken and confused. But there *is* a connection between what you are putting *into* your marriage and what you are getting *out* of it.

The mere suggestion that people need to change their *own* behavior in order to get a better result is often greeted by blank stares. People tend to believe they should have a good marriage for no other reason than that marriage is supposed to be good. They believe they should have a good marriage because that is what they prayed for. They believe they should have a good marriage because . . . well, just because.

An attorney friend of mine told me, "I hit a horrible impasse in my first marriage. I felt I was right and she was wrong, so I cashed out. In my second marriage I saw the same things starting to occur that destroyed my first marriage. At first I thought I had made another bad choice in partner, but I decided to change how I was married, not my marriage partner. It turned everything around. I love my second wife, but I also understand now that I could have loved my first wife and not experienced the hell of divorce and the lifelong awkwardness it creates—especially with kids."

Marriage is not supposed to hurt. The whole thing was a God-idea in the beginning. The Genesis narrative reads, "A man will leave his father and mother and be united to his wife, and they will become one flesh."[2] At first glance, this appears to be a loss: *two* now equals *one.* Perhaps it is this view that causes many men to be hesitant toward marriage. After all, from a logical numbers perspective, if *two* becomes *one,* that usually means one dies; and that is not far from the truth. The *two* must die to their own selfishness in order to become a stronger *one,* and that can be a scary prospect. But the wonderful potential of marriage is that the *one* actually ends up being *greater than the sum of its parts.* Marriage was designed by God to make the human experience *more.*

Does that mean marriage is a free ticket to happiness? Not on your life. Invariably, you get out of it what you put into it. Most unmarried people are clueless about what it takes to make a marriage work. They tend to assume marriage just "works" if you find the "right one" or wait for the "right circumstances" to fall into place. They grossly underestimate the price they will have to pay to move from being an independent, self-centered individual to being an interdependent, selfless one in marriage.

Marriage is a process, not a product. Marriage is not some prepackaged bundle of joy that *plugs-and-plays* after you say, "I do." It is a journey jammed with surprise and paradox, which can lead to disappointment and hurt—but also to wonder and fulfillment. Marriage *really can* be wonderful. But it takes thousands of "I'm sorry's," hundreds of difficult conversations, scores of sleepless nights and weary days, and a willingness to die to selfishness too many times to remember. You will need to pray lots of prayers, use lots of wisdom, and stockpile as much patience, persistence, and guts as your faith can muster.

Don't feel badly if you have become disillusioned in your marriage. But don't be too quick to discard what you have because of incompatibility. Often, opposites attract in marriage. It's not unusual for a love-struck member of my congregation to come to me and say something like, "Oh, Pastor Mark, there is really something *special* about this guy!" I usually reply, "Yeah, he's the *opposite* of you!"

We are typically drawn to a person who thinks differently than we do; who loves and needs love differently; who has different strengths and weaknesses and talents than we do; who may be more logical, while we are emotional; and so on. The

upside is, opposites create a great opportunity for balance. One
partner might be a tad rigid and exacting, while the other is an
embracing, more laid-back person. This can actually make for a
kind of equilibrium or counterbalance.

However, appreciating our differences and making them
work in harmony (versus yielding to the urge to kill each other)
requires great effort and willingness to compromise and/or concede. The *secret-in-the-sauce* of marriage is not so much about
finding compatibility (compatibility is easy), it is about discovering ways to handle and process *incompatibility*. We don't have
to see eye to eye on everything, but we *do* need to set our eyes
in the *same direction*: a loving and mutually fulfilling marriage
relationship.

Learning to do this will greatly increase our human stock
value. When we defer to another or set aside our ego and selfishness in order to focus on another, we grow personally. The
good news *and* bad news is that marriage constantly affords us
the opportunity to learn how to accommodate.

On top of all this, we must face the inevitable stresses of
day-to-day living (underwear left on the floor instead of tossed
into the hamper, dishes in the sink, toilet paper rolling the
wrong way, the thermostat up/the thermostat down, hair in the
sink). These may *appear* to be of no great consequence, but in
reality they can be very stressful to the relationship. And they
demand adjustments and compromises from each partner. This
carries the potential for both greatness and world war.

There is a pot of gold at the end of the rainbow if you will
dare to navigate through differences and the accompanying
conflict to arrive at a place of intimacy—the place where one
knows and is known, the place where one can be open and
naked, and not be ashamed. The place called *marriage*. I believe
a happy marriage is possible for everyone who is willing to

fight for it. And fighting is *not* an option. You will either fight to make your marriage work, or you will just fight, period.

There is great news for those of you who are Christ-followers: He promises to get in the mix of our efforts, to cause us to be "joined together."[3] Nice. The Bible says that our marriages and families have the potential to be "as the days of heaven upon the earth."[4] Pray over your marriage: *Heaven, yes. Hell, no.* But even if you are not a person of faith, championing your marriage is worth the effort.

Selling Divorce

For many severely conflicted couples, divorce seems to promise peace from the infighting, a fresh start, the hope of new love, and a kind of "reset button" for life. Many buy into the idea that ending a marriage is a viable way to *solve* relationship problems.

Besides, you reason, *it will ultimately be better for all, and the kids will make it—kids are resilient.* And you won't have to look far to find voices to side with you. People who love you will give you a biased shoulder to cry on; they want you to feel loved and supported. But don't be quick to listen to your personal fan club. They are not objective; they are out to protect and rescue you. People like this will always urge you to divorce if they believe you are suffering emotionally in your marriage.

But divorce has been oversold. What most fail to acknowledge is the longstanding pain created by a divorce. Contrary to popular belief, statistics show that after divorce children are *not* okay. The "trickle-down effect" causes them emotional trauma that stays with them throughout life. Also, divorced people are less healthy and less happy, and have a higher risk of substance abuse. Depression is three times greater in women who divorce than in those who do not. And divorce severely lowers one's standard of living. In fact, if statistics are to be believed, the one sure way you can guarantee that *you*, your *children*, and your *grandchildren* will live at or below the poverty level for their *entire lives* is simply to get a divorce.[5]

Never mind the religious implications, we should fight for our marriages because divorce sucks. And at the end of the day, it doesn't eliminate the relational dysfunction evidenced in the marriage. Marriage problems are *relationship* problems, they are the result of how two people *interact* with each other. You may abandon a troubled marriage, but you will still bring the *way* you interact with others along with you. *You can run, but you cannot hide* applies here.

And what of the pain you feel when you have to deal with your ex-spouse? You may think you'll be free when you "ex" your spouse, but you will relive the pain and awkwardness of facing that ex at every holiday, every birthday, and every special occasion. Even in divorce, spouses don't disappear.

Author and counselor Michele Weiner Davis shares a letter she received from a client: "I've been divorced for twenty-three years. I realized that my ex and I would be in touch weekly because of our kids, but I guess I thought that when my kids got older, he would just disappear from my life. My grown daughter is about to give birth next week and for the first time, I realized that my ex and I are going to be 'the grandparents' together. What was I thinking? Spouses don't disappear."[6]

The Good, the Bad, and the Ugly

Whether your marriage is good, bad, or just plain ugly, there is always hope to make it great. But great does not come easily.

Great marriages take courage. When we think of courage,
we generally think of the policemen and firemen who ran into
the Twin Towers, or of a person diving into an icy pond to save
a friend, or of a soldier on the front lines of battle. Most of us
don't think of courage when it comes to facing our everyday
stuff, such as our marriage or raising kids. But it takes great
courage to build relational intimacy, which is the oxygen of a
marriage. It takes an enormous amount of courage to say, "This
marriage is in trouble and we need to do something about it."
It's much easier to put your troubles on the back burner, engage in the rough-and-tumble of life, and hope things will sort
of work themselves out. Running from problems is always easier than solving them. But courage is willing to put on the
gloves and say, "Let's fight for this marriage."

It takes courage to work through all the layers of "stuff"
we haul around, from masks to defense mechanisms to the slick
relational cover-ups we've mastered over the years. It takes guts
to face yourself, to say to your spouse, "This is me. I know I'm
wrong and I'm not proud of it."

Great marriages take discipline. When you look at successful
people, you will find one thing in every case: It takes discipline
to become successful at anything. Failure, for the most part, is
due to people letting things slide. There is a lack of *discipline.*

In his book *The Road Less Traveled,* Scott Peck writes,
"Delaying gratification is a process of scheduling the pain and
pleasure of life in such a way as to enhance the pleasure by
meeting and experiencing the pain first and getting it over
with."[7] Discipline is simply a commitment to get the pain out
of the way first.

When Deb and I were first married (we were in our
teens), we decided to wrestle through the hard stuff from the
start. We needed to learn how to fight fair, when to speak up

and when to keep quiet, how to forgive, how to handle money (what little we had), how to love in a language the other one understood, and so on. There were some long nights as we worked through sneers, fears, and unfair judgments. But the long-term benefit has been wonderful.

Over the years I have sat across from many couples in deep conflict. As the problems emerged in their marriage, they chose to ignore them, to let them slither out of sight, refusing to deal with them. Instead of committing to work through the pain early on they ignored it. But ignoring problems in the context of an intimate relationship doesn't work. Eventually it becomes intolerable.

Here is a practical idea: *Don't go to bed mad.* It was the apostle Paul who wrote, "Do not let the sun go down while you are still angry."[8] Decide in advance (a secret to being disciplined) that whenever you get into a spat, you will at least quash the negative emotions associated with the argument. And do it before you fall asleep (this will make for some long nights). You might not get the issue resolved, but you at least get past the hurt of disagreement.

Great marriages take endurance. Endurance refuses to cash it in—it pushes past quitting points. We live in a culture where we have come to expect things instantly. We like fast diets, overnight success, rapid fitness, and a hundred-yard dash to marital bliss. If we don't experience what we want in a reasonable amount of time—say, in a day or two, we think something is wrong. Those of us over fifty were once called the "now generation." We were pretty well known for easily quitting things before the rewards showed up—jobs, educational paths, relationships, pretty much anything complex. Why? It couldn't be had, *now.* Sadly, the generations that follow us expect no less.

Marriage Is a Marathon

Sprints and marathons are two distinctly different races. In a sprint, one of the most critical elements is the start. Runners practice for hours on end getting into those little blocks and bursting out the very nanosecond the gun goes off. Why? Because if you falter in the start, you don't stand a chance of winning the race.

On the other hand, the starts of marathons are not that important at all. Most runners are just standing around waiting for the gun to go off. Truth is, you could fall down, have three guys run over you, get up, and still win the race. It's not the start that is so important; it is the endurance.

Today, many believe marriage is like a sprint, that the *start* is what is critical. I never cease to be amazed at how many struggling couples point to the *start* as the reason for their struggles. "We were too young." "We didn't know each other for very long." "We didn't have enough money." They are convinced that the poor *start* is the reason for their troubles, but they are wrong. Marriage is not a sprint; it is a marathon. It is not the start that leads to a failed marriage, but the unwillingness to endure the race.

You don't do marathons quickly. You have to spread out your energy over time. Endurance is what empowers a couple over the long haul. It will enable you to push through old familiar conflict zones for the ten-thousandth time without quitting; you just keep going and going . . . Scripture urges, "Keep your eyes on Jesus, who both began and finished this race we're in. Study how He did it. Because He never lost sight of where He was headed—that exhilarating finish in and with God—He could put up with anything along the way: Cross, shame, whatever."[9] That's *endurance.* It makes marriages last.

21

The Reset Button

I used to be a video game freak. I *loved* sitting in front of the screen battling aliens from other planets, reliving World War II, or fighting it out on the football gridiron. My son Phillip, who was just barely over being a toddler, would come and sit next to me and watch as I wrestled the joystick, furiously pushed buttons, and giggled and screamed at the screen. He eventually asked, "Daddy, can I play too?" I said, "Of course," and handed him an *unplugged* controller. At first he didn't realize his controller wasn't plugged in and was thrilled to be a part of the game. We spent countless hours together laughing and shouting as we hung out playing video games. But the day came when it started to dawn on Phil that something was amiss.

"Dad?" Phil asked. "I think something is wrong with my controller."

"*Really?*" I said, hoping he wasn't catching on. "Why do you say that?"

"It's not *responding*," he said.

I was pretty impressed that he used the word "responding"; he was a pretty little guy. So I decided it was time to actually plug him in. And as soon as I connected the controller, he immediately lit up, realizing he was now controlling what he saw on the screen. At first, to make things fair, I adjusted the way I played the game to let him get ahead, and then I would catch up. . . . This is what good dads do.

It wasn't long, however, before Phillip excelled and started *beating me*! Though I used to let him stay close to me *scoring-wise* when I was better than him, he felt no such compassion for his old man. He would *kill* me mercilessly! Struggle as I might, he would consistently destroy my attempts to beat him. When things got really bad, and I knew I had no hope catching up with him, I had one recourse at my disposal: *the reset button*. In a desperate struggle to save face, I would quickly reach over and push the reset button, which started the game from the beginning. Though my action was met with great consternation on Phillip's part, the reset button was my best and only hope for staying in the game.

Wouldn't it be grand if marriages came with a reset button? How many times have you fallen behind at something or made a bunch of very stupid choices, knowing you had no chance at coming back from so far behind? At those times, wouldn't it be great to have a reset button that would put everything back *the way it was*—giving you a fresh chance to do better next time around?

The truth is, God *has* given us just such a button.

Killer for Hire

Back in the early 1970s, before I entered the ministry, Deb and I were part of an evangelistic group of young people who traveled from city to city sharing our faith in Christ. We would come into a town, set up camp, and go out during the day handing out flyers announcing our meetings. Then each night we would hold a meeting and share our faith in Christ. We always kept our schedule pretty fluid, extending our stay if the response was good, and shortening it if people were cold to our efforts.

In the winter we would stay south, where the weather was warm. This particular winter we headed for Phoenix, Arizona. I don't know if you have ever been to Phoenix in the summertime, but it is a great way to get a glimpse of what hell is like. But the winter? Ahhh, the winter in Phoenix is like heaven. Being raised in Wisconsin, I had no idea there was any place on earth that could be so wonderful in January.

After getting set up in Phoenix, we began our routine of going downtown to hand out flyers promoting our daily evening meetings. Each night hundreds upon hundreds of people would come and listen as we shared our love for Jesus and what He could do for those who would receive him.

One of our favorite spots to hand out flyers in downtown Phoenix was in front of the local porn shop. It was hilarious handing a guy a flyer about Jesus as he was heading for this store! Ninety percent of the time he would do a huge one-eighty and head off in the other direction. But while *we* were having a good time, the owner of the porn shop was not nearly as entertained. He was losing business. A *lot* of business. And he came to believe we were never going to go away. After six weeks of this, he became desperate; and because desperate people do desperate things, this porn storeowner hired a professional killer to come to one of our nightly meetings to shoot the evangelist who spoke each night. He figured that if the evangelist were dead, we would all leave town and things could go back to the way they were.

That night, the would-be killer came to the meeting with a loaded weapon. Normally, it would have been very easy for him to shoot the evangelist at the start of the meeting as he walked onto the stage. But that evening, the evangelist had told us he wasn't feeling very well and asked if we could just start *without him.* So the hired killer had to sit through the re- vival service waiting for the evangelist he had come to kill. (Kind of a bummer if you are a killer.)

The band started playing (I was the keyboard player) and everyone started to clap their hands and sing. Our killer had to join in in order to fake it as best he could, not wanting to draw undue attention to himself.

At one point we started singing an old gospel song:

> *Give me that old time religion,*
> *Give me that old time religion,*
> *Give me that old time religion,*
> *It's good enough for me. . . .*

After a few verses the band stopped and the leader announced, "Now we are going to sing the next verse that says, 'Makes me love *everybody,'* and we want you to go around and hug as many people as you can."

Suddenly our killer was being accosted by dozens of peo- ple giving him bear hugs and telling him, "Jesus loves you!" Now, I have no idea what people in the world of professional murder understand as "normal," but I would guess hugging is not a big part of their culture. This, no doubt, was the most hugging this man had experienced in quite some time. Indeed, I would assume his own mother never hugged him that much, which may or may not have contributed to his eventual choice of profession.

Soon the hug frenzy was over and everyone was seated. Next, testimonials were shared from the platform by people whose lives had been destroyed by drugs, alcohol, and promiscuous sex, but who now proclaimed hope and joy because of their newfound relationship with Jesus Christ.

Finally our evangelist made his way out to the stage, but by now our killer was in a state of shock. He had never heard, felt, or experienced anything like this in his life. He sat mesmerized as the evangelist shared the old Gospel message that God loved the world so much that He sent His Son Jesus to show us His love. He told the crowd of how Jesus willingly allowed Himself to be crucified on a cross to pay for the sins of mankind. Then at the end of his message, he gave a Billy Graham–like invitation: "If you would like to ask Jesus Christ into your life to forgive you of your sins and give you a new beginning, I want you to stand to your feet and come forward for prayer."

About a hundred to a hundred and fifty people stood up and came forward. Among them came this professional killer. When he got to the front, he fell on his knees and started to weep. He kept saying, "I can't do it. I just can't do it."

The prayer counselor next to him put his arm around him, assuring him and saying, "Sure you can! You can do it! In fact, God *wants* you to do it . . ."

The killer replied, "You don't understand," and then proceeded to pull out the loaded forty-five and confess to his original intentions. In one evening, that man went from a *killer for hire* to having his life dramatically affected by the love of God.

The Ultimate Reset Button

I am sure that most of you would never hire a *hit man*, but one thing is clear: When somebody hurts us we want them to pay for what they have done. Most often, we choose to take our revenge by refusing to forgive the other person. But unforgiveness only hurts the one who refuses to forgive. Unforgiveness is like taking poison in hopes that the *other* guy will die.

I never cease to be amazed by how many people—particularly *Christian* people—struggle with the idea of forgiveness. Many Christians approach forgiveness as some kind of optional road for the believer. You see, there are many *optional* things in the life of the believer that, though these things should be practiced, won't directly affect your eternal soul. Giving money, for example, is something a believer *should* do, but many need to grow in their faith before they come to a place where they are able to give as they should. Going to church is another option. Though it is very important, whether or not you actually go to church this Sunday won't be the final indicator of whether or not you get to heaven.

Forgiveness, on the other hand, is *not optional* for the man or woman of faith. Look at these important words Jesus said right after teaching the Lord's Prayer to his followers: "For if you forgive men when they sin against you, your heavenly Father will also forgive you. But if you do not forgive men their sins, your Father will not forgive your sins."[1]

Whoa! That's pretty strong. God *won't* forgive your sins if you refuse to forgive someone else their sins. And this isn't the only time in the Bible when Jesus taught this concept. Bottom line: If you want God to forgive you, you *must* forgive others. There is nothing *optional* about it.

How to Forgive

Rather than hurt ourselves with bitterness, the best course of action is to simply forgive. Forgiveness is the ultimate *reset button.* Sadly, millions of people struggle with forgiveness, but it is because they don't understand *how* to forgive.

The first thing you have to understand about forgiveness is that is has nothing to do with your emotions. You may feel the emotional pain of what that other person did to you till the day you die—it has nothing to do with forgiveness.

Second, forgiveness has nothing to do with erasing your memory. You may remember what that person did to you till the day you die. Forgiveness is simply this: a decision to let it go. The Greek word that translates to "forgiveness" is *"aphieemi,"* literally "to send off," "to release," or "to let go." This means forgiveness is the act of *sending away* incidents that cause offense to brew in us. It means we can't keep focusing on the wrong done to us. Forgiveness is an act. This is an example of forgiveness: *"I forgive you. I will never use it against you in the future. I will never speak of it again to you or to anyone else."*

When you forgive, you decide to release the person from his or her guilt, period. You may remember the offense repeatedly at first. That's okay. The commitment to forgive a person is a commitment to "send away" the incident every time it reappears in your mind.

Once the apostle Peter asked Jesus, "Lord, how often shall my brother sin against me, and I forgive him? Up to seven times?" Jesus said to him, "I do not say to you, up to seven times, but up to seventy times seven."[2]

That's 490 times.

Luke, in his Gospel, adds the phrase "a day."[3] Imagine forgiving the same person 490 times *a day*! Truth is, it is pretty easy to get consumed by someone's offense. When a person does something that really hurts you, you will naturally think about it *over* and *over* again. Practicing the principle of forgiving someone 490 times a day means every time you think about what that person did to you, you prayerfully give it to God. The choice to forgive means we *keep* forgiving. Over time you will find the incident losing strength.

You must also remember that forgiveness has more to do with your tongue than your head or your heart. If you're still talking about what that person did to you, you haven't forgiven him or her. You need to hush. You need to let it go. The good news is, God will help you do this.

Corrie ten Boom spent a large part of her life as a prisoner in the concentration camps of Nazi Germany during the Second World War. She saw unspeakable acts committed against innocent human beings—including those done to her own flesh-and-blood sister, who was eventually murdered. She writes:

In the concentration camp where I was imprisoned many years ago, sometimes bitterness and hatred tried to enter my heart when people were so cruel to my sister and me. Then I learned this prayer. It's a thank-you based upon Romans 5:5:

Thank you Lord Jesus that you have brought into my heart the love of God through the Holy Spirit who was given to me. Thank You Father that Your love in me is victorious over the bitterness in me and the cruelty around me.

After I prayed it, I experienced the miracle that there was no room for bitterness in my heart anymore. Will you learn to pray that prayer, too? If you are a child of God, you have a great task in your prison. You are a representative of the Lord Jesus, the King of Kings. He will use you to win others for Christ.

You can't, you say? I can't either. But Jesus can! The Bible says, "Be filled with the Spirit." If you give room in your life to the Holy Spirit, then He can work through you making you the salt of the earth and a shining light in your prison.[4]

At the conclusion of my seminars I have the couples stand and apologize to each other. It is the ultimate *reset button.* Without forgiveness, Jesus taught, your very connection to God is doomed. And I can assure you that without forgiveness, your marriage is doomed.

David and Bathsheba

In the Old Testament we read of David and Bathsheba. It is a story of both tragedy and hope. One day King David was meandering on the roof of his house at a time when kings were supposed to be in battle. From the rooftop he saw Bathsheba taking a bath. She must have been one hot babe, because David could not stop thinking about her. While her husband was off to war fighting for King David, David had Bathsheba brought to him and he seduced her. However, the sexual encounter re-sulted in an unwanted pregnancy. (This is where the story *really* gets bad.) To cover his tracks, David arranged to have Bathsheba's husband killed on the front lines of battle and quickly wed Bathsheba to cover up what he had done.

It is a story of lust, lying, adultery, and murder—a total *mess.* There was *nothing* holy about it. God *never* intended it. Yet later, after David repented and asked God to forgive him, God *did.* In fact, the forgiveness was so complete that when it was time to name the next king of Israel, to name the man who would become the wisest king to ever live, to name the one who would oversee the Golden Age in Jewish history, David's son, *Solomon,* was named—the son of *Bathsheba*! Bathsheba became the great-great-great . . . great-grandmother of the Lord Jesus Christ himself.

One could make the argument that, had it not been for lust, lying, adultery, and murder, Solomon would have never been born. One could make the argument that, had it not been for lust, lying, adultery, and murder, the line of David would have never produced Joseph who married Mary, the mother of Jesus. But how could this be?

Did God intend lust, lying, adultery, and murder to take place? Of course not. But the message is clear: God can take your biggest mistake and turn it into something so wonderful, it won't make any sense to anyone. *That* is the power of the reset button.

Despite all the advice I can offer in this book, nobody does marriage perfectly. We all mess up. We all make mistakes. We all create poo that has to be dealt with. *Forgiveness* keeps you from defining your future based on the mistakes of the past. *Forgiveness* is that critical *reset button* essential for *any* marriage to succeed.

You want to give your marriage a chance for success? Get comfortable with this one simple phrase: *Honey, I'm sorry . . .*

Notes

INTRODUCTION
1. David Viscott, *How to Live with Another Person* (New York: Simon & Schuster, 1976).
2. Proverbs 14:4 (NASB).
3. 1 Corinthians 7:1.
4. 1 Corinthians 7:28.

CHAPTER 1
1. Proverbs 13:12.
2. Genesis 24:26–27.
3. James 2:26 (KJV).

CHAPTER 2
1. Genesis 2:25.
2. Genesis 3:12.
3. Charles Stanley, *Forgiveness* (Nashville, TN: Thomas Nelson, 1987).

CHAPTER 3
1. Luke 9.
2. Ephesians 3:20.
3. 1 Corinthians 15:10.

CHAPTER 4
1. Stephen R. Covey, *The 7 Habits of Highly Effective People* (New York: Simon & Schuster, 1989), pp. 30–31.
2. Genesis 2:24 (author's paraphrase).

CHAPTER 5

1. Matthew 7:1
2. John Scalzi, "What Are You Thinking?" www.geocities.com/Wellesley/2052/menthink.html, November 30, 2007.
3. Ibid.

CHAPTER 6

1. Dr. Dave Currie, "You Make No Sense." www.growthtrac.com
2. Ephesians 4:26.
3. 1 Samuel 16:7.

CHAPTER 7

1. Genesis 2:24.
2. Proverbs 14:1.
3. Proverbs 12:4.
4. Rabbi Shmuley Boteach, "What a woman wants." www.worldnetdaily.com/news/article.asp?ARTICLE_ID=50735, June 22, 2006.

CHAPTER 8

1. Luke 6:38.
2. John Gray, *Men Are from Mars, Women Are from Venus* (New York: Harper-Collins, 1992), pp. 267–68.

CHAPTER 9

1. Deuteronomy 11:21. (KJV)
2. Hebrews 13:5–6.
3. Romans 5:8. (NASB)
4. Virginia Lively, *Healing in His Presence* (Grand Rapids, MI: Chosen Books, 1984).
5. Matthew 23:37–38 (author's emphasis). (NASB)
6. 1 John 4:19. (KJV)
7. Proverbs 13:12.
8. Matthew 18:7.
9. Matthew 6:21. (KJV)
10. Philippians 4:8. (NASB)
11. Matthew 5:44.
12. Matthew 19:6–8. (NASB)

CHAPTER 10

1. Romans 12:18.
2. John 3:16. (NASB)
3. 1 Corinthians 11:23–25

4. Matthew 19:6.
5. 1 Corinthians 6:19.
6. Romans 5:5 (author's emphasis). (KJV)
7. John 17:26.
8. 1 Corinthians 15:31. (KJV)
9. John 12:23–25.
10. Philippians 2:9. (NASB)
11. I Peter 5:5–6 (author's emphasis) (NASB).
12. Hebrews 13:21.
13. Philippians 2:13. (AMP)
14. Luke 6:36–38. (NASB)
15. Pat Robertson, *The Secret Kingdom* (Nashville, TN: Thomas Nelson, 1982).
16. Acts 20:35.
17. Romans 12:21.
18. Galatians 6:9. (NASB)
19. 1 Corinthians 13:4–8. (AMP)
20. Proverbs 27:2.
21. 2 Corinthians 5:17.
22. 2 Corinthians 5:14. (NASB)

CHAPTER 11
1. Genesis 3:22.
2. Rabbi Shmuley Boteach, *Kosher Sex: A Recipe for Passion and Intimacy* (New York: Main Street Books, 2000), p. 10.
3. Ephesians 5:31-32.
4. Rabbi Shmuley Boteach, *Kosher Sex,* pp. 35–36.
5. 1 Corinthians 7.
6. Rabbi Shmuley Boteach, *Kosher Sex,* pp. 36–37.
7. Genesis 2:24 (author's paraphrase).
8. Song of Solomon 8:6.
9. 1 Thessalonians 4:3–5. (NLT)
10. 1 Corinthians 7:3–5. (NLT)

CHAPTER 12
1. Michele Weiner Davis, *The Sex-Starved Marriage: A Couple's Guide to Boosting Their Marriage Libido* (New York: Simon & Schuster, 2004), p. 56.
2. Ibid.

CHAPTER 13
1. Desmond Morris, *Intimate Behavior* (New York: Random House, 1971).
2. "The art of kissing a woman." www.farmersalmanac.com/best_days/a/the_art_of_kissing_a_woman, November 30, 2007.

3. Song of Solomon 7:7–8.
4. Song of Solomon 2:8.
5. Song of Solomon 5:4–5.
6. Song of Solomon 4:6.
7. Naomi Wolf, "The Porn Myth," *New York* magazine, October 20, 2003.

CHAPTER 14

1. I John 2:17. (NKJ)
2. Romans 7:5.
3. Romans 7:6.
4. Judith A. Reisman, Edward W. Eichel, J. Gordon Muir, and J.H. Court, *Kinsey, Sex and Fraud: The Indoctrination of a People* (Vital Issues Press, 1990).
5. Naomi Wolf, "The Porn Myth," *New York* magazine, October 20, 2003.
6. Proverbs 5:18-19.
7. Dr. Mary Anne Layden, "The Science Behind Pornography Addiction and the Effects of Addiction on Families and Communities," www.obscenitycrimes.org/Senate-Reisman-Layden-Etc.pdf
8. Ibid.
9. Ibid.
10. Dolf Zillmann, Jennings Bryant, Aletha C. Huston, *Media, Children, and the Family; Social, Scientific, Psychodynamic, and Clinical Perspectives* (Hillsdale, NJ; Lawrence Erlbaum, 1994).
11. Pamela Paul, "The Porn Factor," *Time* magazine, January 19, 2004.
12. "Is the Internet Bad for Your Marriage? Online Affairs, Pornographic Sites Playing Greater Role in Divorces," PR Newswire, November 14, 2002.
13. Robert T. Michael, Edward O Laumann, John H. Gagnon, *Sex in America: A Definitive Survey* (New York; Grand Central Publishing, 10995).
14. Ibid.

CHAPTER 15

1. Dr. Thomas Szasz, www.quotationreference.com/quotefinder.php.
2. New Scientist (print edition), "Sex with a Partner is 400% Better", February 22, 2006.
3. Ibid.
4. Bill Perkins, When good Men Are Tempted (Grand Rapids, MI: Zondervan, 1997), pp. 192-93).
5. "The Science of Dysfunctions of the Male Reproductive System" *http://www.andrology.com/ejaculatorydisorders.htm.*
6. *New Scientist* (print edition), "Semen acts as an antidepressant", June 26, 2002.

CHAPTER 16

1. Eric J. Keroack, M.D., and John R. Diggs Jr., M.D., "Bonding Imperative," A Special Report from the Abstinence Medical Council. As quoted by Abstinence Clearinghouse, 30 April 2001.
2. National Review Online, February 14, 2007, by Patrick F. Fagan.
3. Romans 12:2.

CHAPTER 17

1. Matthew 18:15 (TLB).
2. Bill Hybels, *Who You Are When No One's Looking: Choosing Consistency, Resisting Compromise* (Downers Grove, IL: InterVarsity Press, 1987), pp. 70–71.
3. "Science proves that love is blind," http://news.bbc.co.uk/2/hi/health/3804545.stm.
4. Ecclesiastes 3:2.
5. Galatians 6:1.
6. Leo F. Buscaglia, *Loving Each Other: The Challenge of Human Relationships* (Thorofare, NJ: SLACK Inc., 1984).
7. Ephesians 5:25.
8. Richard B. Stuart, *Helping Couples Change* (New York: Guilford Press, 2003).
9. Charles A. Kiesler, *The Psychology of Commitment: Experiments Linking Behavior to Belief* (New York: Academic Press, 1971).

CHAPTER 18

1. John 12:24 (NKJV).
2. Matthew 16:24.
3. Matthew 16:25 (NLT).

CHAPTER 19

1. Psalms 144:15 (NKJV).
2. Ecclesiastes 5:19.
3. John 16:33. (NKJV)
4. Charles R. Hembree, *Pocket of Pebbles: Inspirational Thoughts on the Fruits of the Spirit* (Grand Rapids, MI: Baker Book House, 1969), p.33.
5. Nehemiah 8:10.
6. Matthew 16:25.

CHAPTER 20

1. Linda Waite and Maggie Gallagher, *The Case for Marriage: Why Married People Are Happier, Healthier, and Better Off Financially* (New York: Doubleday, 2000).

2. Genesis 2:24.
3. Matthew 19:6.
4. Deuteronomy 11:21. (KJV)
5. Linda Waite and Maggie Gallagher, *The Case for Marriage: Why Married People Are Happier, Healthier, and Better Off Financially* (New York: Doubleday, 2000).
6. Michele Weiner Davis, *The Divorce Remedy: The Proven 7-Step Program for Saving Your Marriage* (New York: Simon & Schuster, 2001), p. 27.
7. M. Scott Peck, *The Road Less Traveled: A New Psychology of Love, Traditional Values and Spiritual Growth* (New York: Touchstone, 1998), p. 19.
8. Ephesians 4:26.
9. Hebrews 12:2 (MSG).

CHAPTER 21
1. Matthew 6:14–15.
2. Matthew 18:21–22 (NKJV).
3. Luke 17:4 (NASB).
4. Corrie ten Boom, *God's Plans Are Perfect.* Quest Tape, P.O. Box 16804, Mobile, AL, 36616.

Bibliography

3475 Humboldt Road
Green Bay, WI 54311

www.laughyourway.com

866-52-LAUGH

For booking information contact us
at booking@laughyourway.com.

To order these and other products, please visit us online.

www.laughyourway.com

Bring Mark Gungor and his Laugh Your Way to a Better Marriage seminar into your small group!

Experience Mark's hilarious, practical, and no-holds-barred advice about relationships through this twelve-week study. Laugh and learn as you explore the underlying dynamics of male/female relationships and his practical solutions to common relationship woes.

Through this small-group study, couples will learn Mark's honest and hard-hitting insights, discuss and interact with each other, and be able to make real, positive changes in their marriages. This study guide can also be used by individual couples to strengthen, improve, and enrich their marriage. In addition, it's a great tool for premarital instruction.

Together, you and your group will experience the side-splitting fun of Mark's unique look at love, life, and marriage that has made him one of the courtry's top marriage speakers.

For the first time ever, the entire life-changing Laugh Your Way to a Better Marriage event is available on DVD!

Recently filmed in high definition in Phoenix, Arizona, this 4-disc DVD set includes every minute of Mark Gungor's weekend seminar, as well as extra bonus clips. With more than 6 hours of material, the DVD set captures all the fun and facts of Mark's look at life, love, and marriage—everything from "The Tale of Two Brains" to the funny, hard-hitting, and must-hear information in "The Number One Key to Incredible Sex."

Through this experience, couples will laugh, learn, and be able to make real, positive changes to their marriage. Perfect for couples, singles, and youth.